Narcissism: Socrates, the Frankfurt School, and Psychoanalytic Theory

Narcissism: Socrates, the Frankfurt School, and Psychoanalytic Theory

C. Fred Alford

Yale University Press
NEW HAVEN AND LONDON

Published with assistance from the foundation established in memory of
Henry Weldon Barnes of the Class of 1882, Yale College.

Designed by James J. Johnson
and set in Melior Roman type by Eastern Graphics
Printed in the United States of America by
Halliday Lithograph Corporation
West Hanover, Massachusetts

Library of Congress Cataloging-in-Publication Data
Alford, C. Fred.
    Narcissism : Socrates, the Frankfurt School, and psychoanalytic
theory / C. Fred Alford.
        p.   cm.
    Bibliography: p.
    Includes index.
    ISBN 0–300–04064–4
    1. Philosophical anthropology—History.   2. Narcissism—History.
3. Socrates.   4. Freud, Sigmund, 1856–1939.   5. Frankfurt, school of
sociology.   I. Title.
BD450.A458 1988
128—dc 19   87–31734
                                                              CIP

The paper in this book meets the guidelines for permanence and durability of the
Committee on Production Guidelines for Book Longevity of the Council on
Library Resources.

10   9   8   7   6   5   4   3   2   1

To Elly and to the students in my graduate seminar on narcissism

Contents

Preface

That the psychoanalytic theory of narcissism might illuminate some basic philosophical issues occurred to me only gradually, while teaching a graduate seminar on cultural narcissism. This book is an attempt to elaborate that insight. In the process, it became apparent that the theory of narcissism could also be used to link the concerns of two of my favorite philosophers, Plato and Herbert Marcuse. Both appreciate that philosophy is as much about *eros* as *logos*. It is the merit of the theory of narcissism that it reveals the roots of logos in eros, without reducing the former to the latter.

Anyone who works in this area follows in the footsteps of Christopher Lasch. The subtlety of his insight impresses me more and more each time I return to his work. My colleague Jim Glass is an inspiration; no one has explored the relationship between psychoanalytic and political thought more deeply than he. His work has influenced me greatly, even if this is not always apparent in the citations. Thomas Cimonetti helped me with this book, perhaps even more than with my first. Patricia Stein Wrightson, a student in my graduate seminar on narcissism, pointed out to me the similarity between Alasdair MacIntyre's *After Virtue* and Lasch's *The Culture of Narcissism*.

The second chapter attempts to synthesize a theory of narcissism—one especially suited to philosophical explication—

from a number of different psychoanalytic accounts. The reader wishing to get to the philosophical analysis immediately may wish to skip this chapter; but he or she should be aware that much of my argument depends on the theory of narcissism developed there.

Narcissism: Socrates, the Frankfurt School, and
Psychoanalytic Theory

• Chapter 1   After Virtue, Narcissism

This book is based on the hypothesis that the psychoanalytic theory of narcissism can help us better understand certain basic philosophical issues, by enabling us to distinguish fruitful from sterile modes of philosophical speculation. In order to establish that this is a hypothesis worth considering, the first part of this chapter will be devoted to a comparison of Alasdair MacIntyre's *After Virtue* with Christopher Lasch's *The Culture of Narcissism* and *The Minimal Self*. If we can show that the theory of narcissism, and more generally, the psychoanalytic thought associated with it (the topic of chapter 2), can illuminate aspects of MacIntyre's work, then we will have demonstrated the potential of the theory of narcissism to illuminate philosophical issues.[1] In subsequent chapters we will examine the philosophies of Plato's Socrates, Theodor Adorno, Herbert Marcuse, and Jürgen Habermas from this perspective. Although each chapter stands on its own as a case study, the theory of narcissism is used to explore in new ways what these thinkers share, as well as what divides them. We will also examine which theorist best integrates the insights of the theory of narcissism.

MacIntyre maintains that we do not fully understand the claims of any (moral) philosophy "until we have spelled out what its social embodiment would be."[2] To this a perceptive critic adds: "Neither have we fully understood it until we have seen the kind of social criticism to which it gives rise."[3] The the-

1

ory of narcissism adds a further qualification. Understanding the ideal social embodiment of a philosophy, as well as criticizing aspects of current society that prevent this philosophy's embodiment, requires an understanding of the characteristic self of each of these societies: the ideal society embodied by the philosophy and the real society that stands in the way. In particular, we must ask whether the ideal and the real societies foster mature or immature solutions to the self's longing for narcissistic wholeness and perfection. Of course, the longings of the self are not the primary determinant of society and philosophy. Self, society, and philosophy are interrelated in complex ways. However, the self cannot be left out of the discussion, and a persistent issue faced by the self is how it can achieve narcissistic wholeness and perfection.

But Isn't Narcissism a Psychological Disorder?

The *Diagnostic and Statistical Manual of Mental Disorders* of the American Psychiatric Association (DSM-III) characterizes narcissism as a personality disorder.[4] Indeed, narcissism is usually seen as an infatuation with self so extreme that the interests of others are ignored, others serving merely as mirrors of one's own grandiosity. That narcissism is a disorder is reflected even in the mythological origins of the term. Not only does Narcissus become so infatuated with his own reflection in the still water that he pines away and dies, he is also confused about his identity and the value of his own selfhood. As Ovid's classic account has Narcissus say:

> Am I the lover
> Or beloved? Then why make love? Since I
> Am what I long for, then my riches are
> So great they make me poor.[5]

How, then, can the concept of narcissism have philosophical worth? How can it possess a progressive moment? In a sense, that is what this whole book is about. However, it may be useful

at this point to outline what the answer to these questions looks
like.

DSM-III characterizes pathological narcissism in terms of an
exaggerated concern with power and control, the result of which
is interpersonal exploitativeness. Typical also is an orientation
of entitlement, the notion that one is worthy of great admiration,
respect, and reward regardless of one's achievements. Pathological narcissism is further characterized by relationships that alter-
nate between extremes of idealization and devaluation. Finally,
the pathological narcissist's grandiosity is curiously coupled
with great fragility of self-esteem.[6] Surely these are unattrac-
tive—indeed, pathological—qualities. Yet, they are not entirely
alien to normal experience. Rather, they may be viewed as exaggerated, distorted versions of normal traits. Most individuals
seek power and control over their own lives, and often over aspects of the lives of others. Who has not sought to influence a
friend, a spouse, or a child? In addition, most individuals seek
not only recognition for their achievements, but to be loved regardless of their achievements. Furthermore, most of us seek
others to idealize, and frequently we are disappointed and
change our minds. And who has not suffered a blow to his or her
self-esteem?

Putting it this way suggests that it may be fruitful to see
these common—indeed, mundane—needs, qualities, and experiences as themselves narcissistic. This would be to frame the issue not in terms of narcissism versus something else—for
example, Freud's mature object love—but rather, in terms of
pathological narcissism versus normal narcissism, regressive
narcissism versus progressive narcissism. From this perspective
narcissism is neither sick nor healthy. It is the human condition.
What is sick or healthy, regressive or progressive, is how individuals come to terms with their narcissism, understood as a
longing for perfection, wholeness, and control over self and
world. It is this aspect that lends itself to philosophical speculation, for the quest for perfection, wholeness, and mastery is part
of many philosophical programs, including those of Plato and

the Frankfurt school. This assumption about narcissism—that it can be a normal, as well as a pathological, condition—is shared by all the theorists of narcissism considered in chapter 2, including Freud. It is also central to my own theory of narcissism, developed at the conclusion of chapter 2.

Yet, to call mine a *theory* of narcissism may be misleading. I invoke the term *theory* in only the most casual sense, to refer to a set of themes that are central to the accounts discussed in chapter 2. The authors of these accounts are not merely theorists of narcissism, however; most of them have developed their own psychoanalytic theories, which is what makes them so interesting. Most of these theories stress the importance of the very first years of life—what Freud called the Minoan-Mycenean level of psychological development, a level that Freud uncovered but did not describe in great detail. At this level it is not sexual issues, such as the oedipal conflict, that are central, but rather, issues of dependence, individuation, and separation—that is, issues relating to the very establishment and coherence of the self. Thus, to talk about narcissism is really to talk about issues concerned with the integrity or fragmentation of the self.

Frequently the term *narcissism* is used as a shorthand way of referring to these more general issues. If this is not recognized, the discussion of narcissism, and especially cultural narcissism, can be most confusing. For the key feature of the culture of narcissism is not selfishness or self-love, but the way in which this culture threatens the coherence of the self. This misunderstanding is referred to by Lasch in the very title of *The Minimal Self*, for the minimal self is the narcissistic self, withdrawn not out of selfishness or self-love, but in response to threats to its integrity and coherence. In chapters 3–6 of the present book, in which the theory of narcissism is applied to the accounts of Socrates, Adorno, Marcuse, and Habermas, both the narrow and the broad meanings of the term *narcissism* will be employed: narcissism as a quest for wholeness and perfection, a quest that may find expression in a progressive or a regressive manner, and narcissism as a more general account of the vicissitudes of the self.

As the dualism of the concept suggests, one cannot focus on the progressive aspect of narcissism without analyzing its regressive aspect, and vice versa. In general, however, it is the progressive aspect that I wish to emphasize. Thus, my approach is the opposite to that of Lasch, who focuses on the regressive dimension. I shall argue (in Chapter 3) that the power of Socratic philosophy stems in large measure from its ability to draw on narcissistic strivings for wholeness and perfection and transform them into a quest for virtue and beauty. I shall also argue that Plato's Socrates holds a view of sublimation that is in some respects superior to that of Freud, insofar as Socrates' account recognizes that "higher" pleasures are not only more compatible with civilization, but also hold out the promise of even greater satisfaction. Platonic sublimation heightens pleasure, a view that is supported by the theory of narcissism. This insight, I contend (in chapter 5, on Marcuse), can help us better distinguish between the progressive and regressive aspects of Marcuse's ideal society, without succumbing to "neo-Freudian revisionism," which risks sacrificing happiness to social integration. Despite all its flaws, Marcuse's ideal is valuable because Marcuse, like Socrates, takes seriously the quest for narcissistic wholeness, in contrast to Adorno (chapter 4) and Habermas (chapter 6), who, for very different reasons and in quite different ways, reject the motive power of narcissism, with problematic consequences for their projects. Adorno is almost led to abandon philosophy altogether, whereas Habermas pursues philosophy by abandoning a psychologically robust view of the individual.

Why These Particular Authors?

I have chosen to look at Plato's Socrates because it is he who introduces narcissism into philosophy. Indeed, Socrates' "ladder of love" in Plato's *Symposium* remains the finest philosophical expression of the transformation of immature into mature narcissism. Other aspects of the *Symposium* suggest that Socrates was not entirely immune to the hubris of narcissism. The

Phaedrus is read as the dialogue in which Socrates comes to terms with this fact. The other authors—Adorno, Marcuse, and Habermas—are associated with the Frankfurt school of critical theory, which stands in a particularly interesting relationship to the classical philosophical tradition, in that it seeks to restore something of the legacy of the concept of reason held by Plato and Aristotle, while at the same time being immensely suspicious of reason as itself a tool of domination. This duality is expressed most clearly perhaps in Max Horkheimer and Theodor Adorno's *Dialectic of Enlightenment*, which is discussed in some detail in chapter 4. To esteem reason as the most distinctly human attribute risks not fully appreciating the power of the narcissistic quest for wholeness and perfection, for the narcissistic quest is prerational, originating in the first months of life and remaining largely unconscious throughout life. Yet, to abandon reason for some sort of aesthetic sensibility risks perverting the quest for perfection.

In the work of Adorno, Marcuse, and Habermas, we see three quite different attempts at the difficult balancing act required. Put simply, Adorno recognizes the power of the narcissistic quest for wholeness, and its intensity frightens him, with good reason. Marcuse embraces the narcissistic quest but is unable fully to distinguish between its progressive and regressive moments. Habermas implicitly rejects this quest almost entirely. Thus, within the Frankfurt school, we see a range of orientations to narcissism that we might expect to find only among philosophers of different schools. To be sure, other philosophers might have been considered. Rousseau and Marx (especially in the "Economic and Philosophic Manuscripts of 1844") come to mind as philosophers who recognize the power of the narcissistic quest for wholeness and perfection but embrace it in very different ways. However, my purpose is not to apply the theory of narcissism to as many different philosophers as possible. It is rather, to show that the psychoanalytic theory of narcissism can illuminate traditional philosophical concerns; and for this, a study of the philosophies of Socrates, Adorno, Marcuse, and Habermas is sufficient.

Though the chapters on Socrates, Adorno, Marcuse, and Habermas are of roughly equal length, it is the chapter on Socrates that serves as the linchpin. Socrates illuminates what the theory of narcissism seeks to explain; conversely, the theory of narcissism illuminates aspects of Socrates' project. Much of the discussion in chapters 4–6 concerns how this Socratic conception of sublimation can help overcome certain difficulties in the Frankfurt school's analysis of the relationship between eros and reason.

What Does an Account of Narcissism Add to our Understanding of these Issues?

Some have seen the quest for human wholeness and perfection as a noble undertaking. Aristotle, for example, writes of this quest in terms of the full development of the distinctively human excellences (N. Ethics 1097b22–1103a10). He also states that self-love is the primary source of human action (ibid., 1168a28–1169b1). Nor does he see anything pathological in this. To him it is obvious that people will love themselves and seek to develop themselves as fully as possible. No encouragement is needed in this direction; nor can people be deterred effectively from this path. What is required is instruction, so that they can learn to distinguish genuine full development from its simulacrum. One need not be a philosopher to recognize that self-love and the quest to develop oneself as fully as possible—that is, to become as perfect as possible—lie behind a great deal of human action.

If so, what does my account, which draws upon a depth-psychological theory of narcissism, add to what we already know? It adds the following:

1. An appreciation of the drive-like character of the quest for wholeness and perfection, which is as intense as the quest for erotic satisfaction, to which it is closely related.

2. The recognition that this intensity is reflected in the closeness of the progressive and regressive aspects of the quest, and insight, therefore, into why the quest is so liable to regression.

3. Insight into why the mastery of self and world that characterizes the successful completion of the narcissistic quest—so similar to what Aristotle means by the full development of the distinctively human excellences—is such a compelling ideal.

The narcissistic ideal is compelling because it links pleasure and achievement, erotic passion and creative passion, ego satisfaction and id satisfaction, love and work. This is Freud's insight. It is also Plato's, particularly in the *Symposium*. I shall argue that the theory of narcissism shows Plato's account of eros to be psychologically—not just philosophically or aesthetically—more compelling than Freud's, and that Plato's account of sublimation, as illuminated by the theory of narcissism, can help us to balance a respect for the claims of reason against an appreciation of the intensity of the nonrational demands generated by the narcissistic pursuit of perfection.

What is it that gives the theory of narcissism its philosophical potential, it might be asked. Is its value that it directs us to a lost experience of wholeness and perfection—the state of primary narcissism to which Freud refers—that all seek to recover? Or does it rather stem from its ability to illuminate the content and meaning of the perfection we all seek? The psychoanalytic theorists of narcissism suggest that the answer is both. However, in an important, controversial recent book, *The Interpersonal World of the Infant: A View from Psychoanalysis and Developmental Psychology*, Daniel Stern reviews a number of studies of cognitive development in the infant and concludes that at no time is the infant so cognitively and emotionally undeveloped that it experiences itself as fused with the mother and the world, an experience that for many theorists is the paradigm of narcissistic wholeness and bliss. Rather, this notion is an elaborate secondary construction, albeit an enormously powerful one. Thus, Stern in effect answers no to the first question raised above and yes only to the second.[7]

Stern has been harshly criticized, however.[8] It has not been overlooked, for example, that he leaps from assumptions about the cognitive development of the infant to assumptions about its emotional development. But these modes of development do not necessarily run parallel. The biological organization of the infant, particularly as it pertains to its cognitive capabilities, is not a reliable indicator of its subjective experience of self. It may be that the infant is cognitively able to do things that it is still psychologically unable to make sense of. Yet, much of Stern's argument hinges on this not being the case, as critics have pointed out.[9] Nevertheless, let us assume for a moment that Stern is correct. This would not fundamentally alter my argument. It is not essential that narcissism refer to the archaic memory of an actual state of "oceanic contentment," as Freud put it. The power of the narcissistic quest depends hardly at all on the historical accuracy of the ideal that it represents, but only on the intensity of the ideal. Thus, when Marcuse states that his utopia expresses a "return to an imaginary *temps perdu* in the real life of mankind,"[10] a primitive state of innocence and perfection, a garden of Eden, the intensity of this longing, as well as its effect on history and culture, does not depend on whether such a state ever actually existed. Indeed, the influence of this so-called memory may be all the greater for evoking a state that never was. And the same could be said of the memory of wholeness, perfection, and gratification associated with the theory of narcissism. This would not change the course of the argument. It would require the reinterpretation of much psychoanalytic theory, however. Most psychoanalysts have not chosen to do this. Nor have I.

The Culture of Emotivism as a Culture of Narcissism

Whereas progressive narcissism illuminates the discussion of the good for man, regressive narcissism only obscures it. From this perspective one can read MacIntyre's *After Virtue* as a philosophical version of Lasch's *The Culture of Narcissism*. Both are concerned with how social changes threaten the self by fostering regressive solutions to the problem of identity, solutions that render virtue, as well as any coherent discussion of the good life, almost impossible. Consider MacIntyre's analysis of emotivism.

Emotivism is the doctrine that all evaluative judgments, and especially all moral judgments, are nothing but expressions of attitudes or feelings.[11] MacIntyre sees this as the dominant moral attitude of the modern world, reflected in everything from Max Weber's "decisionism" to the political compromises of the Supreme Court of the United States. The fundamental problem with emotivism, in MacIntyre's view, is that it obliterates any genuine distinction between manipulative and nonmanipulative social relations. Evaluative utterances, as expressions only of my own feelings, can ultimately appeal to nothing but my own needs. In this emotive, manipulative culture, three characters stand out as archetypes: the aesthete, the bureaucratic manager, and the therapist. In calling these archetypes "characters," MacIntyre means to suggest that they are the moral representatives of our culture. "Characters are the masks worn by moral philosophies."[12] These characters are also the primary players in Lasch's account of the culture of narcissism.

Lasch expresses the character of the aesthete in terms of what he calls the "survival mentality," which he defines (much as the aesthete is by MacIntyre) as a withdrawal of interest in the past and the future. The resultant, enfeebled self is capable of doing no more than holding on to the tenuous present. "The everyday survivalist has deliberately lowered his sights from history to the immediacies of face-to-face relationships. He takes one day at a time. He pays a heavy price for this radical restriction of perspective, which precludes moral judgment and intelligent political activity."[13] Compare this view with MacIntyre's characterization of the emotivist self, which "in acquiring sovereignty in its own realm lost its traditional boundaries provided by a social identity and a view of human life as ordered to a given end."[14] The survival mentality is the loss of what MacIntyre calls a "narrative self," the ability to see the events of one's life as connected and as having a meaning that can be projected into the future. All attempts to elucidate the notion of personal identity "independently of and in isolation from the notions of narrative, intelligibility and accountability are bound to fail. As all such attempts have."[15]

Survivalism, as Lasch makes clear, is pathological narcissism, the shrinking of the self back into nothing but the self, a last-ditch effort to protect its integrity. This survival mentality is seen especially clearly in what Lasch calls the "minimalist aesthetic."

> Overwhelmed by the cruelty, disorder, and sheer complexity of modern history, the artist retreats into a solipsistic mode of discourse that represents "not so much an attempt to understand the self," in [Philip] Roth's words, as an attempt "to assert it." He conducts his own struggle for survival as an artist, under conditions that have made it more and more difficult to transcribe any shared experience or common perceptions of the world, undermined the conventions of artistic realism, and given rise to a type of art that no longer seems to refer to anything outside itself.[16]

Such a retreat serves a purpose, however. In abandoning a conception of a self that can influence the world, the minimal aesthetic seeks relief from the burden of selfhood. This is the strategy of pure narcissistic regression, the pathological shortcut to narcissistic perfection.

> An inner agenda nevertheless underlines much of contemporary music, art, and literature, one that seeks to recapture a sense of psychic oneness without taking any account of the obstacles, psychic or material, that lie in the way of oneness. . . . They seek the shortest road to Nirvana. . . . Instead of seeking to reconcile the ego and its environment, [they] deny the very distinction between them.[17]

MacIntyre and Lasch both see bureaucracy as the central phenomenon of the modern age and agree that it is characterized by an orientation of manipulation and control for their own sake—that is, by what Horkheimer and Adorno call "instrumental reason." MacIntyre focuses on why this pure culture of manipulation and control has no choice but to treat people as mere means, since it abandons—as the primary institutional exemplar of emotivism—any hope of rational discourse over ends. Lasch does not ignore this aspect of bureaucracy—indeed, like many others, he points out how readily the emotionally shallow narcissist finds a home in the superficial, manipulative world of the bureaucracy—but he stresses another aspect of it—namely, the way in which it fosters dependence, once again leading the individual toward more regressive modes of satisfaction.

> Modern capitalist society not only elevates narcissists to promi-nence, it elicits and reinforces narcissistic traits in everyone. It does this in many ways: by displaying narcissism so prominently and in such attractive forms; by undermining parental authority and thus making it hard for children to grow up; but above all by creating so many varieties of bureaucratic dependence. This dependence, in-creasingly widespread in a society that is not merely paternalistic but maternalistic as well, makes it increasingly difficult for people to lay to rest the terrors of infancy or to enjoy the consolations of adulthood.[18]

This is a social-psychological characterization of what MacIn-tyre calls the "emotivist culture."

Lasch and MacIntyre view the therapist in almost identical terms—as the representative of the bureaucratic manager within the private sphere. Like the bureaucratic manager, the therapist also abandons rational and moral considerations, teaching adap-tation to the needs of the bureaucratic, industrial system. Lasch, following Talcott Parsons, refers to this as the "production of personality." MacIntyre puts it this way:

> The manager represents in his *character* the obliteration of the dis-tinction between manipulative and nonmanipulative social rela-tions; the therapist represents the same obliteration in the sphere of personal life. The manager treats ends as given, as outside his scope; his concern is with technique. . . . The therapist also treats ends as given, as outside his scope; his concern also is with tech-nique, with effectiveness in transforming neurotic symptoms into directed energy, maladjusted individuals into well-adjusted ones.[19]

The outcome of the activities represented by these three characters is the destruction of the possibility of narrative self-hood. Indeed, we may provisionally define the culture of narcissism as a culture which destroys this possibility by dis-connecting men and women from their past and their future. What remains is an abstract, ghostly self, which retreats further into itself in order to find security, a process which intensifies the very problem it attempts to redress, that of situating the self in the world. MacIntyre's discussion of a self deprived of narrative unity might well have been written by Lasch.

> The self thus conceived, utterly distinct on the one hand from its social embodiments and lacking on the other any rational history of its own, may seem to have a certain abstract and ghostly character.
> . . . For one way of re-envisaging the emotivist self is as having suffered a deprivation, a stripping away of qualities that were once perceived to belong to the self. . . . The particularly modern self, the emotivist self, in acquiring sovereignty in its own realm lost its traditional boundaries provided by a social identity and a view of human life as ordered to a given end.[20]

This process, MacIntyre shows us, has philosophical as well as psychological consequences, which cannot be separated. For the destruction of narrative selfhood destroys not only the meaning of human life, but the very possibility of virtue. No longer is it possible to intelligibly ask questions about the good life, for such questions presuppose that a life has a unity and a purpose, something that is lost when life is seen as no more than a succession of moments.

The virtues, says MacIntyre, are precisely those attributes that will lead us successfully through the risks associated with the quest for narrative selfhood. From the perspective of the theory of narcissism, the prime risk is that the individual will become persuaded that it is not necessary to grow up in order to re-establish narcissistic wholeness. Indeed, this is what the culture of narcissism is all about. It panders to the desire for instant wholeness, via religions that promise instant salvation, therapies that promise instant happiness, and commodities that promise love and feelings of power and control. From this perspective, the virtues of which MacIntyre writes are attributes associated with maturity. For, as the psychoanalyst Janine Chasseguet-Smirgel points out, it is maturity that allows the individual to postpone and delay narcissistic satisfaction, as well as to accept less than complete satisfaction, in the knowledge that in the long run such satisfaction is more gratifying to the self than regressive satisfaction.[21]

This perspective recognizes the importance of a pair of Aristotelian virtues that MacIntyre does not stress: temperance and moderation.[22] MacIntyre seeks to combat liberal—what he calls "bureaucratic"—individualism, which leads him to stress the social and cooperative aspects of the self. Aristotelian moderation and temperance, on the other hand, are primarily concerned not with the orientation of the self toward others, but with its orientation toward objects of consumption and enjoyment.[23] In this respect the theory of narcissism comes closer to Aristotle than to MacIntyre, for it accepts a certain fundamental selfishness in human beings, even the most generous. As Aristotle puts it, "One will wish the greatest good for his friend as a human being. But perhaps not all the greatest goods, for each man wishes for his own good most of all" (N. Ethics 1159a10–13). What divides individuals, making them less than perfect communitarians, is not merely capitalism, possessive individualism, and emotivism (as MacIntyre sometimes seems to imply), but the stubborn facts of human separateness and difference.[24] This, too, philosophy and social theory must come to terms with.

The connection between *After Virtue* and *The Culture of Narcissism* is apparent. Immature or pathological narcissism makes virtue impossible, because it disconnects man from his past and future. For the minimal self it is senseless even to consider what the excellent performance of a human life—the classical definition of virtue—might entail. What are the implications of the connection between these two books for the theory of narcissism? Does the theory tell us about the good for man or only about what feels good? As we shall see, the answer lies somewhere in between. The mature, progressive narcissist is not necessarily a virtuous man. However, the theory of narcissism is far more than just an explanation of the sources of human pleasure, for it links pleasure with the pursuit of humanity's highest values.

Can Narcissism Be a Cultural Phenomenon?

It may be useful here to address an issue that cannot help but have troubled the thoughtful reader, that of whether it makes sense to talk of a psychoanalytic category, narcissism, as though it were also a cultural, indeed a philosophical, category? If it does not, then the demonstration that Lasch's work can illuminate MacIntyre's is not helpful, for Lasch's work would itself be a misguided attempt to apply psychoanalytic schemes to non-psychoanalytic issues. In the last analysis this question is best answered by the entirety of my book. Does its use of the psychoanalytic category of narcissism reveal aspects of culture and philosophy that might otherwise have been overlooked, aspects that upon consideration seem important? The proof of the pudding is in the eating. However, it may be helpful here to explain why it is at least possible that a psychoanalytic category could be meaningfully applied to cultural and philosophical phenomena, and that so doing is not to be involved in some sort of category mistake.

It might be asked whether in applying the concept of narcissism to cultural phenomena, we do not face a levels of analysis problem analogous to trying to explain large-scale historical events strictly in terms of the beliefs and actions of individuals, while ignoring the larger social and economic changes to which these individuals were subject. The answer is that, in principle, there is no philosophical barrier to the concept of cultural narcissism, since nothing in the issues dealt with by the philosophy of science under the categories of reductionism, emergence, and composition laws suggests that large-scale social changes could not affect individual psychological development, which in turn would further affect this social change.[25] Indeed, this is precisely what the Frankfurt school argues under rubrics such as the "end of the individual" and the "obsolescence of the Freudian concept of man" (see chapter 4).

In a particularly harsh criticism of Lasch's attempt to apply the psychoanalytic category of narcissism to social and cultural phenomena, Colleen Clements nevertheless agrees that while the concept "could lead to a significant reductionist error, confusing metaphors (or models) from different levels of organization," it need not do so.[26] That it could lead to such an error is because macro-level events are often not merely the additive consequence of individual micro-level phenomena. Clements's cautions are well taken. However, the moral is surely not to abandon the attempt to discover relationships between social and psychological changes, but rather, to take care to specify precisely the links between individuals and society. Otto Kernberg's speculations on the relationship between social change, family change, and personality change are a case in point, as we shall see in the next chapter. Kernberg is most careful to distinguish social changes that might reach sufficiently deep into the psyche to affect basic personality from those that are unlikely to do so. He is not necessarily correct, of course, but he does exemplify how this issue can be approached in a sophisticated and self-conscious fashion.

Clements's primary objection is more fundamental, however. She argues that to call a culture "narcissistic" is to transform a clinical diagnostic term into a moral judgment, and a harsh one at that. On this issue she seems to be correct. Indeed, this is why it was suggested that the theory of narcissism becomes a powerful analytic tool only when linked with a philosophical account of the human good. It is this philosophical account, not the theory of narcissism per se, that supports the moral judgment about the culture. Presumably Clements does not mean that it is inappropriate to make moral judgments about individuals and societies, though sometimes she seems to imply this.[27]

Even if all this is granted, one might argue that it is not appropriate to apply the theory of narcissism to philosophy, that the theory is little more than a metaphor. Yet, this in itself is not a criticism. Many explanations, including scientific ones, employ metaphor. As Max Black puts it in *Models and Metaphors*: "Perhaps every science must start with metaphor and end with algebra; and perhaps without the metaphor there would never have been any algebra."[28] Since even the strictly psychoanalytic theory of narcissism has not yet reached the stage of algebra, the key question would seem to be not whether narcissism as applied to philosophy is a metaphor, but whether it is a useful one.

This question cannot be answered in advance. Whether the theory of narcissism can reveal neglected aspects of philosophical thought that are worth pursuing can be determined only by applying the theory and seeing what happens, which is what this book seeks to do.

It would be a mistake, however, to assume that the theory of narcissism can be nothing more than a metaphor when applied to philosophy. As MacIntyre showed in *After Virtue*, how people live and what their lives are like affect how they think about philosophical matters. For example, do they see their lives as possessing a unity over time such that they can take moral responsibility for their own actions? To demonstrate that the individual's sense of self might make a difference in this regard was my purpose in comparing Lasch and MacIntyre. From this perspective social changes may well affect philosophy, by affecting how individuals understand the meaning of their own lives. Nor is this an unusual claim. Karl Marx made a similar one. Once it is admitted that social change might affect philosophy, and that psychological change might affect social change, the possibility of a relationship between psychological and philosophical change is readily established—via the property of transitivity, one might say.

The Ethnopsychiatric Paradigm

In *Basic Problems of Ethnopsychiatry*, George Devereux distinguishes between two components of the unconscious: a part that was never conscious, the realm of the id, and a part that contains material that was once conscious but has since been repressed. This second portion, which Devereux calls the "ethnic unconscious,"[29] also includes most of our defense mechanisms and a substantial portion of the superego. Each culture permits certain impulses, fantasies, and so forth to become and remain conscious, while requiring that others be repressed. "Hence, all members of a given culture will have certain unconscious conflicts in common."[30] A particularly interesting element of the ethnic unconscious consists of what might be called "directives for the misuse of cultural material"—what others have called "patterns of misconduct." It is as though the group says to the individual, "Don't do this, but if you do, go about it in this way, and not that."[31]

In terms of its relationship to the ethnic unconscious, mental illness may take two forms. The most severe illness will be idiosyncratic, for the individual will be unable to utilize the culture or to follow the "directives for the misuse of cultural material." Such an individual is fundamentally isolated and schizophrenic. One reason for this, according to Devereux, is that the traumas causing the most severe psychoses occur very early in life, mostly at the oral stage, when the infant does not yet have at its disposal the cultural resources that could be drawn on as a defense. Hence, it must improvise defenses, which will always retain their improvisational character, even if, later, they come to utilize superficially the symbols of the culture. In general, however, emotional illness will follow the "directives for misuse." As examples, Devereux mentions a Malayan running amok and an American Indian becoming a shaman. Of the shaman Devereux says, "He is quite often like everyone else—'only more so,'" which is why his performance strikes normal people as uncanny, "as something that their unconscious experiences as 'disturbingly and unexpectedly familiar.'"[32]

The relevance of these considerations to the phenomenon of cultural narcissism is clear. It is the culture, mediated first by the parents and later by schools, television, and so forth, that "instructs" the individual that the way to deal with the stresses associated with this culture is to withdraw into the self. Prime among the stresses, as Lasch points out, is the sense of isolation in the midst of others, alienation in a mass society. From this perspective, the ethnic illness of modern industrial society—schizoid withdrawal—is especially problematic, since it fosters the very problems against which it is a defense. Indeed, this is the thesis of *The Culture of Narcissism* and *The Minimal Self*. This vicious circle is characteristic of much mental illness, as

Devereux points out. More evidence that withdrawal is indeed the ethnic illness of modern industrial society is found in Richard Sennett's *The Fall of Public Man: On the Social Psychology of Capitalism*, particularly the sections on narcissism.[33] The *locus classicus* of this discussion, of course, is the second volume of Alexis de Tocqueville's *Democracy in America*.

From this perspective, Devereux's chapter entitled "Schizophrenia: An Ethnic Psychosis, or Schizophrenia Without Tears," is intriguing.[34] He argues that a mild form of schizophrenia (what W. R. D. Fairbairn and Harry Guntrip call "schizoid disorder") is characteristic of the United States today. Its symptoms are withdrawal, emotional aloofness, hyporeactivity (emotional flatness), sex without emotional involvement, segmentation and partial involvement (lack of interest in and commitment to things outside oneself), fixation on oral-stage issues, regression, infantalism, and depersonalization. These, of course, are many of the same designations that Lasch employs to describe the culture of narcissism. Thus, it appears that it is not misleading to equate narcissism with schizoid disorder. This is important, as a key argument of chapter 2 is that it is helpful to understand narcissism in just this fashion. Devereux goes on to argue that such cultural schizophrenia is the mark of a sick and declining civilization. Less sick societies have less severe modal ethnic neuroses. As an example, he mentions hysteria in Periclean Athens.[35] In this, Devereux seems to be mistaken, or at least fails to give the complete picture, for, as we shall see in chapter 3, narcissism appears to have been the modal ethnic neurosis in ancient Greece. Indeed, Devereux's "Greek Homosexuality and the 'Greek Miracle,'" will be employed to support this claim.

The preceding considerations do not, of course, demonstrate that cultural narcissism is a useful analytic concept. Nor do they show that one of the most abstract aspects of culture, philosophy, can fruitfully be viewed from the perspective of the psychoanalytic theory of narcissism. What they do reveal is that it is neither incoherent nor merely metaphorical to say of a culture or its philosophy that it exhibits symptoms and characteristics usually associated with individual emotional states. Indeed, to regard such speech as incoherent would itself reflect a sense of the individual as isolated and alienated, a monad whose mentation operates independently of the culture. Yet, there remains a danger associated with the concept of cultural narcissism. Because the culture influences the unconscious, and vice versa, does not mean that these two entities stand in some sort of mirror relationship. The influence of culture on the unconscious and the reverse thereof may be very indirect, as we will see in part 3 of chapter 4.

One further methodological issue needs to be clarified: at no point will it be argued either that any individual philosopher had difficulty in coming to terms with his own narcissism, or that he was particularly successful in so doing. This level of analysis, akin to so-called psycho-biography, is excluded.

• Chapter 2 The Psychoanalytic Theory of Narcissism

In this chapter, we will examine the accounts of narcissism given by Freud, Melanie Klein, W. R. D. Fairbairn and Harry Guntrip, Heinz Kohut, Otto Kernberg, Béla Grunberger, and Janine Chasseguet-Smirgel. These theorists, all of whom are psychoanalysts, represent diverse theoretical perspectives. The basic disagreement is between those who hold to a conception of narcissism influenced by classical Freudian drive theory and those whose conception is more strongly influenced by object relations theory. The drive perspective sees primary narcissism as an original objectless state—the libidinal cathexis of the self. The object relations perspective denies the very possibility of an objectless state, viewing narcissism as though it were a schizoid disorder, characterized by an exaggerated attachment to archaic internal objects. Yet, these differences may be less profound than first appears. We will see that not only is there considerable agreement on the symptoms of narcissism, but that the theoretical differences can sometimes be bridged. Though drive theory and object relations theory may be incommensurable, their accounts of narcissism are not necessarily so.

The stress throughout this chapter will be upon what these theorists share, and how they can sometimes be interpreted as building upon each other's work, even when they do not explicitly state that they are doing so. Indeed, an effort is made to theoretically bridge the differences. The goal is not theoretical reconciliation for its own sake, but to establish that there exists an account of narcissism shared by a number of theorists, even if there is no shared theory of psychoanalysis. Little in this chapter is original, except the way in which very different theorists are brought together. My goal is an account that draws together a number of widely shared assumptions regarding narcissism and that stresses the continuity between pathological and normal narcissism. This view of narcissism is similar to Freud's view of neurosis as an intensification of developmental conflicts faced by every individual.[1] It emphasizes how narcissism stands behind almost every human action, in that it connects almost every action with its consequences for self-esteem. As Grunberger puts it, "One could regard all the manifestations of civilization as a kaleidoscope of different attempts by man to restore narcissistic omnipotence."[2]

Grunberger states dramatically what should already be apparent. *Narcissism* is not merely a label for a pathology that seems to have become more common in recent years.[3] It is also a world view—an account of the meaning of human action as it affects self-esteem and the quest for human perfection generally. It is precisely because narcissism is such a rich, multidimensional concept that it lends itself to elucidation by philosophical speculation. But in order to undersand the philosophical dimension of narcissism, it is first necessary to turn to a rather detailed discussion of its place in psychoanalytic thought. To short-circuit this aspect by turning too quickly to its philosophical dimension would be to rob the concept of narcissism of its depth. The impatient reader, however, may wish to turn directly to the conclusion of this chapter, where the results of my study are summarized, and my theory of narcissism is outlined.

As with most psychoanalytic concepts, the place to begin—and to a considerable degree to end—is with Freud. But first, one point must be clarified. Though a number of different theorists are considered and considerable effort is made to bridge their differences, this is not a universal account of narcissism. It could not be: there is simply too much divergence among the various theorists. The result is that I emphasize some themes and theorists at the expense of others. Thus, narcissism as a quest for fusion is emphasized over narcissistic rage. Narcissism as a quest for wholeness and perfection is emphasized over narcissism as an attitude toward others characterized by exploitation and devaluation. Envy is emphasized over projective identification. In general, the closeness of narcissism to schizoid phenomena is emphasized, possibly at the expense of narcissism as a particular orientation of the drives. As far as theorists are concerned, it is the object relations theorists, as well as Kohut, and the French psychoanalysts Grunberger and Chasseguet-Smirgel who are given most attention. Less attention is paid to the so-called Freudian Kleinians, such as Joan Riviere, Margaret Mahler, and Edith Jacobson.

It might be argued that the account of narcissism given here is biased, in that, from the beginning, it is designed to explain the most abstract philosophical expressions of narcissism. However, I am not sure that this constitutes a valid criticism. In general I stress the metapsychology of narcissism—what the theory of narcissism has to say about the human condition, what men and women most seek, what they most fear, and why. Thus, I downplay more symptom-oriented accounts.

The account of narcissism given by Kernberg possesses a somewhat anomalous status in this chapter. Because his is such a theoretically influential and profound account, it is given considerable attention. However, this attention is not fully reflected in the theory of narcissism developed at the conclusion of this chapter, which has a more philosophical orientation. Kernberg's theory stresses the great distance between normal and pathological narcissism, not the continuity that makes it possible to apply theories of pathological narcissism to "normal" cultural and philosophical phenomena. Yet, important aspects of Kernberg's theory are adopted, nevertheless, in part, by drawing on Arnold Rothstein's study (*The Narcissistic Pursuit of Perfection*) of the continuities between normal, neurotic, borderline, and psychotic expressions of narcissism.

Is the Metapsychology of Narcissism a Science?

In *The Foundations of Psychoanalysis: A Philosophical Critique* Adolf Grünbaum charges that at this point in its history psychoanalysis is a failed science. Earlier, Karl Popper argued that psychoanalysis is a pseudoscience.[4] These charges deserve to be taken seriously, especially since so many psychoanalysts still refer, sometimes in a tone of desperation, to "their science." However, my focus here is upon the most abstract, philosophical, metapsychological aspects of the psychoanalytic theory of narcissism. At this level psychoanalysis is more akin to a metaphysics, a world view, or literary account of the meaning of life. In claiming this, I am not suggesting that a "hermeneutic" account of psychoanalysis somehow bypasses the normal demands of scientific rigor, only that the metapsychology of narcissism can be fruitful even if it is not (yet) testable.

Popper never intended that the falsifiability criterion, by which he sought to distinguish science from non-science, be seen as distinguishing meaningful from nonmeaningful statements. The demarcation criterion was aimed at the Vienna Circle and sought to demonstrate quite the opposite: that the class of testable statements was not identical with the class of meaningful ones.[5] Even Grünbaum ignores Freud's metapsychology (focusing instead on the theory of repression), agreeing that Freud understood this aspect of his work as speculation rather than science.[6] It is in this spirit that the theory of narcissism is considered here: as speculation about the deepest sources of what makes human life worth living and worth living well. Whether this speculation yields dividends will depend on whether it can illuminate more traditional philosophical accounts concerned with this issue. It is in this spirit that we now turn to Freud.

Freud

In the beginning, says Freud in "On Narcissism" (1914), the human being has two sexual objects: "himself and the woman who tends him, and thereby we postulate a primary narcissism in everyone, which may in the long run manifest itself as dominating his object choice."[7] Primary narcissism is not a perversion, of course, but the first stage of psychosexual development, in which the young child's libidinal interests are centered upon himself and his own body. Earlier, in his account of the Schreber case (1911), Freud distinguished between an even earlier stage of autoeroticism and narcissism per se.[8] Though Freud conceptualizes narcissism in various ways, calling it, for example, "the libidinal complement to the egoism of the instinct of self-preservation," the underlying model is that of the amoeba and its pseudopod. The amoeba represents pure libido, the energy associated with the erotic drives. ("We call," says Freud, "by that name [libido] the energy . . . of those instincts which have to do with all that may be comprised under the word 'love'."[9]) The more the amoeba extends a pseudopod of libidinal energy out toward objects, the less is available to the amoeba itself. Narcissism can be represented by an amoeba with no pseudopod at all; it directs none of its libido outward toward objects but keeps it all for itself. The state of being head over heels in love, on the other hand, is represented by an amoeba as virtually pure pseudopod; there is no libido left for the amoeba itself, all is given over to object love.

Freud regards the development of the ego as in large measure a matter of abandoning one's primary narcissism and with it the libido's investment in the self. In place of self-love comes love of human objects, so-called anaclitic (literally, leaning-up-against) relations. However, as the amoeba model makes clear there is a cost involved: in object love the self is depleted of libido, and there is a necessary decrease in narcissistic satisfaction. While being loved in return may provide considerable narcissistic gratification, it is not sufficient to compensate for the loss. It is in this context that Freud introduces the concept of the ego ideal. "As always where the libido is concerned, here again man has shown himself incapable of giving up a gratification he has once enjoyed. He is not willing to forgo his narcissistic perfection in his childhood. . . . That which he projects ahead of him as his ideal is merely his substitute for the lost narcissism of his childhood—the time when he was his own ideal."[10]

In Freud's later work the ego ideal is almost completely absorbed into the concept of the superego, but here the ego ideal is conceptualized as an ideal standard of perfection, one that is compelling because it draws on the unconscious memory of the first, most complete state of perfection, when the infant was source and object of all the good in the world: the state of primary narcissism. As the individual matures, so too does the ego ideal, which comes to include social and cultural ideals. To the extent that the individual is able to live up to these ideals, thereby reducing the distance between ego and ego ideal, narcissistic satisfaction ensues. To be sure, the satisfaction that stems from living up to a mature ego ideal is highly modulated, or sublimated. It remains narcissistic satisfaction, however, insofar as the gratification is obtained not from external objects, but from a relationship with oneself, that is, between ego and ego ideal.

Because the mature ego ideal is modeled on ideals available in the society, it stands in a close relationship to conscience, the psychic agency that internalizes parental and societal standards. The mature ego ideal thus imposes conditions upon the gratification of libido, censoring modes incompatible with itself and thereby civilizing narcissism. Indeed, in "The Ego and the Id" (1923), Freud treats the ego ideal as indistinguishable from the superego.[11] The narcissistic aim of being loved and approved of by one's self becomes merged with the desire to be loved and approved of by the ideal internalized parent, the superego.[12]

Freud argues that the ego ideal is of great importance in understanding group psychology. In "Group Psychology and the Analysis of the Ego" (1921), he says that narcissism could be an almost insuperable barrier to the formation of groups, but that if members of a group share a common ego ideal, their narcissistic self-love can be redirected toward this ideal, thereby binding them together.[13] As Freud puts it, "A primary group of this kind is a number of individuals who have substituted one and the same object for their ego ideal and have consequently identified themselves with another in their ego."[14] It is this aspect of narcissism that Adorno describes as "among Freud's most magnificent discoveries."[15]

Several of the analysts whom we will consider reject key assumptions of Freud's argument. Some reject the claim that primary narcissism constitutes an original objectless state and therefore reject the sharp dichotomy between narcissistic and object love proposed by Freud. Most also reject the hydraulic, amoeba model, in which more libido available for object love means less available for self-love. Indeed, there is probably no Freudian assumption that is more widely rejected, with the possible exception of the death drive. Nevertheless, many of the basic themes outlined by Freud continue to dominate contemporary discussions of narcissism. Prime among these is Freud's insight that narcissism is never overcome, but only rechanneled, because it represents an especially complete and profound mode of gratification, and man is loath to abandon a pleasure once experienced. If the ego ideal is immature (which means, in effect, not well integrated with the superego), this rechanneling will be ineffective and will lead to perversion: the quest for immediate gratification regardless of the appropriateness of the setting or the object. If the ego level is mature, on the other hand, narcissism may serve as a stimulus for the achievement of the highest ideals. For in striving to realize socially valued ideals, the ego moves closer to becoming one with its own ego ideal, thereby recapturing something of the perfection that the individual knew when he was the source and object of all the good in the world. In this formulation one sees the source of the dualism of narcissism noted by so many analysts: that it connects the most primitive and selfish desires with the highest achievements of mankind, motivating the saint as well as the sinner.

Christopher Lasch suggests that the two conceptions of narcissism in Freud's 1914 essay are not readily integrated. Narcissism as described by the amoeba model, in which libido is drawn into the self, is not the same thing as primary narcissism, which is prior to all object relations (from which libido could be withdrawn)—indeed, prior to the awareness of separate objects altogether.[16] Lasch would seem to be correct. This "blissful state of mind" in which the infant is "possessor of all perfections" seems characterized more by an oceanic dispersal of libido, than by its withdrawal. This is perhaps explained by the fact that at the stage of primary narcissism the infant has not yet differentiated itself from the world. Thus, the distinction between extension and withdrawal of libido is not pertinent. From the infant's perspective, the infant and its libido are all that exist. This point makes a difference, we shall see, in how Grunberger's theory of narcissism is interpreted. Lasch goes on to suggest that it may have been Freud's growing interest in narcissism that led him to the nirvana principle—the longing for absolute equilibrium, for the cessation of all stimulation. This is certainly the path that Marcuse follows, transforming narcissism into the nirvana principle, thereby avoiding the theoretical problems associated with seeing nirvana as the goal of the death instinct.

Though subject to various interpretations, Freud's later work certainly evinces an increasing concern with a part of the mind that seeks rather than instinctual gratification, a primordial, oceanic contentment beyond pleasure, beyond desire. One sees this especially in *Beyond the Pleasure Principle* (1920) and *Civilization and its Discontents* (1930). Lasch points out that this line of thought converges with Freud's discovery of the Minoan-Mycenean stage of psychological development, preceding the oedipal stage. At this stage the fundamental issues are not the jealousy associated with a three-way relationship, but the infant's earlier dyadic relationship with its mother. As Freud puts it in "Female Sexuality" (1931):

> Since this phase [the pre-oedipal phase in women] allows room for all the fixations and repressions from which we trace the origin of the neuroses, it would seem as though we must retract the universality of the thesis that the oedipus complex is the nucleus of the neuroses. . . . Our insight into this early, pre-oedipus, phase in girls comes to us as a surprise, like the discovery, in another field, of the Minoan-Mycenean civilization behind the civilization of Greece.[17]

It was Freud's growing interest in the earliest stages of emotional development that seems to have led him to see separation anxiety as the prototype of all other forms of anxiety.[18] But it is not decisive for our purposes whether Lasch's interpretation attributes more coherence to the development of Freud's thought on these issues than was actually the case.[19] What is important is that it is this general line of thought that characterizes so much post-Freudian work on narcissism. In general, this line runs from narcissism as a libidinal stage to narcissism as a doorway to a range of issues concerned with separation, individuation, and a search for satisfaction that lies beyond libidinal gratification.

Melanie Klein

Melanie Klein, who was a follower of Freud, began her work in 1919, when she was nearly forty. Although she stressed the continuity between her work and Freud's, others have seen her work as profoundly revisionist. Indeed, the controversy between her and Anna Freud almost split the British Psychoanalytic Society during the early and mid-forties. The Society maintained its institutional coherence only by separating into the so-called A and B schools.[20] Today Kleinian and non-Kleinian analysts generally agree that Klein's work diverged more sharply from Freud's than she was prepared to admit. Klein worked mostly with children, some as young as two and three-quarters.[21] She was among the very first to employ genuine psychoanalysis—as opposed to educative techniques—with children. Her method was to provide the child with little toys and to interpret the child's play to him or her. One result of her focus on young children was to push back the beginnings of Freud's psychosexual stages to earlier and earlier in life. For example, she came to set the beginning of the oedipus complex at about six months of age.

Perhaps her most fundamental difference with Freud lies in her assumption that the ego is present at birth.[22] This, of course, is contrary to the Freudian position that the ego is a later outgrowth of the id, concerned with mediating the demands of the id with the constraints and opportunities of the environment. The nascent ego, according to Klein, is terribly weak and unintegrated, with a propensity to fragment and disintegrate through anxiety. Indeed, fear of disintegration is perhaps the deepest human fear. In this regard, too, she disagrees with Freud, suggesting that because the infant possesses an ego, it is capable of fearing total disintegration—that is, death. Freud, on the contrary, argued that neither the infant nor the small child had any concept of death, and that the fear of death is a later outgrowth of the fear of castration.[23] But according to Klein, disintegration anxiety stems from the operation of the death drive within the infant. From the beginning of life, says Klein, the infant experiences a vast conflict between its life and death drives. Splitting, projection, and introjection are its first defense mechanisms. In order to cope with the anxiety generated by its own aggression, the ego splits that part of itself off and projects the death drive outward. The libidinal (life) drive is also split off from the ego and projected outward. Klein is unique among psychoanalysts in transforming Freud's metapsychological speculations about the death drive into a working clinical hypothesis.

The infant experiences his world in a Manichaean fashion, which Klein describes in terms of the good breast and the bad breast; the latter becomes a devouring persecutor (paranoid projection). The aim of the infantile ego is to introject and identify with the good object, while keeping the devouring persecuting bad objects at bay. It is the good breast that becomes the core of the ego, the grain of sand around which the pearl that is the ego is formed.[24] While the good object is felt to be whole and intact, the bad object is generally perceived as fragmented. Why is explained by Hanna Segal, a student of Klein's. "This is so partly because it is a part of the ego fragmented by the death instinct which is projected, and partly because the oral sadism which expresses itself in biting leads to the hated object being perceived as being bitten up into pieces."[25]

The infant's fundamental anxiety is that persecutors will destroy him and his good objects. The primary defense is a series of schizoid (splitting) mechanisms, such as exaggerating the difference between the good and the bad objects. Here Klein introduces a new psychological mechanism: projective identification, which as Segal points out, evolves from primitive projection. In projective identification it is not merely the impulse, but also parts of the baby's body, such as the mouth and the penis, as well as its bodily products, such as its urine and feces, that are in phantasy projected into the object. This is why the bad breast does not merely withhold milk, but also bites, penetrates, and soils the infant. Not only the infant's vast rage and aggression, but also those bodily parts capable of expressing aggression, are projected onto the bad breast.[26] Thus, what is involved in the paranoid-schizoid position is not only a projection of aggression outward, where it becomes the persecutor, but also splitting of the ego—a schozoid phenomenon—in which parts of the self (including the physical self, the primitive body ego) are also projected outward, in the mode of projective identification.

However terrifying—and in Klein's case studies the young child's unconscious world reads like a nightmare, filled with devouring breasts, poisonous feces, and dismembered bodies—the paranoid-schizoid position is a necessary developmental stage. It allows the infant to cope with its fears of disintegration and annihilation by projecting them outward and provides it with an entirely good object with which to identify. Obviously, however, the paranoid-schizoid position must be transcended, lest the individual remain permanently vulnerable to schizophrenia and other disorders characterized by the fragmentation of the self. To explain how the paranoid-schizoid position is transcended, Klein introduces the depressive position. The term *position* is important. It suggests not only that the events characterized by a position may be contemporaneous with those associated with other positions (as opposed to the sequence of stages), but also that the positions are never entirely given up. Thus, the depressive position comes into existence very shortly after the emergence of the paranoid-schizoid position—Klein sets the emergence of the depressive position as early as the third month of life—and alternates with it, generally in quite modulated or toned-down form, throughout life.

The depressive position commences when the infant comes to realize that the good and the bad breast are one, and that they belong to an integrated object, its mother. The result is feelings of guilt that the murderous aggression against the bad breast was in fact directed at an object that is also the source of goodness and anxiety lest the good object be harmed through the infant's own aggression. Feelings of loss are also involved, stemming from the recognition that the source of goodness is outside the infant's self, beyond its omnipotent control. The depressive position is the working through of this situation, which gives rise to the desire to make reparation to the object, to make it whole again, after having murderously destroyed it in fantasy a thousand times. While the depressive position evokes sadness and mourning, it is at the same time the path to wholeness. For in recognizing that mother, father, and others are independent whole objects, the infant begins to experience his own wholeness. Whether this is cause, effect, or both is not entirely clear from Klein's writings, but the process itself is quite clear: it is only by a splitting of the ego that the infant is able to hold the good and the bad object rigidly apart. Recognition that the object is whole, good, and bad, requires a relatively integrated ego. Although this recognition may begin as early as three months of age, it is a lifelong process, in which paranoid-schizoid and depressive elements are frequently mixed. Klein suggests, for example, that in the early stages of the depressive position the guilt experienced by the infant over its own aggression may also take the form of phantasies of persecution.[27]

If the anxiety associated with the paranoid-schizoid position is not too great, the depressive position will be entered into naturally. However, it is not only anxiety, but also envy, that constitutes a barrier to the integrative process associated with the depressive position. Indeed, Klein is the first psychoanalytic theorist to make envy—such an important experience in everyday life—a key psychoanalytic concept. For Klein, envy is an

THE PSYCHOANALYTIC THEORY OF NARCISSISM   33

oral and anal-sadistic expression of the destructive impulses and thus has a constitutional basis.[28] Klein makes a series of careful distinctions among envy, jealousy, and greed. Envy is more primitive than jealousy. Jealousy seeks to exclude another from the source of the good, its psychoanalytic paradigm being the oedipus conflict. Envy is far more destructive, for it seeks to destroy the good itself, frequently out of sheer spite: if the envious person cannot have all the good himself, if he cannot be the good itself, then no one else shall have it either. Envy thus serves a defensive function; for, if the good is destroyed, then there is no reason to feel the discomfort of envy. Greed, by contrast, aims at possessing all the goodness of the object, and any damage done to the object, or even a third party, is incidental.

Envy is damaging primarily because it empties the world of goodness. Excessive envy interferes with the primal split between the good and the bad breast. The building up of a good object becomes virtually impossible, because even the good is spoiled.[29] The individual finds himself alone in a world of persecutors, with no good objects to fall back on, around which to consolidate the ego. It is for this reason that Klein states:

> There are very pertinent psychological reasons why envy ranks among the seven 'deadly sins.' I would even suggest that it is unconsciously felt to be the greatest sin of all, because it spoils and harms the good object which is the source of life. This view is consistent with the view described by Chaucer in *The Parsons Tale*: 'It is certain that envy is the worst sin that is; for all other sins are sins only against one virtue, whereas envy is against all virtue and against all goodness.'[30]

Just as important, envy interferes with reparation, the process associated with the depressive position. Because envy recoils from good itself, it does not feel guilt and loss on account of aggressive impulses directed at the good-bad object. Envy is incompatible with the goal of restoring the object to a state of wholeness, for that would only enhance envy. By standing as a barrier to working through the depressive position, envy thus stands in the way of consolidation and integration of the ego. Indeed, excessive envy gives rise to a vicious circle: the more the good internal object is spoiled, the more impoverished the ego feels, which increases envy still further.[31] Perhaps the most ironic expression of envy occurs in what is called "negative therapeutic reaction." Sometimes, says Klein, patients are unable to accept the analyst's help precisely *because* they see the analyst as having something good to offer. It is as though the patient must remain ill in order to deny the worth of the analyst and his technique.[32]

Although Klein does not develop the point, it appears that there is a relationship between envy and narcissism.[33] Indeed, envy is frequently associated with narcissism, as in *DSM-III*.[34] Klein sees envy as rage at the recognition that the source of good is outside oneself and that one lacks control over it. Narcissism defends against this recognition, via phantasies of omnipotence and total control which in effect deny that there is any good outside oneself. At one level, narcissism serves as a defense against the unpleasant experience of envy; but at a deeper level, it may protect the individual not just against envy, but against a total loss of goodness in the world. Since envy seeks to destroy all that is good, were it successful, it would literally make life worthless. For the individual would then live in a world filled only with bad objects, a world of his own making. By supporting the phantasy that the individual is the source of all goodness and worth, narcissism can act as a defense against an enraged and envious self that would make life on earth a living hell. As we shall see, Kernberg seems to build on this insight. These considerations are supported by the striking similarity between envy and what is frequently called "narcissistic rage": a vast hatred and aggression directed toward persons and circumstances that fail to support fantasies of narcissistic omnipotence.[35]

The possibility that narcissism may serve as a defense against envy is not the only impact of Klein's work on the theory of narcissism. It has a more theoretical impact as well. Klein rejects Freud's view that narcissism constitutes an original objectless state.

The hypothesis that a stage extending over several months precedes object-relations [i.e., the stage of primary narcissism] implies that —except for the libido attached to the infant's own body— impulses, phantasies, anxieties, and defenses are not present in him, or are not related to an object, that is to say, they would operate in vacuo. The analysis of very young children has taught me that there is no instinctual urge, no anxiety situation, no mental process which does not involve, objects, external or internal; in other words, object-relations are at the centre of emotional life . . . from the beginning.[36]

As Greenberg and Mitchell point out in *Object Relations in Psychoanalytic Theory*, Klein's rejection of a state of primary narcissism is of considerably more theoretical importance than might appear at first glance.[37] Narcissism has been invoked to explain a wide variety of clinical phenomena, ranging from tics (Sandor Ferenczi) to schizophrenia (Freud), and as a key to understanding rigid resistance within the psychoanalytic setting (Karl Abraham).[38] Klein and her associates took issue with these explanations, all of which assume that narcissism reflects an original objectless state. They argued that such apparently narcissistic manifestations as tics and schizophrenia reflect, rather, an intense relationship to internal objects—namely, images and phantasies.[39] Klein thus replaces Freud's distinction between narcissistic and object libido with a distinction between internal and external object relationships. This move opened the door to the development of object relations theory, which, as we shall see, puts object seeking at the center of emotional life.

Narcissism or Schizoid Phenomenon?

Klein's reinterpretation of the relationship between narcissistic and object libido in terms of the relationship between internal and external objects allows us to see more clearly the relationship between narcissism and schizoid phenomena. Although Freud saw a connection, as noted above, he saw it almost entirely in terms of their both being characterized by a withdrawal of libido from the world.[40] Klein allows us to characterize this relationship between narcissism and schizoid phenomena more precisely. However, *relationship* may not be the most accurate term. Greenberg and Mitchell suggest that the difference between narcissism and schizoid disorder is less a matter of clinical differences than of terminological ones.[41] The term *narcissism*, they note, despite its drastic revision in recent years by analysts such as Edith Jacobson and Otto Kernberg, suggests a particular orientation of the drives. The term *schizoid*, on the other hand, refers to a splitting of the ego, a response to early and later object relationships.

> The term "narcissism" tends to be employed diagnostically by those proclaiming loyalty to the drive model (Kernberg) and mixed model theorists (Kohut), who are interested in preserving a tie to drive theory. "Schizoid" tends to be employed diagnostically by adherents of relational models (Fairbairn, Guntrip), who are interested in articulating their break with drive theory. . . . These two differing diagnoses and accompanying formulations are applied to patients who are essentially similar, by theorists who start with very different conceptual premises and ideological affiliations.[42]

Klein's work stands as a bridge between these two conceptions. By in effect reformulating libidinal issues in terms of the individual's relationship to his objects, she connects narcissism (seen classically as an orientation of the drives) to schizoid phenomena (seen by Fairbairn and Guntrip as a retreat from a world of external objects to a world of internal ones).

Recognizing the essential similarity between narcissism and schizoid phenomena helps us to connect the phenomenology of narcissism with its theory. In the symptomatology of narcissism, feelings of fragmentation, diffusion, unreality, and emptiness are central. These symptoms, difficult to explain entirely in terms of libido theory, become more readily explicable in terms of the splitting of the ego from itself (fragmentation and diffusion) and its detachment from the world of external object relations (unreality and emptiness). The latter account lends itself to theory building. Kernberg (whose allegiance to the drive model does not prevent him from drawing heavily on object relations theory), for example, goes on to characterize the turning inward associated with narcissism as a fusing of the ego (self-representation) with idealized, grandiose images of the parents, so that the self becomes defensively confused with these grandiose images. That is, narcissism is characterized in terms of a particular relationship to internal objects. In the subsequent discussion of narcissism its essential similarity with schizoid phenomena will be stressed.

Klein has been sharply criticized, especially, perhaps, by those who developed her insights into what has come to be known as object relations theory. It is frequently noted, for example, that real people often play a relatively small role in her accounts. It is not the child's actual parents, but his images and phantasies of them, that are central. The possibility that the behavior of the actual parents might vastly heighten the child's anxiety and aggression plays a surprising small role in her system. Rather, parents are screens against which a child projects his rage and love. It is also argued that Klein has no real conception of how psychic structure develops in a child. Although she presents a marvelously rich, colorful, variegated picture of a child's phantasy life, how these phantasies interact to help build psychic structure is unclear. It is often argued that these defects in Klein's system stem from her failure to recognize how thoroughly she had revised Freud's system. In particular, while she writes of drives in much the same language as Freud, she in effect redefines them. For Freud, drives are psychic representations—ideas—of bodily stimuli; they are not the bodily stimuli themselves.[43] For Klein, however, drives are not directionless, tension-producing stimuli that only secondarily become attached to objects, which serve as the vehicle of gratification. Rather, they are object-related from the start. As Greenberg and Mitchell put it, "Drives, for Klein, are relationships."[44] Libido and aggression are aimed at particular objects in particular ways —for example, the good and the bad breast—from the very beginning. It is this ambiguity in Klein's system that makes her such a useful transitional figure; for she serves as a link to Freud, even as her work leads away from drive theory, toward a focus on relationships.

Fairbairn and Guntrip

W. R. D. Fairbairn and Harry Guntrip are the purest representatives of the British object relations school. Fairbairn's work is strongly informed by the work of Klein (Fairbairn wrote in Scotland in the 1940s and 1950s, when Klein's influence there was particularly strong), and he used her language, especially that referring to internal object relations, throughout his life. Yet, he transformed her work even more thoroughly than she transformed the work of Freud. For Fairbairn, objects are no longer screens against which the individual projects his own impulses; they are real people. But Fairbairn never became a social psychologist; he remained a depth psychologist. Although Guntrip is perhaps better known than Fairbairn, his work is an elaboration of Fairbairn's, and we will focus here on Fairbairn.

Fairbairn makes explicit what is only implicit in Klein: namely, that drives, especially the libido, are object-seeking. The goal of the drives is not pleasure, but relationships. The erogenous zones are not ends in themselves, as Freud would have it, but what Fairbairn calls "signposts to the object," paths to relationships. Their satisfaction is not the goal of relationships, but the means to relationships.[45] Ernest Jones succinctly captures the difference between Freud and Fairbairn in his introduction to Fairbairn's *An Object-Relations Theory of the Personality.* "Instead of starting, as Freud did, from stimulation of the nervous system [due to drives and excitation] . . . Dr. Fairbairn starts at the centre of the personality, the ego, and depicts its strivings and difficulties in its endeavour to reach an object where it may find support."[46] To be sure, some individuals appear to seek only libidinal pleasure, and the relationship with the object of pleasure is strictly instrumental. Such a pursuit is a form of pathological compensation, however, a "means of mitigating the failure" in the pursuit of genuine relationships.[47]

Fairbairn sees the earliest months of life not as a state of self-absorbed primary narcissism, but in terms of the infant's merger with the mother, a "state of identification with the object."[48] The infant is intensely involved with others, but at the same time he is not fully differentiated from them. This is the psycho-dynamic of infancy. In a certain sense one may say that for Fairbairn, as for Freud, the beginning is also the end or, at least, sharply influences the end. In Freud's view, the individual begins life as a narcissist, detached from all object relationships, and remains a pleasure-seeking monad all his life. While the infant quickly becomes object-oriented, objects are primarily a means for satisfying drives, even though the way in which objects are employed is brought under the control of the ego and the superego. For Fairbairn, on the other hand, individuals are born into object relationships and remain in them until they die. The fundamental issues are not the vicissitudes of the drives, but independence versus dependence, separation versus fusion. The goal is mature dependence on realistically perceived external objects.

Fairbairn stresses the continuity between his view and Freud's. He maintains that his distinction between immature and mature dependence "is identical with Freud's distinction between the narcissistic and the anaclitic choice of objects."[49] This does not seem quite right, however, for it downplays the way in which Fairbairn fundamentally transforms Freudian drive theory into a theory of relationships. Nevertheless, Fairbairn's point is clear enough: immature dependence involves not only dependence on external objects, but dependence on internal objects as well. It is the dependence on internal objects that Fairbairn identifies with narcissism. Why a dependence on internal objects is pathological if carried on into later childhood and adulthood will be discussed below.

Fairbairn sees the infant as beginning life with a "unitary, dynamic ego," which possesses its own libidinal energy, and seeks relationships with real objects. Were these relationships perfect, the ego would remain whole and intact. To compensate for its frustrations in actual relationships with real external objects, however, the infant and child establish compensatory internal objects. The unitary ego is split in this process, as different portions of the ego are attached to different objects. As Guntrip, Fairbairn's foremost follower and popularizer, puts it, Fairbairn's concept of the ego is not "the superficial, adaptive ego of Freud . . . formed on the surface of a hypothetical impersonal id as its adjustment to outer reality. Fairbairn's 'ego' is the primary psychic self in its original wholeness, a whole which differentiates into organized structural patterns under the impact of object relationships after birth."[50] This view of the ego closely resembles the concept of the *self* in the work of analysts such as Kohut.

Fairbairn's structural model of the psyche stems from his assumption that the original libidinal ego follows a particular pattern as it splits into three parts (see figure 1). According to Fairbairn, the child has three different experiences of mother: mother as gratifying the child's need; mother as enticing or tantalizing the child with promises of satisfaction that are never fulfilled; and mother as depriving the child. These three aspects are internalized in such a way that they are held separate in the mind (much like Klein's good and bad breast). Furthermore, since each of them has a piece of the ego attached to it—an essential principle of Fairbairn's structural system is that ego and object are always linked, or "twinned"—this means that different aspects of the ego are held separate. Thus the ego becomes fragmented. The consequence is what one might describe as a developmentally normal—or at least unavoidable—schizoid state. Psychopathology is understood by Fairbairn primarily in quantitative terms: How fragmented is the ego? How much of the original libidinal ego is given over to internal objects? As Greenberg and Mitchell put it, for Fairbairn, "psychopathology results from this fragmentation of the ego and the devotion of the resulting portions of the ego to their internal objects at the expense of relations with real people."[51] This is why excessive devotion to internal objects is bad, for such devotion is inseparable from a fragmentation of the ego. Maturity is largely a matter of an indi-

Figure 1. *Fairbairn's System, with Guntrip's Addition*

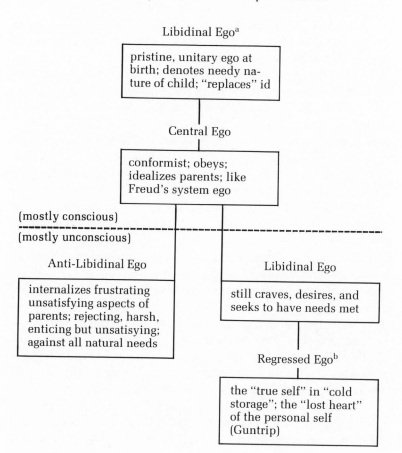

Libidinal Ego[a]

> pristine, unitary ego at birth; denotes needy nature of child; "replaces" id

Central Ego

> conformist; obeys; idealizes parents; like Freud's system ego

(mostly conscious)
- -
(mostly unconscious)

Anti-Libidinal Ego

> internalizes frustrating unsatisfying aspects of parents; rejecting, harsh, enticing but unsatisying; against all natural needs

Libidinal Ego

> still craves, desires, and seeks to have needs met

Regressed Ego[b]

> the "true self" in "cold storage"; the "lost heart" of the personal self (Guntrip)

Note: All parts of the psyche are ego. This is the pure object relations theory view.

[a]Splits under pressure of reality
[b]Guntrip's addition

vidual renouncing his attachment to the compensatory internal objects which once provided him with the security and satisfaction that he missed from his real parents but which have come to exact too great a toll on the integrity of his ego.

Fairbairn, with his focus on separation from the mother, makes the oral stage of development central. But whereas for Klein the central issues of the oral stage concern aggression and hate, for Fairbairn they concern dependence and frustrated love. The child needs parents who are responsive, fair, and reliable. If the parents do not have these qualities, the child internalizes their bad aspects in the form of internal objects, such as the enticing mother and the depriving mother. These bad objects are then repressed, along with corresponding portions of the ego. This allows the child some control over the bad aspects of the parents. In terms of long-term psychological consequences, however, the child has jumped out of the frying pan into the fire, because his parents' badness has not merely become internalized; it has become bound up with his own ego. Though this occurs in all children to some degree, much larger portions of the ego are bound up with bad internal objects in the emotionally disturbed individual. For Fairbairn, therapy becomes an even longer and more arduous process than it was for Freud, since it must promote what the individual most seeks to avoid: the release of bad internal objects. "It becomes evident, accordingly, that the psychotherapist is the true successor to the exorcist, and that he is concerned, not only with 'the forgiveness of sins,' but also with 'the casting out of devils' [i.e., bad internal objects]."[52]

Fairbairn does not make any sharp distinction between neurosis and psychosis, suggesting that schizoid phenomena—ego splitting—originating in the oral stage of infancy lie behind most neurotic, as well as psychotic, disorders. The severity of the disorder depends primarily on the degree of splitting, not on whether it occurs at all. Such a view suggests that the oedipal conflict, arising well after the oral stage, is quite secondary as a source of neurosis. Fairbairn puts it bluntly: "All psychopathological developments originate at a stage antecedent to that at which the super-ego develops and proceed from a level beneath that at which the super-ego operates."[53] We recall that, according to Freud, the oedipus conflict is the crucible of superego development, as the male child (partly in order to defend against castration anxiety) internalizes the father's authority as representative of the morality of the larger world.[54] For Fairbairn, neurosis is primarily about the conflict between dependence and independence, a conflict that becomes pathological only when attachment to compensatory internal objects is too strong.

For both Fairbairn and Guntrip, conflict over separation, particularly as it assumes the form of intense ambivalence over the desirability of maturity, is the fundamental emotional conflict.[55] At an abstract, theoretical level, this conflict can be expressed in terms of a reluctance to abandon internal compensatory objects. While Fairbairn exaggerates his continuity with Freud when he equates this reluctance with narcissism, the general idea remains valid: that what is called narcissism can usefully be seen (even if one must switch from drive to object-oriented theories to do so) as a schizoid phenomenon, characterized by emotional withdrawal to a world of internal objects and by ego splitting. Of equal importance is the recognition that narcissistic disorders have their origin prior to the oedipus conflict, even if they sometimes find an oedipal expression, because they concern disturbances not in sexual identity, but in identity per se—that is, disturbances at the very core of what it means to be an individual person, separated from others, yet bound to them in relationships. It is this aspect of narcissism—that it is concerned, ultimately, with what it means to be a self in the world—that is taken up by Kohut and Kernberg and also by Grunberger and Chasseguet-Smirgel, who return to a more Freudian concept of narcissism.

Heinz Kohut and Otto Kernberg

Kohut and Kernberg are the principal theorists of narcissism in the United States today. In a special edition of the *Journal of the*

American Psychoanalytic Association of 1974 devoted to narcissism, virtually the entire discussion focused on their work.[56] Other theorists barely figured. Indeed, not only are Kohut and Kernberg *the* theorists of narcissism, but the debate between them circumscribes the field of narcissism for most practitioners. Kernberg explicitly links his thinking to the tradition of object relations theory, particularly as it developed along roughly Kleinian lines in the work of Joan Riviere, Edith Jacobson, and Margaret Mahler,[57] that is, to a strand of object relations theory that retains strong ties with drive theory, just as Klein's work does. Kohut, a past president of the American Psychoanalytic Association, has been especially concerned with accommodating the classical Freudian tradition. However, it seems fair to say that both are fundamentally theorists of the self (Kohut calls his contribution "self psychology"), concerned with how the self is formed or deformed in interaction with others.

Kohut and Kernberg are in general agreement regarding the symptoms of pathological narcissism, and they agree that one of the remarkable things about narcissism is how grandiosity and fragile self-esteem can exist side by side in the same individual. The individual may be aware of both sets of feelings, but they are never integrated, never seen as different aspects of the same experience of self in the world. Also symptomatic of narcissism are detachment and withdrawal. The narcissist is frequently morally corruptible, lacking the rigid superego of "classical" neurotics. Feelings of emptiness and isolation, of not being real, of being an observer of one's own life, are also common. The narcissist is frequently cold and detached, using his often not inconsiderable charm for strictly instrumental purposes. He frequently functions very well in social settings, such as on the job. It is in the realm of private and personal relationships that his coldness and emptiness become apparent. In a word, the narcissist is schizoid.[58] Kohut and Kernberg also agree that narcissism stands between the psychoses and the neuroses. However, Kernberg sees it as a special version of a borderline disorder, Kohut as a somewhat less severe disturbance. In fact, it is not entirely clear how much this difference is due to their different theoretical assessments of narcissism, and how much to their different definitions of the term *borderline* (Kernberg stresses the maintenance of reality testing in borderline cases, whereas Kohut views these cases as unanalyzable veiled psychoses). Many commentators see the difference between Kohut and Kernberg as less a theoretical matter than a consequence of their different clienteles, in that Kernberg worked with a sicker group of patients.[59] However, we shall see that their disagreement on the diagnostic location of narcissism reflects more fundamental theoretical differences as well.

While Kohut and Kernberg agree that narcissism represents a fixation on a grandiose self, they disagree as to whether the grandiose self in question was once part of a normal developmental sequence that became frozen in time (Kohut), or whether it was always pathological (Kernberg). Kohut argues that the source of narcissistic personality disorder is a failure of empathy by the parents, who did not respond appropriately to the child's need for recognition, particularly the child's need for a "selfobject"—that is, recognition of his own nascent self. Selfobjects serve to shore up the self by acting as a virtual substitute self. It is the parents' ability to respond to the child as though he possessed a coherent, integrated self that teaches the child that he is such a self.

In Kohut's view, therapy is not primarily a matter of interpreting the analysand's feelings, for "it is not interpretation that cures the patient."[60] Nor does therapy have to do with the expansion of the realm of the ego. Rather, the empathy of the analyst for the analysand substitutes for the failed relationship with the parents.[61] However, this should not be understood as achieving a cure by love. Rather, empathy cures by "transmuting internalization," a process in which the analyst's recognition of the analysand's self creates psychic structure, building a self where none existed previously, by allowing the analysand to use the analyst as a selfobject.[62] In particular, Kohut encourages the analyst to respond empathically to the analysand's fantasies of grandiosity and splendor, thereby bringing these images out from deep concealment in the unconscious and allowing their integration into the superego, where they form more modulated images of success and achievement.

Kernberg accuses Kohut of helping the analysand only to temper his grandiosity. The basically pathological structure of such grandiosity is never fully confronted.[63] While there may be some truth in this accusation, we are dealing here with what is really a larger disagreement. Kohut stresses that individual development cannot be understood in terms of a move from narcissism to object love or from selfobjects to love objects. Narcissism follows an independent line of development, accompanying every strata of experience, giving experience additional meaning, as it reflects back on the self. As Kohut puts it, in normal development "we see a movement from archaic to mature narcissism, side by side and intertwined with a movement from archaic to mature object love; we do not see an abandonment of self-love and its replacement by the love for others."[64]

It is this mature narcissism that gives meaning to our successes and achievements, by relating them to some of the deepest needs of the self: to be grand, sublime, magnificent, and recognized as such by all. Unsublimated, such needs lead to great unhappiness and gross perversion—pathological narcissism at its worst. The goal of maturity is not to abandon such needs, but to integrate them realistically with one's skills and talents, on the one hand, and one's opportunities on the other. From this perspective it is quite clear that all Kohut would even *wish* to do would be to temper archaic grandiosity. Its therapeutic elimination would be tantamount to eliminating one of the deepest sources of human fulfillment.

Little influenced by Kohut, apparently, Grunberger and Chasseguet-Smirgel also address the continuity of narcissism. Like Kohut, each suggests that while untempered narcissism is the source of some of the most severe emotional disturbances, mature narcissism can be the source of the greatest human achievements, because it gives energy, meaning, and purpose to

almost every human action, by relating such action to its consequences for self-esteem.

Kernberg argues that the grandiose self which Kohut seeks
to temper is a pathological self. He supports this claim by his intriguing observation that "the coldness and aloofness of patients
with pathological narcissism . . . are in marked contrast to the
warm quality of the small child's self-centeredness."[65] By the
age of two or three years, the future pathological narcissist often
displays not only grandiosity, but also the schizoid features associated with adult pathological narcissism, which suggests that
pathological narcissism is more than just fixation at a normal developmental stage. He expresses his difference with Kohut thus:
"Pathological narcissism does not simply reflect libidinal investment in the self in contrast to libidinal investment in objects, but
libidinal investment in a pathological self-structure."[66] He characterizes the nature of this pathological self in terms of an integrated, but pathological, condensation of three aspects of the
grandiose self: (1) aspects of the real self (for example, the "spe-
cialness" of the child as reinforced by the projection of parental
narcissism onto the child; (2) the ideal self (for example, self-
images of power, wealth, and beauty that compensated the small
child for the experience of severe frustration, rage, and envy);
and (3) the ideal object (for example, the fantasy of an omnipotent and ever-giving, ever-loving mother).[67]

It is this integrated, but pathological, self that accounts for
one of the most striking features of the pathological narcissist:
his relatively high level of social functioning, despite his basically borderline personality organization. The cost of such functioning is a remarkably rigid self-structure, which is most resistant to change. This obviously does not make such individuals
particularly good candidates for analysis. Yet, like Kohut, Kernberg believes that analysis of narcissistic persons should be
undertaken whenever possible, in large measure because of the
"devastating effects of unresolved pathological narcissism
during the second half of life." Basic conflicts associated with
ageing, chronic illness, physical and mental limitations, and

above all, separation, loss, and loneliness are heightened for most individuals during the second half of life; but for the narcissist, they are specially intense, for such experiences make it more and more difficult for the grandiose self to deny the frail, limited, and transitory character of human existence.[68]

The links between Kernberg's views and those of Klein are especially suggestive, although Kernberg rarely mentions her, but rather, those associated with her, such as Riviere, Jacobson, and Mahler. The links are seen clearly in Kernberg's discussion of narcissism as a defense. Associated with Kernberg's view that the narcissistic self is pathological is his view that this self serves as a defense against even more primitive object relations, centered around rage and envy, fear and guilt because of this rage, and yet coupled with a desperate longing for a loving relationship that will not be destroyed by hate.[69] In the analysis of persons with narcissistic disorders, it becomes apparent that the analysand's apparent aloofness and lack of involvement with the analyst is a defense against "paranoid fears related to projection of sadistic trends onto the analyst (representing a primitive, hated, and sadistically perceived mother image), and against basic feelings of terrifying empty loneliness, hunger for love, and guilt over the aggression directed against the frustrating parental images."[70]

Though their views are not identical, it would not be fundamentally misleading to say that Kernberg regards narcissism as a defense against the emergence of the paranoid-schizoid position described by Klein. Such an emergence would, of course, be totally psychotic in an adult. If narcissism does indeed serve as defense against the emergence of a basically psychotic organization of the self, it seems correct to label it a borderline phenomenon. Yet, severe as the disorder is, Kernberg believes that in many cases the patient can be helped by a therapy that is also Kleinian in its basic approach. The goal is to help the patient experience his own split-off contempt, rage, and envy, in the hope that the analyst's interpretation of the negative transference (as it is called) can help reduce the patient's fear of his own destructiveness and his doubts about his own goodness.[71]

Kernberg's is widely, but hardly universally, considered to be the more acute and profound theoretical account. It has been reinforced by Kohut's rather clumsy attempts to save a place for Freudian theory via the assertion of a psychoanalytic version of the "complementarity principle"—namely, that classical Freudian drive theory is the explanation of choice in the case of neurosis, whereas "self psychology" best explains the increasingly common disturbances of the self. However, in his recent work, Kohut seems to have abandoned this salvage project, noting that in using Freudian language he was merely "attempting to make new ideas appear less radically new and more acceptable not only to my fellow analysts, but above all to myself . . . . I shared my colleagues' reluctance to face openly the fact that our theories needed a radical change."[72]

Yet, while Kohut is not as rigorous or as systematic a thinker as Kernberg, his conception of narcissism is fruitful in understanding its cultural manifestations. This is so for reasons already suggested—namely, his greater emphasis on the continuity between pathological and normal narcissism—and also because Kernberg's view of narcissism as a borderline disorder, while powerful theoretically, lacks obvious cultural implications. Many of the patients whom Kernberg describes seem so ill that any links between them and average "cultural narcissists" are hard to see. By contrast, Kohut focuses on modern art and literature and the way in which they express the fragmentation of the self characteristic of the contemporary (twentieth-century) world. In *The Restoration of the Self*, he quotes from Eugene O'Neill's *The Great God Brown*: "Man is born broken. He lives by mending. The grace of God is glue."[73] "Could the essence of the pathology of modern man's self be stated more impressively?" asks Kohut. How this view of narcissism lends itself to cultural explanation will become apparent in the next chapter, where we consider Aristophanes' account, in Plato's *Symposium*, of the great god Zeus' bisection of the human race.

Although Kernberg devotes far less attention to the social and cultural implications of his account, it would be misleading to suggest that he ignores these issues altogether. In *Borderline*

Conditions and Pathological Narcissism, he asks whether social changes, especially the increasing alienation characteristic of modern society, could contribute to narcissistic symptoms, such as a decline in the capacity to become deeply involved with others. He answers that things like changing social and sexual mores probably do not reach this deeply into the psyche, but he speculates that fundamental changes in family structure, particularly when perpetuated over several generations, probably could reach this deeply.[74] We will see in later chapters that it is precisely this change in family structure that the Frankfurt school addresses, using such provocative language as "the end of the individual" and the "obsolescence of the Freudian concept of man."

Arnold Rothstein

In *The Narcissistic Pursuit of Perfection*, Arnold Rothstein argues that both Kohut and Kernberg fail "to differentiate narcissism from ego, superego, and ego-ideal development."[75] The result is that each sees narcissism as a particular disorder, rather than as an organizing principle of mental life. Rothstein argues that Kernberg's understanding of narcissism in terms of a fused self structure—that is, a pathological condensation of real self, ideal self, and ideal object—applies to only one type of narcissist. Treating this limited understanding as a virtual definition of pathological narcissism results, according to Rothstein, in a "static conceptualization that is prone to pejorative elaboration."[76] Kohut's view of narcissism, albeit broader, as we have seen, comes in for the same criticism. Kohut regards a narcissistic *behavior* disorder as more serious than a narcissistic *personality* disorder because the former is likely to give rise to sadistic behavior, rather than just fantasy. In fact, says Rothstein, a judgment of relative health can be made only from an assessment of the subject's integration of his defensive activity, which does not necessarily correspond to the distinction between behavior and fantasy. It is frequently the sickest narcissists, particularly those

with strong schizoid characteristics, who confine their narcissistic pursuits to fantasy.[77]

At issue here are not particular claims made by Kernberg
and Kohut, which are mentioned only as examples, but rather,
the tendency of Kohut (particularly in his earlier work) and of
Kernberg to an even greater degree to transform narcissism into a
unique pathology requiring special methods, theories, and assumptions. But some of their claims regarding narcissism fail
to correspond to more general, widely held psychoanalytic insights. Rothstein's alternative, "investment" account avoids this
extreme specialization. Rothstein defines narcissism both more
narrowly and more broadly than either Kohut or Kernberg, as the
illusion of perfection, which protects the ego from fully recognizing its own finite limits and hence its lack of mastery over self
and world.[78] Narrow in one respect, this definition is broad
enough that it can be applied to normal, neurotic, borderline,
and psychotic expressions of narcissism. From this perspective,
narcissism is not itself a disorder; even entirely normal people
will protect themselves by narcissistic illusions. Disorder concerns the way in which narcissistic illusions are integrated with
the rest of the psyche, what Rothstein calls the "mode of narcissistic investment."

The analyzable (that is, neurotic) narcissistic patient, says
Rothstein, has an image of himself, often unconscious, as perfect
and vastly admired in some way. In the course of analysis, he
will come to mourn the loss of both the illusionary aspect of the
self-representation and the admiring object. More seriously disturbed analysands, on the other hand (generally borderline and
psychotic), will not be able to relinquish and, consequently,
mourn the loss of their narcissistic defenses. Narcissistic investment in an idealized self-image is required to preserve the very
coherence of the self.[79] To illustrate how one might determine
the mode of narcissistic investment, Rothstein asks whether the
"subject's ego has developed the degree of differentiation associated with well-integrated ego-ideal and superego structuraliza-
tions" such that it can invest its narcissism in abstract ideas,

rather than in concrete images of self and object?[80] It is from this perspective that Chasseguet-Smirgel approaches the ego ideal.

Rothstein's perspective has two advantages, the second more significant than the first. First, it suggests an underlying continuity between the accounts of Kohut (narcissism as fixation at a normal developmental stage) and Kernberg (narcissism as fixation at a pathological expression of a normal developmental stage). If we assume, as many do, that their disagreement reflects their different clienteles, then the *theoretical* difference between them may be interpreted as a difference in the mode of narcissistic investment. To characterize narcissism, as Kernberg does, as the pathological condensation of real self, ideal self, and ideal object is perhaps not so much to offer a new theory of narcissism as to describe its expression in patients previously thought to be nonanalyzable, patients whose inner world is distinguished by abridged, concrete images of self and object. These patients must invest their narcissism in these images, because there is nowhere else for it to go.

This does not mean that the substantial differences between Kohut and Kernberg disappear altogether. It is rather to suggest that different modes of narcissistic investment, associated with different degrees of coherence of the self (normal, neurotic, borderline, or psychotic), are readily confused with different theoretical entities, especially if we lack hard information about client mix. Within the discipline of psychoanalysis, as in most other disciplines, most of the rewards go to those who originate new theories, rather than to those who integrate old ones. It is possible that the proliferation and divergence of theories of narcissism belie the actual theoretical differences involved. This suspicion is supported, though of course not corroborated, by the very substantial agreement between Kohut and Kernberg over the symptoms of narcissism.

The second, greater advantage of Rothstein's perspective is the implication that it is probably not very fruitful to conceptualize narcissism as a unique disorder requiring a new psychoanalytic theory or as a disorder along the lines of compulsive hand washing, hysteria, or phobia. In fact, narcissism is not a disorder at all per se, although it may become one if it is invested by a neurotic, borderline, or psychotic ego as a defense, in which case it takes on the status of the disorder in whose service it is employed. Narcissism is more akin to a stage of development, albeit a stage that is never superseded. Like every stage of development, narcissism can be seen as posing a set of problems that the individual must confront. These problems vary according to the actual level of development. At every level, however, there remains one constant. Narcissism is concerned with how the individual integrates his libidinal needs with the needs of the self for wholeness and self-respect. It is from this perspective that both Grunberger and Chasseguet-Smirgal approach narcissism, thereby transforming it from a disorder into a question about the meaning and purpose of human life.

Grunberger and Chasseguet-Smirgel

Béla Grunberger and Janine Chasseguet-Smirgel are contemporary French psychoanalysts. Lasch turns to them frequently, and with good reason; for although they themselves do not stress the cultural aspects of narcissism, their formulations are especially well suited to explaining its cultural expression. In part this is because they stress the ubiquity of narcissism: that it is expressed in almost every aspect of human experience. Both stand closer to Freud than the other theorists we have been examining. Neither draws explicitly on object relations theory, although an object relations perspective on their work, especially on Chasseguet-Smirgel's concept of the ego ideal, can be most fruitful. For each, narcissism functions as what one might call a drive theory version of the self, a concept more usually addressed from the perspective of object relations theory. Although Grunberger argues that his scheme can be interpreted in Kleinian terms, the links are abstract.[81] It seems best to approach his scheme, as well as that of Chasseguet-Smirgel, as a modification of classical Freudian theory, since this is how they understand their own work. Whereas Kohut and Kernberg are best under-stood in terms of the dispute between them, Grunberger and Chasseguet-Smirgel are best approached as complementary to one another. In particular, Chasseguet-Smirgel's use of Freud's concept of the ego ideal completes Grunberger's speculations on narcissism by more thoroughly characterizing its puzzling dual-ity: that narcissism at once seeks fusion and autonomy.

Grunberger

Grunberger views narcissism as having the attributes of a psychic agency (such as the ego, the superego, or the id), as well as of an instinct. Like an instinct, it is present at birth (Grun-berger is operating from a Freudian perspective; for many object relations theorists the ego is itself present at birth). But like a psychic agency, it has a life of its own, pursuing its own inde-pendence line of development—for example, it may support the ego or attack it (as in depression). For Grunberger, the key fea-ture of narcissism is its dualism. In this, he follows closely Lou Andreas-Salomé's "The Dual Orientation of Narcissism," which seeks to explain the contradictory character of narcissism: that it seeks individuality at all costs and yet cannot live apart from a state of continuing fusion with another.[82] Other key features of narcissism, according to Grunberger, are:

1. The memory of a unique and privileged state of elation, which Grunberger associates with the experience of the infant shortly before and after birth
2. A sense of well-being associated with this memory, accompa-nied by a sense of wholeness and omnipotence
3. A sense of pride stemming from this experience and also from the illusion of uniqueness
4. A lifelong desire to recapture this paradise lost[83]

Grunberger's phenomenology of narcissism recalls Freud's brief discussion in *Civilization and its Discontents* of that oce-anic feeling that might be the foundation of religion: "a sensation of 'eternity,' a feeling as of something limitless, unbounded—as

it were, 'oceanic.' " Grunberger would perhaps agree. "The superego is the Bible," Grunberger says, "but narcissism is God Al-
mighty."[84] Like Kohut, he emphasizes the degree to which narcissism operates as an independent principle throughout life.
Once more he turns to Andreas-Salomé, who states that "narcissism accompanies all the strata of our experience, independently of them. In other words, it is not only an immature stage
of life needing to be superseded, but also the ever renewing companion of all life."[85] The goal of maturity is not the abandonment of narcissism for object love, as Freud maintained, but the
integration of narcissism with the various stages of psychosexual
development. Grunberger nevertheless agrees with Freud that
narcissism represents an original objectless state.[86] Indeed, for
Grunberger, the paradigm of narcissism is the womb, in which
the fetus is coincident with eternity, knowing nothing outside itself. Is there any way to make this view compatible with object
relations theory's insight that no objectless states exist? Margaret
Mahler's "On Human Symbiosis and the Vicissitudes of Individuation" provides a clue. Mahler defines narcissism as the
cathexis of a still merged image of self and object. The libidinal
cathexis of the self—Freud's definition of narcissism—is at the
same time the libidinal cathexis of an object; or rather, the original narcissistic cathexis precedes the distinction between self
and object. At the stage of primary narcissism the boundaries between self and object are indistinct.[87] Hence the self's feelings
of grandiosity and wholeness are inseparable from the grandiosity and wholeness of the object. More precisely, the self's feelings of grandiosity and wholeness are inseparable from these
feelings as they derive from an experience of merger with another who is perceived to be grand and whole. This helps to explain that key feature of narcissism: that it confuses autonomy
and dependence. This confusion stems from the unconscious
recollection of a narcissistic state in which the other's power is
an extension of one's own to such an extent that one's dependence on it is not recognized: a contradictory state of total freedom and total dependence.

Grunberger takes pains to stress that he does not see primary narcissism in terms of fusion with the mother. "The primal narcissistic state, to my way of thinking, is not the narcissistic child-mother fusion, which in a way tends to be maintained for a while after birth, but the fusion of the child with *his* world, which for him is *the* world."[88] However, his distinction may be more subtle than is warranted, given the diffuse ego of the infant. Why should we not assume that for the infant the mother *is* the world? The distinction between the infant's fusion with the mother and its fusion with his world is then superfluous. It seems reasonable to conclude that the phenomenology of narcissism that Grunberger develops can be interpreted in terms of the fusion of a diffuse ego with a not fully differentiated object, even if Grunberger does not quite see it this way. Mahler has written of the infant's symbiosis with its mother in a way that clearly reveals the continuity between her conception of narcissism and Grunberger's: "One could regard the entire life cycle as . . . an eternal longing for the actual or fantasied 'ideal stage of self,' with the latter standing for a symbiotic fusion with the 'all good' symbiotic mother, who was at one time part of the self in a blissful state of well-being."[89]

For Grunberger, emotional development is about the integration of narcissism with the drives and later with the ego and the superego. In the beginning the drives are incompatible with narcissism. As Freud states in a footnote to "Instincts and their Vicissitudes," the disturbance of the primary narcissistic state is linked with the infant's incapacity to help himself.[90] The demands of the drives challenge the narcissistic principle that the infant is omnipotent, without need of anything outside himself. As Grunberger puts it, the infant is an outcast in two worlds: he is unable to satisfy his instinctual urges in a satisfactory manner, and he is unable to achieve narcissistic satisfaction. The result is a humiliating sense of powerlessness, which is frequently referred to as "the narcissistic wound," or "the narcissistic injury." A quotation from Kafka serves as an epigram for Grunberger's discussion of this theme:

A fine wound is all I brought into the world; that was my sole endowment.[91]

What will ultimately compensate for this injury to some extent is a sense of "object mastery": the ability to control one's environment and oneself. The goal of mastery is narcissistic wholeness, the synthesis of instinct and narcissism. What narcissistic wholeness looks like depends in large measure on the stage of psychosexual development. At the oral stage the instinctual gratification of feeding is accompanied by megalomaniacal narcissistic gratification: "I was satisfied, for I am the universe." (Obviously, says Grunberger, such an experience is virtually ineffable; words are but a crude approximation.) At the anal stage the megalomania is far more tempered. Narcissistic satisfaction typically derives from the satisfaction of having a fit body that functions well and is under the control of individual (for example, bladder and bowel control), which enhances one's sense of self-worth.[92] The goal of mature narcissism is to bring this interaction of instinct and narcissism under the reign of the ego and the superego—for example, by fulfilling one's needs in a socially acceptable manner. It is the ability to do this that helps overcome the humiliation of narcissistic injury. As Marion Oliner puts it, "The role of the narcissistic factor within psychosexual development rests on its bestowing a sense of worth on strivings that have their foundation in biology."[93] Conversely, a neurotic, according to Grunberger, is one "who has failed to recover his lost narcissistic integrity in the different opportunities that arise at the various levels of his *instinctual development*."[94] Indeed, Grunberger interprets melancholy and even suicide as attacks on the ego by the narcissistic agency for not getting enough pleasure.[95]

Grunberger reinterprets the problem which Freud confronts in *Civilization and its Discontents* in a most intriguing way. Freud argues that civilization is painful because it requires far more instinctual renunciation than is ever compensated for by the creation of more secure, regular channels of satisfaction.[96] Grunberger notes that Freud ignores the narcissistic factor: "In my view, there is no doubt that the instinctual sacrifices that man must make to become civilized are painful in large part because they have the nature of narcissistic injury, which is compensated for in only very small measure by the cathexis of civilization as a value in itself."[97] This perspective is illuminating because it suggests that the cost of civilization is not the lessening of gratification per se, but the fact that the loss of gratification is coupled with narcissistic humiliation, rather than compensated for by mastery. This consideration will be central to our discussion of Marcuse's *Eros and Civilization*, for part of the reason why Marcuse is driven to such utopian extremes as to posit a society without labor is that the only alternatives he sees are instinctual satisfaction or its repression. The possibility that in a properly organized society the narcissistic gratification available in meaningful labor might be profound allows us to revise Marcuse's ideal without trivializing it. Similarly, Grunberger suggests that the knowledge that one can fulfill a need is often more important than actually doing so. This knowledge by itself gratifies one's narcissism, by communicating that one is worthy of satisfaction and capable of achieving it. Grunberger's insight allows a reinterpretation of Marcuse's concept of nonrepressive sublimation, which is the psychological basis of his utopia. It also explains why Plato's theory of sublimation is in some respects superior to Freud's (as we shall see in the next chapter).

Like virtually all theorists of narcissism, Grunberger sees the oedipal conflict as secondary, though by no means unimportant. He writes of it as a "displacement of the subject's narcissistic wound to his conflict with father."[98] What he means by this is revealed by his argument that the incest taboo protects the child from its own inadequacy, the recognition of which would only intensify narcissistic injury. Because the young child does not wish to face the humiliating fact that he is too immature to be an adequate sexual partner for his mother, he feels guilt at his own desires as a defense. It is as if he were saying to himself, "I am not able; therefore I should not (lest the fact of my inability overwhelm me with shame and fright)."

Grunberger concludes that a pathological narcissist is not one who becomes enmeshed in the oedipal conflict, but one who avoids it. The narcissist "shrinks from Oedipus and identification because of the visceral connotation of the process, which he sees as a penetration of his boundaries."[99] It is this retreat that is the real threat to maturity. Frequently it takes the form of the adolescent narcissist (and Grunberger suggests that all adolescents are pathological narcissists to some degree) refusing to identify with the adult world and becoming "fixated at the level of counteridentification." It is not a question of taking the father's place but of acting as if the father had never existed. By refusing all identification with the adult world, the adolescent becomes not a unique individual, but simply a carbon copy of his peers. Though to some degree a normal developmental process, this refusal of identification is exacerbated by a society that increasingly isolates its children and its adolescents from the adult world.[100] It is this theme that Lasch develops in *The Culture of Narcissism*. In the next chapter of this book, I will develop a related theme. Alcibiades' failure to internalize the lessons taught him by Socrates will be explained in terms of his narcissistic fixation at the level of counteridentification. Indeed, it will be suggested that this fixation characterized much of Athenian society.

Chasseguet-Smirgel

Chasseguet-Smirgel's concept of the ego ideal elaborates Grunberger's analysis. The ego ideal is Freud's concept. First introduced by name in "On Narcissism" (1914), it quickly became absorbed into the superego, so that by "Group Psychology and the Analysis of the Ego" (1921), Freud seems to be equating the ego ideal with the superego.[101] In "On Narcissism," however, Freud treats the ego ideal as a unique entity that inherits and carries forward the individual's primary narcissism. About the ego ideal, he says:

> As always where the libido is concerned, here again man has
> shown himself incapable of giving up a gratification he has once

enjoyed. He is not willing to forgo his narcissistic perfection in his childhood. . . . He seeks to recover the early perfection, thus wrested from him, in the form of an ego-ideal. That which he projects ahead of him as his ideal is merely his substitute for the lost narcissism of his childhood—the time when he was his own ideal.[102]

As the avatar of primary narcissism, the ego ideal is projected before the individual as a hope or a promise: that one day he may recover something of the perfection and wholeness he once experienced. Indeed, Chasseguet-Smirgel sees all life as about man's attempt to redeem this promise by realizing a reconciliation between the ego and the ego ideal. This reconciliation may take two forms: one progressive, one regressive. Progressive reconciliation involves the hope that through postponement and hard work one may eventually achieve a level of mastery over self and world that approximates what the ego ideal desires— namely, the wholeness and perfection associated with the state of primary narcissism. Chasseguet-Smirgel expressly notes the similarity between her concept of progressive reconciliation with the ego ideal and Grunberger's concept of object mastery, which acts in a similar fashion to help heal the narcissistic wound.[103] In progressive reconciliation the ego ideal becomes closely allied with the superego. Regressive reconciliation, on the other hand, seeks immediate, complete reconciliation, often via attempts at fusion with powers greater than the self.

Chasseguet-Smirgel, like Grunberger, stays close to Freudian drive theory. Yet, an interesting interpretation that would make her work more compatible with object relations theory suggests itself. Fairbairn notes that Freud's superego is an internal object, with which the individual has an internal object relationship.[104] Chasseguet-Smirgel's discussion of the ego ideal, including its relationship to the superego, suggests that one may also regard the ego ideal as an internal object. However, whereas Fairbairn would see maturity in terms of the gradual abandonment of an internal object relationship with the ego ideal, Chasseguet-Smirgel sees it as involving a change in both the content of the ego ideal and the relationship of the ego ideal to other internal objects. The ego ideal would gradually be drawn under the sway of the superego, so that *how* one achieves reunification with the ego ideal would become part of the ideal itself. Although Chasseguet-Smirgel does not seem interested in reconciling her account with that of object relations theory, the preceding considerations suggest that it would not be impossible to do so.

Like Grunberger—indeed, like virtually all theorists of narcissism—Chasseguet-Smirgel reinterprets the oedipus conflict. For her too, it becomes secondary, but not unimportant. She makes the simple, but powerful, point that there is no oedipal instinct, only a sexual instinct. It is therefore not obvious or given that the child's sexual instinct will become exclusively and intensively directed toward the mother. It happens, she says, because the child's oedipal wishes are carried along by the search for his lost omnipotence. The child directs his sexuality almost exclusively toward the mother because sexuality is a vehicle and a symbolic expression (and in this sense akin to what Fairbairn calls "signposts to the object"—that is, a means to an object relationship) of the narcissistic quest for re-fusion with what can make him whole. Chasseguet-Smirgel writes: "I do not wish to minimize here the role of sexuality in oedpial wishes. I simply want to underline that . . . the wish to penetrate one's mother also includes that of rediscovering the boundless and the absolute, the perfection of an ego whose wound, left gaping by the tearing out of its narcissism, finds itself healed at last."[105] Although she is not explicit on this point, it appears that her concept of the primary narcissistic state comes closer to that of Margaret Mahler than that of Grunberger. Thus, it is an expression of fusion with mother *qua* mother, not *qua* world.

Chasseguet-Smirgel uses the oedipal conflict, thus reinterpreted, to explain the development of the ego ideal. The ego ideal implies the idea of a project, a hope, and a guide. But project, hope, and guide imply postponement and delay, which are characteristic of a mental state under the rule of the reality principle. The hope is that in growing up one can gain some recompense for the lost perfection of the state of primary narcissism. What at first gives this project its energy is an illusion: that in growing up to be like father one will come to deserve his privileges, including sexual access to the mother. The oedipal conflict and narcissism are here tightly intertwined. But in the course of growing up, the illusion is transformed. This transformation involves recognizing that it is reconciliation with one's own ego ideal, not re-fusion with the mother, that constitutes the best, most acceptable, and most realistic hope of narcissistic fulfillment. (At the unconscious level it appears that re-fusion with the mother may remain the "best" hope; at the conscious level, however, the reality principle holds sway, and what is most realistic comes to be equated with what is best.) Mature reconciliation with the ego ideal takes the form of object mastery, the ability to exert substantial control over oneself and one's environment and in so doing become worthy of being one's own ideal, by becoming capable of providing for one's own instinctual and cultural needs. It is object mastery that heals, or at least soothes, the narcissistic wound.

Chasseguet-Smirgel writes of the mature ego ideal as embodying "all the pregenital ego ideals in the same way, so to speak, as Hegel writes of 'going beyond yet preserving' (aufheben)." It is, she says, "no doubt inaccurate to say that the ego ideal becomes less demanding. The goal pursued is still equally grandiose (that is to say incest), but the subject is no longer bound by the law of all or nothing, by the necessity for immediate and total gratification."[106] This is important, for it suggests that while the ego ideal may be brought under the reign of the superego, it remains demanding and not easily satisfied. At some level it still wants it all, even if the ego is willing to accept less. In chapter 5 I will suggest that the ego ideal may be substituted for Marcuse's conception of eros, which wants complete and total gratification and wants it now. One frequent objection to suggestions like this is that they have reformist implications, in that they reveal a willingness to compromise with repression and unhappiness. It is apparent, however, that the ego ideal makes demands all its own, demands that are at least as uncompromising as those made by eros (to which the ego ideal is tightly bound in any case). Chasseguet-Smirgel may have had the demands made by revolutionary political traditions in mind as an analogy when she wrote that "in general it would seem that even a well-established superego is not sufficient to provide man with the food he requires for his narcissism. . . . Man needs both bread and roses. The ego ideal can live in friendship with the superego when it has itself acquired the maturative quality that I have spoken about and effected a certain number of instinctual integrations."[107]

The threat to maturity takes the form of the temptation to take shortcuts to reconciliation between ego and ideal, to seek immediate reconciliation via regressive modes of satisfaction. The "pervert's mother," says Chasseguet-Smirgel, plays temptress when she leads the child to believe that he has no need either to grow up or to identify with his father in order to be her perfect partner. This allows the child's ego ideal to become fixated at a level at which archaic ideals of fusion and oedipal victory predominate. One sees analogs of the pervert's mother in certain ideological groups. Chasseguet-Smirgel interprets Hitler, for example, not as a father figure, but as like the pervert's mother, the promoter of an illusion, because he activated the primitive wish for instant fusion of ego and ideal. "As far as Nazism is concerned, the return to nature, to ancient Germanic mythology represents an aspiration to fusion with the omnipotent mother."[108] This observation is enriched by Kohut's claim that groups may also succumb to narcissistic rage, particularly against those who seem—or have been made to seem—to stand in the way of the fulfillment of narcissistic illusion.[109] Nor did it escape the notice of Adorno, though he did not make the argument in quite this form, in "Freudian Theory and the Pattern of Fascist Propaganda," that the appeal to regressive narcissism constituted a key element in the success of national socialism.

Although there are obviously vast, profound, and far-reaching differences between national socialism and the contemporary culture of narcissism, they nevertheless share this tendency to appeal to the regressive moment of narcissism. Indeed, one might define the culture of narcissism as simply the cultural analog of the pervert's mother. For like the pervert's mother, the culture of narcissism suggests that there is no need to work hard and postpone gratification in order to become worthy of one's ego ideal. One can have it all right now. One can see this aspect of the culture of narcissism particularly clearly in the way that it at once encourages dependence and the demand for immediate gratification. As Lasch puts it:

> Since modern society prolongs the experience of dependence into adult life, it encourages milder forms of narcissism in people who might otherwise come to terms with the inescapable limits on their personal freedom and power—limits inherent in the human condition—by developing competence as workers and parents. But at the same time that our society makes it more and more difficult to find satisfaction in love and work, it surrounds the individual with manufactured fantasies of total gratification. The new paternalism preaches not self-denial but self-fulfillment. It sides with narcissistic impulses and discourages their modification by the pleasure of becoming self-reliant, even in a limited domain, which under favorable conditions accompanies maturity.[110]

One sees the quest for a shortcut to reconciliation in surprising places, including the experience of scientific and technological progress, according to Chasseguet-Smirgel. Scientific progress demands extensive, sophisticated methods of reality testing, an expression of secondary process (conscious) thinking under the rule of the reality principle. However, at a primary process (unconscious) level, scientific progress is frequently experienced as magic.[111] This is especially true, perhaps, for the lay public, who are presented with the results of science by the media in gee-whiz fashion, utterly divorced from any discussion of the scientific method—that is, the reality testing—that made them possible. The outcome is that scientific and technological progress encourages the illusion that anything is possible, including immediate, effortless reconciliation of ego and ego ideal. It is not necessary to control our needs and desires, to practice self-restraint, to grow up. Science and technology can do it for us, by providing all we ever wanted right now. We shall see later that neither Adorno nor Marcuse is entirely immune to this illusion, though each succumbs in a different way. It should also be apparent how this illusion supports the culture of narcissism.

A Theory of Narcissism

Although a number of thematic continuities among the preceding accounts of narcissism are apparent, there are discontinuities as well. The primary discontinuity does not stem from disagreement over narcissism per se, but concerns the framework within which it should be studied: whether of drive theory or object relations theory. As Greenberg and Mitchell point out, these perspectives are ultimately incommensurable. Object relations theory argues that it is relationships with other people that build psychic structure, and that it is from these that people retreat in mental illness. Drive theory, on the other hand, sees pleasure seeking and aggression as central, the relationship of drives to objects being secondary. The goal of psychic development is then an accommodation between the internal demands of the drives and the external demands of reality, an accommodation made especially difficult by the intensity of anxiety and guilt associated with early experiences of drives.[112] The incommensurability between the two theories is particularly manifest in the theory of narcissism; for drive theory sees narcissism as an original objectless state, whereas object relations theory argues that no such state exists and sees narcissism in terms of an intense attachment to internal objects.

Yet, in seeking to understand the experience and manifestations of narcissism, both accounts are useful. Indeed, they can often be fruitfully combined, as Kernberg demonstrates so well. Ultimately, the goal is neither theoretical consistency nor elegance, but an explanation of the data, in this case, the narcissistic themes in the philosophies of Socrates and the Frankfurt school. For this, it is necessary to draw on and combine several different traditions. The theoretical purists may decry such eclecticism, but my present task will have been accomplished if I can identify common themes in the various theories of narcissism and show how these are manifested in the philosophies of Socrates and the Frankfurt school.

There is, of course, no theory of narcissism as such, but only theories or partial accounts. The term *theory* is used here in an almost rhetorical sense: to emphasize the thematic continuities among the diverse accounts, for it is these continuities that constitute the theory, so-called.

Not surprisingly, Freud's "On Narcissism" is the basis of almost all subsequent discussions of the topic. The alternatives of narcissistic and object love are established by Freud. He also recognizes the similarity between narcissism and severe emotional disorders in which interest is withdrawn from the external object world altogether. An object relations theorist would add that this does not mean that the individual has withdrawn from all objects, only that he has traded external for internal objects. Nevertheless, Fairbairn states that his distinction beween immature and mature dependence "is identical with Freud's distinction between the narcissistic and the anaclitic choice of objects" (see above, p. 39). Freud also establishes that narcissism is not a perversion, but a normal phase in sexual development, the "libidinal complement to the egoism of the instinct of self-preservation." Though we have seen that theorists such as Grunberger challenge Freud's particular formulation of this assumption (stressing instead narcissism's separate line of development), Freud's remains a key assumption because it establishes the continuity of narcissism throughout life. This continuity is reinforced by his observation that the ego ideal inherits the memory of narcissistic perfection, a memory that is powerful because it recalls perhaps the greatest pleasure of all, the experience of narcissistic wholeness. We have seen what a fruitful concept the ego ideal is, for it explains the connection between immature and mature narcissism. In both, fusion with an ego ideal is involved, but in mature narcissism the ideal is tempered by its integration with the superego. In this respect even Freud's later, somewhat casual equation of ego ideal and superego is fruitful, insofar as it suggests their extremely close connection.

Melanie Klein, who laid the foundations of object relations theory, developed the theoretical basis for the assumption that narcissism—understood as a retreat into fantasies of utter self-sufficiency—serves as a defense against a vast envy and rage, which threaten to destroy the good as well as the bad. With Klein we have the first mapping of the Minoan-Mycenean level of psychic development—the early oral stage—that Freud unearthed but did not develop. This is important because pathological narcissism is a disorder of this stage, at which the earliest relationships are established and the earliest conflicts over separation and individuation played out.

Fairbairn and Guntrip represent the purest expression of object relations theory, which is characterized by the insight that real relationships with real people build psychic structure. Although they rarely mention narcissism, they see a schizoid split in the self as characteristic of virtually all emotional disorder. It is Greenberg and Mitchell, in *Object Relations in Psychoanalytic Theory*, who establish the relevance of Fairbairn and Guntrip to our concerns, by pointing out that what American analysts label "narcissism," British analysts tend to call "schizoid personality disorder." This insight allows us to connect the symptomatology of narcissism—feelings of emptiness, unreality, alienation, and emotional withdrawal—with a theory that sees such symptoms as an accurate reflection of the experience of being split off from a part of oneself. That narcissism is such a confusing category is in large part because its drive-theoretic definition, the libidinal cathexis of the self—in a word, self-love—seems far removed from the experience of narcissism, as characterized by a loss of, or split in, the self. Fairbairn's and Guntrip's view of narcissism as an excessive attachment of the ego to internal objects (roughly analogous to Freud's narcissistic, as opposed to object, love), resulting in various splits in the ego necessary to maintain these attachments, allows us to penetrate this confusion.

Kohut and Kernberg develop the insight that pathological narcissism is a disorder involving the enfeeblement and fragmentation of the self. Kohut provides the valuable perspective that narcissism represents a separate developmental principle, not destined to be superseded by object love, but rather to accompany it. Though he does not quote Andreas-Salomé on this point, he could have done so. Narcissism, says Andreas-Salomé, "accompanies all the strata of our experience, independently of them. In other words, it is not only an immature stage of life needing to be superseded, but also the ever-renewing companion of all life."[113] *This is the first of four key themes regarding narcissism that will appear again and again in our analysis: that narcissism persists throughout life and is not superseded by object love, but follows its own developmental line.*

At first sight, Grunberger's work might seem difficult to integrate into this chapter's account of narcissism, because Grunberger appears to hold to Freud's formulation of narcissism as a pure objectless state. But by recalling Margaret Mahler's insight that for an infant still merged with its mother the libidinal cathexis of the infantile self will simultaneously involve the libidinal cathexis of an object (mother), Grunberger's work can be rendered compatible with object relations theory. It is the source of two key insights: first, *that narcissism may be progressive or regressive, mature or immature, and that it can support humanity's greatest achievements or its most regressive follies. A related aspect of this duality is that because primary narcissism does not fully distinguish self from other, it confounds opposites, such as freedom and dependence. This is the second key theme regarding narcissism, one that will also appear again and again in our subsequent discussions.* Sometimes this duality will be referred to as the bridge-like character of narcissism, in order to emphasize how narcissism connects the base with the sublime.

Grunberger also develops the insight that *narcissistic injury stems from the infant's recognition of his own helplessness. Much of human life can be explained as an attempt by individu-*

als to achieve a level of mastery and control over self and world sufficient to compensate for their lost omnipotence. This is the third key theme regarding narcissism: that object mastery helps heal narcissistic injury. Also important is Grunberger's suggestion that his understanding of narcissism as a psychic agency is but another way (more compatible with drive theory) of talking about the self. This links Grunberger's formulations with those of Fairbairn, Guntrip, Kohut, and Kernberg.

Chasseguet-Smirgel's focus on the ego ideal as avatar of primary narcissism is valuable because it gives us a more precise way of talking about object mastery. The ego ideal also clarifies the relationship between mature and immature narcissism. Further, it allows us to understand better *the fourth key theme that characterizes narcissism: that narcissism seeks fusion and wholeness by merging with something complete and perfect— namely the ego ideal.* It is the content of this ideal (especially whether it is integrated with the superego), as well as the path taken to reach it (especially whether this path passes through object mastery), that determines whether the quest for fusion, wholeness, and perfection is progressive or regressive. The concept of the ego ideal thus helps us to distinguish mastery from what Theodor Adorno calls "wild self-assertion" (*verwilderte Selbstbehauptung*).

These four key themes all emphasize the continuity between normal and pathological narcissism. There are also themes common to most of these accounts concerning the strictly pathological dimension of narcissism. Prime among these is that narcissism is a disorder of the self, stemming from difficulties with separation and individuation. Indeed, most theorists (not just those, such as Kernberg, who are strongly influenced by Klein) seem to see narcissism as a defense, a way to deny that the self needs the constant recognition of others in order to feel real and whole. Conversely, narcissistic rage, so closely associated with Klein's concept of envy, can be seen as aggression directed against those who fail to support the individual's fantasies of omnipotence and total control. Directed at those who fail to mirror perfectly the narcissist's every need, narcissistic rage is intense because it is a response to a perceived threat to the core of the self, and the very survival of the self is at stake. Thus, narcissism is concerned with pre-oedipal issues concerning fundamental distinctions between self and other. Klein's description of this stage in terms of the paranoid-schizoid position, characterized by primitive defense mechanisms such as splitting and projection or introjection, accurately captures the primitive quality of narcissistic personality disorder.

Although pathological narcissism sounds so sick, mature, healthy narcissism shares many of the same characteristics: continuity, duality, mastery, and fusion. This is explained by a presumption, sometimes tacit, shared by almost all theorists of narcissism that there is a continuum between pathological and normal narcissism, and that even the most extreme manifestations of pathological narcissism are not entirely alien to normal narcissists. Just as Freud assumed that the study of neurosis could illuminate the psychic life of normal men and women, so pathological narcissism illuminates normal narcissism. This is so even for Kernberg. Because he assumes that pathological narcissism represents a fixation on a pathological self-structure does not mean that he sees no continuity between normal and pathological narcissism. Quite the contrary, he tells us.[114] To be sure, it gets complicated, because some theorists, especially Kohut and Kernberg, posit a category of what might be called "pseudo-narcissism," in which an apparently pathological narcissism defends against less severe disorders, generally oedipally based neurosis. But in general, it is fair to say that all the theorists we have examined, including Freud, view the distinction between pathological and normal narcissism on a continuum. Therefore it can be enlightening to focus on even quite pathological aspects in order to explain the appearance of normal—and not always normal—narcissism in the culture and in philosophy. Rothstein's "mode of investment" account serves as a metapsychological justification of this assumption of continuity.

THE PSYCHOANALYTIC THEORY OF NARCISSISM   71

The phrase "theory of narcissism" will be employed frequently in subsequent chapters. Unless qualified, it refers to the key themes summarized here. The less frequently employed phrase, "the psychoanalytic theory associated with the theory of narcissism," unless qualified, refers to the insight shared by many of the psychoanalysts considered in this chapter that narcissism is a disorder of the self. As such it is best understood by focusing on the most primitive experiences of the self—those concerned with separation from the mother and the establishment of personal identity. These are the fundamental concerns of the first two years of life (although they persist throughout life), the so-called Minoan-Mycenean stage of psychological development.

• Chapter 3   Socrates, Eros, and the Culture of Narcissism

In pre-Socratic philosophy, eros (ἔρως) is generally the enemy of human reason. In Hesiod's *Theogony*, Eros is one of the three primordial gods, the others being Chaos and Earth. Of the three, Eros has the greatest power, including the power to overcome the reason and courage of gods and man (lines 115–25).[1] A similar conception of eros is found in Sophocles' *Antigone*. In the chorus that follows Creon's announcement that Antigone must die, Eros is addressed as the god who has caused Antigone's destruction (lines 782–97). An even stronger denunciation of erotic love is found in Euripides' *Hippolytos*. Aphrodite states that "the power I possess is sex, passion, love" (that is, eros), and the play seems to warn that whether one surrenders to love or rejects it, one is doomed (lines 1–64). Phaedra becomes the prototype of a woman ruined by love. There are, to be sure, exceptions to this overall negative evaluation of eros. Empedocles sees love as a universal force that opposes strife (fragments 115, 128, 130). And Parmenides of Elea attributes peace and harmony to the goddess Aphrodite (also Empedocles' name for love) (fragments 12–13). Nevertheless, the basic pattern in pre-Socratic philosophy is that eros is the enemy of reason and hence of what is most distinctly human.[2] This line of thought is certainly found in much of Plato's philosophy: not only eros versus reason, but a whole host of related dualisms, such as body versus soul, appearances versus reality, the transitory versus the perma-

72

nent, dualisms that are expressed most strongly, perhaps, in the *Gorgias, Phaedo,* and to a somewhat lesser degree the *Republic.* In these works the body is a virtual prison of the soul, and the goal of the true lover of wisdom is to transcend the body by denying its claims. By contrast, in the *Symposium* and the *Phaedrus,* the body and its eros, far from being the enemy, are a source of energy and inspiration that lead man higher, thereby acting as a bridge to the sublime. One sees this most dramatically in Socrates' (Diotima's) discussion of the "ladder of love" in the *Symposium* (210a–211b), which posits the love of beautiful bodies as the first step toward the love of absolute Beauty. Hans Kelsen expresses it this way:

> What a transformation of views lies between the *Gorgias* and the *Phaedo* on the one hand, and the *Symposium* and the *Phaedrus* on the other. The body with its sensuality is no longer the simple earthly evil . . . which he has to leave as soon as possible. That body is now the indispensable presupposition for attaining the goal; the love of it is already the first, the most significant step on the way to the good.[3]

It should also be noted that Plato's ambivalent attitude toward reason and eros is seen not only by comparing dialogues, but also within them. In the *Phaedrus,* Socrates, following the lead of Phaedrus, praises friendship over love, for love is so passionate and wild as to be destructive (237c–241d). But immediately after, he asks the god of eros to forgive him, and he goes on to treat eros as heaven-sent madness (244a–b).

In *Eclipse of Reason,* Max Horkheimer (a close associate of Adorno and intellectual co-leader with Adorno of the Frankfurt School), states that objective reason is both a structure inherent in reality and an orientation to this structure—that is, a human faculty. Horkheimer argues that this structure "is accessible to him who takes upon himself the effort of dialectical thinking, or identically, who is capable of eros."[4] Such a view of eros comes close indeed to Socrates' understanding of the term. Eros is a motive force, as well as a bridge, or path, to objective reality. Eros serves reason. Nevertheless, eros is first of all of the body, and

Plato's Socratic dialogues are works of art designed to persuade us to question our beliefs. In this chapter we will be considering how Plato artistically exploited narcissistic motifs in Athenian culture, transforming aspects that were potentially regressive— indeed, infantile—in their narcissism into the foundation of mature narcissism. It is this mature narcissism that is the ground of the philosopher's eros.

Though the eros of Socrates and his philosophy are apparent in many of the Platonic dialogues, it is in the *Symposium* that Plato establishes the theoretical connection between eros and narcissism, especially in Aristophanes' praise of the unifying power of love. It is a primary characteristic of narcissism that it seeks unity, ultimately with the cosmos itself. However, the transformation of narcissism that Socrates is able to achieve remains primarily an artistic one. The final speech in the *Symposium*, that of Alcibiades, reveals not only the strength of regressive narcissistic elements in Greek culture, but also that Socrates himself may not be entirely immune to their influence. I am not, of course, arguing that Plato had an explicit theory of what today is called narcissism, but rather, that the theory of narcissism expresses a profound and timeless human truth. A great thinker's insight into this truth, regardless of what it is called, can be illuminated by the theory of narcissism; and conversely, aspects of psychoanalytic theory can be illuminated by a great thinker's insight into this truth, a point that did not escape Freud's notice.

A word regarding what I am *not* trying to do may be helpful at this point. Hans Kelsen, in "Platonic Love," attempts to psychoanalyze Plato. He sees Plato's interest in eros, which he interprets almost entirely in terms of pederasty (homosexual eros directed at youth), as an attempt to come to terms with his own homosexuality, which Kelsen argues was much more intense than was the norm in Athens. The problems with such an argument are apparent. We have very little evidence regarding Plato's private life, and what evidence there is, such as the seventh letter, may not be reliable. Hence Kelsen must make a number of assumptions regarding the relationship between Plato's work and life. Further, he assumes that we can know how Socrates differed from Plato, in spite of the remarkably difficult issues raised by any attempt to distinguish Socrates from Plato. Finally, Kelsen's argument that Plato's homosexuality was abnormally intense—an argument that hangs on slender threads in any case—is difficult to evaluate without knowing what might have been normal, an issue that Kelsen only begins to address.[5] I have used none of Kelsen's arguments or approaches here, although I refer to aspects of his nonetheless interesting work. Nor do I go as far as Gomperz, who suggests that there may have been a connection between Socrates' theoretical attitude toward ethical problems and his pederastic inclinations.[6] My approach in this chapter is very much on the surface, as it were. I seek merely to show that narcissistic elements were present in Athenian culture (which is widely recognized), and that Plato sometimes exploited these elements artistically in his attempt to make eros serve philosophy. The historical Socrates and Plato's Socrates are assumed to be identical. While it is unlikely that this was actually the case, there is insufficient evidence to support any other line of argument.[7]

The Agonal Culture and Homosexuality: Evidence of Narcissism?

It is widely recognized that narcissism in classical Athens was intense. But closer examination reveals considerable confusion regarding the relationship between what appear to be cultural manifestations of narcissism and the psychoanalytic theory of narcissism. In *The Glory of Hera: Greek Mythology and the Greek Family*, Philip Slater argues that the system of weak, diluted marriage in classical Athens led mothers to relate to their sons in a profoundly ambivalent manner, alternating between seductive behavior and hostile ridicule. The result was men with a fragile sense of themselves, especially of their masculinity. This fostered a culture in which invidious displays of aggression and unrestrained competition in every aspect of life were common, as men sought to bolster their fragile egos by overcoming other men. It is this agonal culture that Slater equates with narcissism.[8]

In *The Culture of Narcissism*, Christopher Lasch is also concerned with the relationship between competition and narcissism. However, he disagrees with Slater, seeing narcissism as a manifestation of a decline in genuine competition. The narcissist dares not compete, says Lasch, because his rage is boundless, for competition implies struggle according to rules, within limits, something that the narcissist, who seeks to obliterate all who stand in his way, cannot come to terms with. Thus, the narcissist refrains from competition, wanting rewards without competition, fame without risk, celebrity without concrete achievement. Lasch describes this as the orientation of narcissistic entitlement and contrasts genuine competition among the ancient Greeks with the entertainment spectacles that frequently pass for sport in our culture.[9] Thus, we have one author who sees pervasive competition as evidence of Greek narcissism and another who sees the decline of genuine competition as evidence of narcissism and contrasts our culture with that of the ancient Greeks in order to highlight the narcissism of our culture.

The theory of narcissism can help us to evaluate the relationship between Greek competitiveness and Greek narcissism. But in order to truly appreciate Greek competitiveness, a factor not considered by Slater must be taken into account: the extraordinarily high death rate among adult men in classical Athens. One historian estimates that only one in five young men of twenty reached sixty years of age, and other historians set the death rate at comparably high levels.[10] Early death, from combat or disease, was thus to be expected. So what we might today regard as an exaggerated pursuit of physical mastery may have been functional on two counts: first, by enhancing an individual's chances of survival in combat, and second, by helping an individual deny his own mortality and vulnerability in what was in fact a remarkably threatening world. However, as Alvin

Gouldner suggests in *Enter Plato*, most people cannot seek mastery constantly; it is too exhausting and denies the real need for secure dependence.[11] The path of regressive narcissism must therefore have been a constant temptation for the ancient Greek.

Drawing upon A. W. H. Adkins's reinterpretation of the so-called Greek "shame culture" as actually a "results culture," Gouldner argues that in ancient Greece enormous emphasis was placed on effective action. Only results counted; good intentions were never enough. The outcome was an excessive concern with potency and strength, which competed with an unacknowledged desire to be passive, dependent on the strength of another, and secure. In this context, Gouldner suggests that we view Greek male homosexuality as an institutionalized opportunity for men to enjoy respite from their constant competition.[12] From this perspective the *Symposium* contains an interesting remark by Pausanias, who praises homosexual eros as especially conducive to democracy.

> The reason why such [homosexual] love, together with love of intellectual and physical achievement, is condemned by the Persians is to be found in the absolute nature of their empire; it does not suit the interest of government that a generous spirit and strong friendships and attachments should spring up among their subjects, and these are effects which love has an especial tendency to produce. [182b–c]

Perhaps Pausanias's remarks can be interpreted this way. It is widely recognized that Greek competitiveness, the agonal culture, threatened democracy. The virtues of the proud Homeric warrior were not merely out of place in the democracy of the fifth and fourth centuries, but were positively disruptive of a settled, cooperative society. Adkins's famous studies of the transformation of the meaning of terms such as ἀρετή (excellence, or virtue), which originally referred to excellence in battle, but which in the fifth century came to refer to more cooperative excellences, are exemplary.[13] Greek male homosexuality—particularly its idealization, perhaps—may have provided a psychological basis for the cooperative excellences, by physically symbolizing the depth of satisfaction available via mutuality. In *The Use of Pleasure*, the second volume of his *History of Sexuality*, Michel Foucault develops a related point. The reason why Greek philosophical "erotics," as he calls it, so thoroughly "problematized" male homosexual courtship had little to do with the moral status of homosexuality per se, but rather with the political problem of how free men might engage in homosexual courtship and relations without submitting to the power and control of another.[14] That is, the extensive concern with male homosexuality in Greek philosophy served not merely an intellectual, but also a social and political function. It addressed how homosexual courtship might be separated out from the agonal culture and thus made less disruptive.

It is apparent that there is no simple answer to the question of the relationship between Greek competitiveness and Greek narcissism. In such a very different world from our own, high levels of competitiveness may have been psychologically functional for the individuals involved. At the same time it is quite apparent that such competition was most disruptive when carried over into all aspects of social life, as it frequently was. Rather than label the agonal culture narcissistic or not, it may be more useful to turn our attention further to the concept of (homosexual) eros that sometimes tempered the agonal culture, the concept on which Socrates builds in his attempt to overcome the conventional meaning of virtue as excellence in competition.

Socrates talks freely of his erotic responses to young men (*Charmides* 153b–155e; *Phaedrus* 227c). Yet, although he frequently speaks "as if his own heart were almost continuously thumping at the sight of beautiful youths and boys," as K. J. Dover puts it, he rejects the physical acting out of homosexual eros.[15] Though he says that he is constantly in love (Xenophon *Symposium* 8.2) and that eros is the only subject he understands (Plato *Symposium* 177d), Socrates' eros moves rapidly from youths to philosophy (*Gorgias* 481d–482a) to the virtuous in the city (Xenophon *Symposium* 8.41). Indeed, this seems to be the point. Socrates often employs physical eros as a parable, as a way of rendering concrete its more abstract manifestations (*Protagoras* 309b–d). He frequently contrasts a thoroughly sublimated homosexual eros, aimed at producing men with good souls, with heterosexual eros, which produces mere children (Plato *Symposium* 208e–209a; *Phaedrus* 250e). Nor should it be overlooked that a thoroughly sublimated homosexual eros is highly compatible with the Socratic method of teaching: an emotionally intense dialectic between an older, wiser man and one or a few younger men.

Eros and Narcissism: Freudian or Platonic Sublimation?

Before proceeding further, we must address the question of relationship between eros, particularly homosexual eros (and more particularly still, pederasty), and narcissism. But to answer this question, we must first address another: that of the relationship between Plato's view of eros and the psychoanalytic view, especially that of Freud. Freud himself was aware of a relationship between his view and Plato's. Against those who objected to his stretching of the concept of eros to include nonsexual relations, he responded: "As for the 'stretching' of the concept of sexuality . . . anyone who looks down with contempt upon psychoanalysis from a superior vantage point should remember how closely the enlarged sexuality of psychoanalysis coincides with the Eros of the divine Plato."[16]

Though qualifications are necessary, it seems fair to state that Plato and Freud shared the assumption that eros is a powerful Protean force, which can be expressed in a wide variety of fashions, from sexual love to love of parents to love of virtue to love of beauty, culture, and philosophy, as Socrates demonstrates so clearly.[17] George Boas argues that there is only a "verbal difference" between the views of Plato and Freud on this subject.

> The libido, as a term for generalized desire . . . by reintegrating humanity and its strivings into the natural world . . . has revived in a

new form the kernel of Diotimas' speech in the *Symposium*. Freud, along with most Platonists, would deny this. However, since love in the *Symposium* is found not only in sexual attraction but also in scientific research and philosophic meditation, there is only a verbal difference between the two philosophies. . . . Although [Freud] may have said that the scientist is dominated by an anal-erotic urge, he did not deprecate science in those terms; rather, he explained what he thought was its general etiology.[18]

However, F. M. Cornford seems closer to the mark when he notes that while eros, like libido, is generalized desire, which can flow either upward or downward, into the physical or the spiritual, there remains a decisive difference between Plato and Freud. For Plato, man is drawn upward, and the self-moving energy of the soul resides in the highest, not the lowest, part of man.[19]

Although Freud and Plato both see the presence of erotic elements in the most rational and sublime pursuits, their attitude toward these elements is quite different. Freud tends to see the most primitive and direct expression of eros, organ satisfaction, as the fundamental reality. Aim-inhibited (sublimated) activities may be satisfying, but they are nevertheless inhibited, a detour from genuine gratification. Plato, on the other hand, sees the ultimate goals of eros, such as the creation of virtue and the experience of beauty, as the fundamental reality, to which physical eros is drawn. That eros is drawn in this direction is in large measure because this is the path of greatest pleasure; for such "sublimated" pursuits are more—rather than less—gratifying, in part because they draw on a wider range of human capabilities. A key reason why the philosopher king is happier than the tyrant is because he experiences the pleasures of reason *and* desire, whereas the tyrant experiences only the pleasures of desire —that is, he draws on only a restricted, pathologically deformed range of capabilities and talents (*Republic* 582a–b).

The theory of narcissism favors Plato's view of sublimation over Freud's, though it is not this simple. Eros may be fundamental biologically, but its role in human experience is not adequately grasped in terms of the quest for infantile pleasure per se. Rather, eros is most fully understood in terms of how it serves

narcissistic needs, needs that ultimately express the desire for
wholeness and the perfection of the self. Conversely, narcissism
draws on and uses eros in this pursuit of perfection. As Marion
Oliner puts it, "The role of the narcissistic factor within psychosexual development rests on its bestowing a sense of worth on
strivings that have their foundation in biology."[20] Nevertheless,
the goal of narcissism cannot be fully expressed in terms of eros,
for it is in some ways more primitive (not pleasure per se, but
pleasure in union and merger with the All: Dionysian pleasure,
Freud's "oceanic contentment"), in others more sublime (to become whole in oneself: narcissistic perfection). Eros serves the
goal of narcissistic reconciliation and gives its pursuit a special
intensity, but it is not the goal itself and cannot explain the goal.
The goal is explained by man's quest to heal his narcissistic
wound. As we shall see shortly, Aristophanes understands that
it is the things that men and women do in the name of eros that
must be explained, and that such an explanation must look beyond—not only deeper into—eros, but without rejecting eros or
leaving it behind. Though Freud draws on Aristophanes' account, he does not see this as its lesson.

Adorno's view of eros and narcissism will be examined
in the next chapter, and Marcuse's in the subsequent chapter.
There we will see how a more Platonic view of eros, especially
as expressed in terms of the theory of narcissism, can help us
to understand, as well as correct, their projects, particularly
Marcuse's. In other words, the theoretical advantages of the Platonic theory of sublimation over the Freudian theory will thus be
tested.

Eros and Narcissism

It remains to establish the relationship between eros and
narcissism. When one considers that Freud sees eros as never
losing its archaic traits, but only building on them, and that narcissistic self-love is the most archaic expression of eros, it is not
surprising that eros and narcissism are closely linked. Love, says

Freud, "originates in the capacity of the ego to satisfy some of its instincts autoerotically. . . . It is primarily narcissistic, is then transferred to those objects which have been incorporated in the ego, now much extended, and expresses the motor striving of the ego after those objects as sources of pleasure."[21] Thus, love is originally narcissistic: it is self-love. This is what Freud's postulation of a stage of primary narcissism means (Socrates takes a more object-relational perspective, arguing that love is always love of something [Symposium 199e, 200e]). Only later is love extended to objects, as a convenience to its satisfaction, one might say. However, the narcissistic origins of love remain. One sees this most dramatically, according to Freud, in the blind love that parents often have for their children; their ability to overlook any faults in their children shows that parental love is a projection of the parents' own narcissism onto the child: "'His Majesty the Baby,' as once we fancied ourselves to be."[22]

Freud also argues, as we have seen, that one of the attractions of reciprocated romantic love is that being loved provides narcissistic gratification, gratification otherwise depleted by loving another. From this perspective, an interesting explanation of the intensity of narcissism at Athens suggests itself. Raymond Larson notes that the distinction between "lover" (erastēs) and "loved one" (erōmenos) was important in ancient Greece. Whereas we tend to see a similarity and an equality between them (we say, for example, "a pair of lovers"), the Greeks emphasized the difference, conceiving the relationship as resembling that of master and slave, in which the loved one is the master, taking all that the lover gives him, but giving little in return.[23] This may have been because the modal erotic relationship was that between a man and a youth, and that while it was considered appropriate for an older, not yet married man to pursue a youth with feverish intensity, it was thought vulgar for the youth to respond in kind (not entirely unlike the Victorian double standard for heterosexual romantic love).[24] Expressed in terms of libido theory, the loved one depletes the lover of narcissistic libido but gives little back in the form of reciprocated love, thereby causing the lover to be especially in need of narcissistic satisfaction, perhaps leading him to seek it with special intensity elsewhere—for example, in constant contests with others. Needless to say, this is an especially speculative explanation of Athenian narcissism.

If all eros has narcissistic roots, this is particularly true of homosexual eros, especially that directed at youth. Indeed, such an object choice is narcissistic by Freudian definition. The homosexual chooses the youthful image of his own sexuality, rather than the maternal image, as his love object; which is to say that homosexual eros is narcissistic rather than anaclitic.[25] Thus it is not theoretically farfetched, but, on the contrary, most orthodox, to posit a close relationship among Plato's concept of eros, Freud's concept of eros, and narcissism. According to Plato, eros seeks wholeness, completion, and healing of a fundamental wound in the self brought about by separation. Here the connection between eros and narcissism becomes especially close and fruitful. For the theory of narcissism can be used to elaborate upon and explain this quest of eros for wholeness. It is to this task that we now turn.

Aristophanes' Account of Narcissistic Injury

It is instructive here to consider Aristophanes' account of Zeus' bisection of the human race in Plato's *Symposium* (189c–193d). No other literary account of the experience of narcissistic injury and longing is as direct and as profound. Aristophanes states that originally each human being was a rounded whole, with four arms and legs and two faces. These original beings came not in two, but three, sexes: male, female, and hermaphrodite. The strength and vigor of such a race made it formidable, but also arrogant, and Zeus decided to punish it by bisecting its members, so as to make them weaker. The outcome was men and women with the form that men and women have now. But ever since its injury, humanity has been searching for its other half. Eros is the feeling that arises between two lovers when each recognizes the other as the missing complement of him or herself. While all human beings, even lesbians and heterosexuals, seek their complement, the highest form of eros is that between halves who were originally whole males. It is thus male homosexual eros. The proof of this, according to Aristophanes, is that such men are the most active in public life (191a–b).

Aristophanes' speech raises an interesting point. There is considerable scholarly debate over the significance of the speeches of Phaedrus, Pausanias, Eryximachus, Aristophanes, and Agathon in the *Symposium*. Some, such as Léon Robin, argue that in these speeches Plato is laying out common, but mistaken, positions on love, in order to reject them.[26] Others, such as Jaeger, see Plato as trying to extract the greatest possible truth from each position.[27] Still others, such as Stanley Rosen, see Plato as making an elaborate and sometimes intentionally abstruse—indeed, hermetic—argument, in which even seemingly straightforward speeches contain a remarkable variety of subtle and sophisticated references.[28]

My inclination is to follow Jaeger's lead. From this perspective (which is not incompatible with Rosen's), it becomes clear that many of the speeches serve a common purpose: namely, to show that eros is not an enemy of civilization, but its friend. Phaedrus talks about how an army consisting entirely of lovers and their beloved would be virtually invincible, because the lover would always prefer death to disgrace in the eyes of his beloved (179a–b). Pausanias, as we have seen, shows how homosexual eros fosters democracy (182a–e). Eryximachus seems to agree, arguing that it is through healthy eros "that we are capable of the pleasures of society, and friendship even, with the gods our masters" (188d). Though Agathon's praise of eros should perhaps be discounted (for the pompous and conventional Agathon, eros is the source of everything good), he too mentions its civilizing force (197c–d). Yet, while the civilizing aspect of eros seems to be a theme that Plato would have us strongly consider, it would be a mistake to follow Agathon in seeing eros as merely a force for moderation. Eros remains a demanding daemon, one that wants complete satisfaction, now and forever.

Why this is so is addressed by Aristophanes, who argues that his elaborate account of love is necessary because the physical pleasure associated with eros is insufficient to explain its hold and the lengths to which it drives man.

> No one can suppose that it is mere physical enjoyment which causes the one to take such intense delight in the company of the other. It is clear that the soul of each has some other longing which it cannot express but only surmise and obscurely hint at. Suppose Hephaestus with his tools were to visit them as they lie together . . . and ask: "What is it, mortals, that you hope to gain from one another? . . . I am ready to melt and weld you together, so that instead of two, you shall be one flesh. . . . Would such a fate as this content you, and satisfy your longings?" We know what their answer would be; no one would refuse the offer; it would be plain that this is what everybody wants, and everybody would regard it as the precise expression of the desire which he had long felt but had been unable to formulate, that he should melt into his beloved, and that henceforth they should be one being instead of two. The reason is that this was our primitive condition when we were wholes, and love is simply the name for the desire and pursuit of the whole (ὅλον).
> [192c–193a]

The way in which eros may serve narcissistic goals has never been more clearly expressed.

Freud recognized the relevance of Aristophanes' speech to his account of eros. He introduces it in a discussion of repetition compulsion, in which he is attempting to explain the regressive character of the drives, the fact that they continually seek to return to their first expression. He states that Aristophanes' account "traces the origin of an instinct to a need to restore an earlier state of things." It is this focus—to understand eros by uncovering its most primitive expression, which is also assumed to be its most essential—that distinguishes Freud's approach. After elaborating on the myth recounted by Aristophanes, Freud asks in a tentative manner, "Shall we follow the hint given us by the poet-philosopher, and venture upon the hypothesis that living substance at the time of its coming to life was torn apart into small particles, which ever since have endeavored to reunite through the sexual instincts?"[29] He concludes by suggesting that after life had evolved to a multicellular condition, it "transferred the instinct for reuniting, in the most highly concentrated form, to the germ cells."[30]

Freud sees the connection between the most primitive and the most sublime expressions of eros but explains the latter in terms of the former. Plato (assuming for a moment that Aristophanes' account accurately represents an aspect of Plato's view) sees this connection too; but, as the dialogue unfolds, it becomes quite apparent that he sees the sublime as more fundamental, drawing the primitive toward it, as it were (the salutary influence of teleology may be apparent here). In some respects the Platonic view is closer to the theory of narcissism. Aristophanes explains that eros cannot be understood adequately in purely physical, sexual terms. Physical pleasure is important, but not so important as to be capable of explaining all that is done in its name. One fully understands eros only when one sees it as the way in which an individual seeks to heal his wounded self, by uniting with another who seems to embody all that he lacks. Aristophanes' account reveals that eros, while having undeniably powerful biological roots, is not best understood by tracing these roots back further and further, ultimately to the fission and fusion of one-celled animals (and their human somatic correlates, sperm and ovum). Rather, eros is best understood in terms of how it becomes integrated into higher—that is, more complex, manifold, sophisticated, and abstract—human needs and purposes. It is in this context that it is most instructive to consider the so-called ladder of love.

The Ladder of Love

Toward the beginning of the *Symposium*, Agathon asks Socrates to come and sit next to him, so that he may partake of Socrates' wisdom. Socrates replies: "It would be very nice, Agathon, if wisdom were like water, and flowed by contact out of a person who has more into one who has less, just as water can be made to pass through a thread of wool out of the fuller of two vessels into the emptier" (175c–d). Agathon wishes to be filled with Socrates' goodness as though he were an empty vessel. The regressive narcissistic motif of gaining wholeness through fusion with the strength of another is too prominent to be missed in Socrates' interpretation of Agathon's desire to be relieved of his emptiness. But Agathon, in a speech praising eros, which falls between the speeches of Aristophanes and Socrates, talks of eros like a romantic schoolgirl: eros is supreme in beauty and goodness, richly endowed with self-control, and fosters calm and respite from sorrow (195a–197e). Because he is unable to accept Aristophanes' insight that eros gains its power from the most regressive needs for fusion, Agathon's understanding of eros remains stylized and empty. It is precisely Socrates' appreciation of its regressive roots that gives his account of eros such power.

By eros Socrates means not merely need or desire, but a universal principle.[31] Eros bridges the gap between the mortal and the immortal, and "prevents the universe from falling into two separate halves" (202e–203a). Earlier, Phaedrus said that Eros is the oldest of the gods, preceded only by Chaos (178a–b). One may read Socrates as suggesting that the separation of the mundane from the spiritual would constitute a comparable level of disorganization, utterly disrupting the wholeness that is the universe. Socrates has an intuitive command of narcissistic imagery. Eros, the vehicle of narcissism in Aristophanes' account, comes in Socrates' speech to connect not merely bodies, but the physical and the spiritual, thereby preserving the wholeness and integrity of the cosmos. Eros, in Socrates' hands a philosophical principle, comes to serve a philosophical version of narcissism, concerned not merely with the wholeness of individuals, but with the integrity of the universe. We shall see that it is precisely this aspect of eros that Adorno rejects and Marcuse embraces.

Socrates goes on to employ an interesting personification. The parents of Eros, he says, are Contrivance (Πόρος) and Poverty (Πενία). For this reason, Eros is always poor and, far from being sensitive and beautiful, is hard, weather-beaten, shoeless, and homeless, taking after his mother. However, as his father's son, he schemes to get what is beautiful. He is bold, always devising tricks, a lover of wisdom, a magician, and a true sophist (203b–e). This account captures well the universal experience of narcissistic weakness and what man must do to overcome it. Man is born poor, unable to meet his most basic instinctual needs. Throughout his life he will have to struggle for their fulfillment in a sparse world, which will require boldness, even trickery. However, the need for trickery may not stem merely from the need to outfox others for scarce resources—love, money, prestige, goodness, security, and so on. It may also stem from an inner anxiety that one is not truly worthy of narcissistic wholeness. Thus, it is necessary to trick oneself.

Here we might recall Chasseguet-Smirgel's claim that mature narcissistic satisfaction derives from successful efforts to reduce the distance between ego and ego ideal. In these terms, the trickery that Socrates refers to can be interpreted as an attempt by eros to obtain satisfaction regardless of whether the distance between ego and mature ego ideal is thereby reduced. The cunning of eros seeks satisfaction, free not only of the judgment of others, but also of the judgment of the ego ideal. Yet, such a strategy is ultimately self-defeating, for just as the unconscious knows every guilty impulse, so the ego ideal never sleeps. It is perhaps for reasons such as this that Socrates concludes: "When he [Eros] wins he always loses" (203e). Yet, eros need not forever lose. The father of Contrivance, says Socrates, is Invention (Μήτιδος, connoting practical wisdom, as in a craft or skill). Eros embodies, albeit twice removed, not merely contrivance, but creativity: the potential to make something new. It is through hard-won mastery of this creative potential that eros can become worthy of its own satisfaction.

What is to be made, of course, is beauty. Indeed, Socrates stresses the active, creative, making aspect. The goal of love, he says, is to procreate (τίκτειν) beauty, to bring it forth, to cause it to appear (206c–e). Preparation for this task is best begun in youth, when a young man falls in love with a beautiful gentleman. Later, he will learn that it is the beauty of the soul that is truly to be cherished, and that physical beauty is a fickle guide to spiritual beauty. Ultimately, he will turn his attention to absolute beauty, beauty per se (211a–212a). "This is the right way of approaching or being initiated into the mysteries of love, to begin with examples of beauty in this world, and using them as ascending steps to ascend continuously with that absolute beauty as one's aim" (211c). This process has come to be known as the "ladder of love" (ἐπαναβαθμοῖς, literally "steps of a stair"). It should not be overlooked, however, that a ladder is also a bridge, symbol of the connection between regressive and mature narcissism. The ladder of love is the path from immature to mature narcissism: from love of the image of one's physical self (beautiful young man) to love of that activity in which one seeks to be worthy of identifying with one's highest values.

Immature narcissism seeks immediate gratification via fusion with the sexual mirror image of itself. As we have seen, such a focus is narcissistic by (Freudian) definition: male libidinal cathexis is fixated on the image of its own sexuality, rather than being directed toward an external (anaclitic) object choice. Mature narcissism, on the other hand, recognizes that sublimation and hard work (object mastery) can lead to even greater gratification: reconciliation between ego and ego ideal at the highest level, at which the ego, rather than seeking shortcuts, aspires to become worthy of its mature ideal. Yet, as Chasseguet-Smirgel points out, even mature narcissism is driven, at some level, by sexual desire, the legacy of the oedipal conflict. One finds an expression of this in the passage immediately following that quoted in the preceding paragraph (211c). Socrates uses the word συνεῖναι (suneinai, the ordinary term for sexual relations) to characterize not only sexual intercourse (211d6), but also intellectual intercourse with the beautiful and the virtuous (212a2). Indeed, intellectual intercourse appears to have a distinct advantage over its physical counterpart, in that it does not depend on the presence and willing cooperation of others. Its object is always beautiful, always available, and always ready to be loved. Thus, intellectual intercourse exercises omnipotent control over its objects. The last section of this chapter will consider the possibility that Socrates' quest for intellectual control does not wholly avoid the temptations of regressive narcissism.

The Cunning of Eros

Some surprising aspects of eros have been revealed in the preceding considerations. Most important for our consideration of the Frankfurt school is that eros cannot be sharply separated from instrumental reason. Eros, as demonstrated most dramatically in its mythological lineage, is in part cunning and trickery. The scarcity of love and beauty—and the sheer neediness of mortal men and women—require eros to be shrewd: "All's fair in love and war." Eros thus resembles—indeed, is embodied in—the wily Odysseus, the figure whom Horkheimer and Adorno invoke to represent the cunning of instrumental reason. To be sure, eros opposes instrumental reason in important respects. For instrumental reason breaks things down into substantively meaningless uniform parts (fungible units of experience), in order to manipulate and control them, thereby disrupting an essential wholeness and objective order in the world. It does not let things be or reveal themselves, seeing them only in terms of human purposes. Eros is quite different, in that it seeks to know and possess the whole (Republic 474–475).[32] The whole is thus the telos of eros, which is what links eros so closely with narcissism.

Yet, eros shares something of the cunning of instrumental reason. It is also hubristic. To seek to know and possess the whole is to go beyond the mean, to transcend human limits, the nomos; not even the Greek gods knew the whole. This hubris is expressed mythically in the circular creatures bisected by Zeus. In Aristophanes' account, they are punished for their hubris, which is expressed by their wholeness (190b). Yet, although weakened by their punishment, they still seek the whole, perhaps more urgently, even as Zeus threatens to divide them once again. Indeed, Rosen suggests that not merely hubris, but criminal hubris, is the dominant theme of the *Symposium*. "The daimonic aura of the banquet is one of criminal hybris."[33] One sees this in the fact that three of the main speakers—Phaedrus, Eryximachus, and Alcibiades—are accused of taking part in the defamation of the mysteries and Hermae. Another aspect of this hubris is reflected in the orientation of eros towards its goal, beauty. Beauty is seen as the prey of eros, which wants not merely to experience beauty, but to own and possess it all, now and forever. This, too, is hubris. Adorno writes of an instrumental reason that sees the world as prey. Eros may have higher goals than merely wresting a comfortable existence from nature; but its attitude to beauty is similar to the attitude of instrumental reason to nature. Both seek total possession and control, thereby exemplifying something of the devouring attitude of the infant toward the good breast, as described by Klein. Indeed, Lasch has equated narcissism with Greek hubris, thereby emphasizing the strong presence of envy and oral greed.[34]

Harry Neumann's fascinating interpretation of the *Symposium* reinforces these considerations. Most commentators, even those who stress the hubris of eros, such as Rosen, have seen the absolute beauty described in the *Symposium* (210d6–212a7) as virtually identical with the idea of the Good.[35] Accordingly, the ultimate reality for Plato has been viewed either as an object of reason (the Good) or as the goal of love (the Beautiful). This virtual equation of Beauty and the Good, were it valid, would support an interesting argument regarding the relationship of eros to narcissism. For the language that Plato employs in the *Republic* to characterize knowledge of the Good stresses imitation of the Good: copying and becoming like it (mimesis).[36]

> For surely, Adeimantus, the man whose mind is truly fixed on eternal realities . . . will endeavour to imitate [μιμεῖσθαί, literally mimic] them and, as far as may be, to fashion himself in their likeness and assimilate [ἀφομοιοῦσθαι, literally to become like] himself to them. Or do you think it possible not to imitate the things to which anyone attaches himself with admiration? "Impossible," he

said. Then the lover of wisdom associating with the divine order will himself become orderly and divine in the measure permitted to man. [500c–d; Shorey trans.]

The *Republic*'s language is thus not unlike that of the theory of narcissism, which refers to the ego ideal in terms which suggest that the unconscious goal is to merge with it, to become like it, and so share in its perfection by partaking of it. If the Beautiful were indeed equivalent to the Good, one could connect the narcissistic eros of the *Symposium* with Plato's larger project in a very straightforward fashion: narcissistic eros would then be the model for all philosophical knowledge, an interpretation suggested by several remarks in the *Republic* regarding the eros of the philosopher (475a–476c).

But the situation is not so simple. In answering Socrates' questions about eros, Diotima reveals a crucial difference between the good and the beautiful (204d1–205a8). The goal of Diotima's love is not the beautiful, but the acquisition of happiness by creating something beautiful. Lovers are not in love with their beloved: their real object is their own happiness. The eros described by Diotima does not share the yearning for ultimate union with its object that the love described by Aristophanes does. The object is attractive solely as a medium in which the lover may give birth to something beautiful out of himself. Diotima stresses the radical separation of lover and beloved: "Basically sophistical, this eros had little of the grandeur leading Aristophanes' love to sacrifice everything for a kind of mystical union with its beloved."[37] Jaeger is mistaken, says Neumann, in describing Diotima's love as a reinterpretation of Aristophanes' love from a new and higher standpoint. He is also mistaken when he goes on to consider Diotima's reinterpretation of Aristophanes as closely resembling Aristotle's definition of the self-love that is the highest expression of moral perfection (N. *Ethics* 1168a28–1169b2). He is justified in regarding Diotima's eros as a form of self-love; but it is a very selfish self-love, quite unlike Aristotle's conception.[38]

The selfishness of eros is like the selfishness of the virtuous man (not necessarily that of a philosopher king) in the Republic. Whereas the philosopher king is expected to sacrifice some of his individual happiness to the common good by returning to the cave (520a–b), the virtuous man is required to tend his soul well, to make himself the best individual he can be—that is, to found the Republic in his own heart (592a–b). Almost as a side effect, one might say, such a man will also be virtuous in a socially conventional sense. He will be the last person to lie, to steal, to commit adultery, and so forth, because to do so would disrupt his happiness, which stems from the harmony of reason, spirit, and desire (Republic 442b–443c). Mature eros is also like this insofar as it is the most enlightened form of selfishness. Like spirit in the Republic, eros can serve either reason or desire. It all depends on natural inclination, upbringing, and education. In the language of narcissism, it all depends on how well the ego ideal is integrated with the superego.

The Persistence of Regressive Narcissism

While mature narcissism may serve virtue, the forces of regressive narcissism at Athens were perhaps even more powerful. This is captured well in Alcibiades' speech at the end of the dialogue. Alcibiades loves and admires Socrates with feverish intensity; yet, he is unable to avail himself of the goodness of Socrates, because he cannot internalize it or model himself after it. He is utterly charmed by Socrates, but the effects never last (216a–c). Nor is it a matter of mere forgetfulness. Alcibiades talks as if he must protect himself from Socrates' goodness, as if Socrates were a Siren against whom Alcibiades must stop his ears and take flight, lest he be destroyed (215b–216c).

Grunberger writes that narcissism "is in principle opposed to introjection,"[39] the active mental process by which, inter alia, the values of others are internalized and taken over as one's own. It is largely through introjection that the conscience (superego) is formed, and in this respect the capacity for introjection is a sign of maturity. A less mature alternative is identification,[40] a process represented by Agathon, who wishes merely to absorb Socrates' goodness (175c–e). Identification involves "borrowing" the goodness of another, rather than making it one's own. But Alcibiades resists both introjection and identification. Grunberger argues that both processes are seen by the narcissist as a visceral intrusion, which challenges the fantasy of narcissistic omnipotence. As a result, the narcissist becomes "fixated at the level of *counteridentification*."[41] Not only does he fail to identify with and introject the values of the adult world; he pursues the opposite course, as though to deny that the adult world might have anything to offer him. For to admit that it might be tantamount to admitting his own imperfection and incompleteness. Counteridentification, a normal part of adolescent protest, represents a last-ditch effort to hold onto one's primitive narcissism. In Alcibiades, it is especially intense and is never overcome.

This is one of the reasons why the relationship between Socrates and Alcibiades is so fascinating. Socrates exemplifies mature self-control, Alcibiades the opposite. Socrates accepts willingly his city's verdict of death, rather than betray his values. Alcibiades serves no values, but only his own self-glorification. The idea that he might betray his city by defecting to Sparta, rather than stand trial at Athens, is inconceivable to Socrates; it is his city that has betrayed him (Thucydides *History* vi.92). This is the viewpoint of the consummate narcissist, for whom even the normal relationship between an individual and his country is inverted. Alcibiades sees himself, it appears, as the true *polis*. Yet, Alcibiades' arrogance, like that of most narcissists, is coupled with a profound vulnerability to narcissistic injury and humiliation, which is why he can learn nothing from Socrates. Socrates, says Alcibiades, "compels me to realize that I am still a mass of imperfections. . . . So against my real inclination I stop up my ears and take refuge in flight, as Odysseus did from the Sirens. . . . He is the only person in whose presence I experience a sensation of which I might be thought incapable, a sensation of shame" (216a–b).

Alcibiades represents the regressive pole of the Athenian "culture of narcissism." At this pole the strength of narcissistic elements is so intense and so unmodulated that identification with and introjection of mature ideals is compromised. In such an environment men compete with each other to inflict narcissistic injury and humiliation on each other, rather than suffer it themselves. This is the agonal culture at its worst. Plato possessed marvelous intuitive insight into the psychological sources of the "Greek disease," as it has been called; and, rather than seeking to obliterate Greek narcissism at its roots—an impossible task, in any case—he sought to transform its expression. The speeches of Pausanias (182b–c) and Aristophanes suggest that Plato found enough precursors of mature narcissism in the culture to work with and build on—for example, in Aristophanes' claim that "if we conduct ourselves well in the light of heaven," Eros is more likely to "make us blessed and happy by restoring us to our former state and healing our wounds" (193d). In other words, it is the pursuit of narcissistic wholeness under the reign of the superego—that is, the integration of narcissistic needs with the demands of morality and society—that is most likely to lead to genuine fulfillment. The progressive pole of narcissism was thus not unrepresented in the culture. It was extremely vulnerable, however; and in the end Plato seems not to have been optimistic. Regressive narcissism is not merely resistant to mature values; it seems set on their rejection. Socrates' teachings frequently fall on intentionally deaf ears.

The Hubris of Socrates

Plato's Socrates does more than merely express the virtues of mature narcissism. He is himself a narcissistic ideal: complete and whole in himself, utterly without need for individual, personal others. As such, he reveals how close progressive narcissism stands to its pathological counterpart. The primary purpose of the second half of Alcibiades' speech (beginning at about 218c), according to Rosen, is to charge Socrates with hubris.

Socrates spends his entire life playing with mortals. Although he pretends to be constantly attracted to young men, he secretly scorns human eros (216d2ff., 219c4–5, 222a8). In his complete and perfect temperance he denies the human order, just as Alcibiades does with his extravagance. "The hubris of Alcibiades is overreaching ambition, whereas Socrates' hubris is temperance or moderation."[42] Socrates is unique. He drinks but is never drunk. He flirts with boys but never falls in love. Even his wife and family seem to be a social convenience, an expression of his willingness to meet the conventions of Athens halfway. At least, there is no evidence that his attachment to them is erotic, and some evidence to the contrary (*Phaedo* 116b). As Rosen puts it, "Socrates is wholly wonderful because he is whole or complete if only in the negative sense of being unique and not needing anyone."[43] But it is precisely in this that Socrates is hubristic. He transcends the normal human order, which is to need real individual others and in this sense, at least, to be always incomplete.

To be whole, complete, and unique, never needing anyone, is the narcissistic ideal. Many strive for this ideal, including Alcibiades, but only Socrates succeeds. That he succeeds so perfectly is what angers Alcibiades; the tone of resentment in Alcibiades' speech is too prominent to be missed (217e, 218d, 219b–d, 222a). Yet, Alcibiades is not only resentful; he admires Socrates profoundly and has no wish to spoil and devalue his goodness. In other words, there are limits to Alcibiades' pathological narcissism. It is important to be clear about why Alcibiades is resentful, however. It is not simply that Socrates has spurned his advances; it is also because Socrates needs no one. (He may need the attention of some of the young gentlemen of Athens in order to practice his calling, but he does not need them *qua* individuals.) The autonomy of Socrates reveals, by contrast, Alcibiades' own neediness. But Socrates exemplifies not only progressive narcissism, but also the hubris of narcissism. The implicit claim to completeness and perfection that Alcibiades sees in Socrates' scorn of human eros avoids hubris only because Socrates is a little more than human. Socrates' incompleteness can be measured only against higher, divine standards—which it sometimes is, by Diotima, for example (207b–208c). Others have to come to terms with their own incompleteness and dependence in this world. But perhaps this way of putting it lets Socrates off the hook just a little too easily.

The Acceptance of Contingency

Martha Nussbaum, in *The Fragility of Goodness: Luck and Ethics in Greek Tragedy and Philosophy*, takes quite a different view of Alcibiades' speech. She sees it as marking a turning point in Plato's philosophy, the point at which Plato comes to recognize the costs of his attempt to transcend the constraints of worldly contingency. From this point on in his work, says Nussbaum (making certain not especially controversial assumptions about the order of composition of the dialogues[44]), Plato becomes far more open to the value of the unique, the particular, the individual. She sees the *Phaedrus* as the culmination of this development.[45] Since the quest to transcend contingency (τύχη, tuchē, which means not merely luck, but all that happens to a man that is beyond his control) and thereby achieve utter mastery over self and world is a central feature of narcissism, Nussbaum's is an argument worth pursuing.

In fact, argues Nussbaum, the attempt to control contingency, to transcend tuchē, is hardly unique to Plato's work. It was a cultural ideal. Echoing Gouldner and Slater, she argues that among the ancient Greeks there was a terrible fear of passivity and a consequent agonal relationship to everyone and everything. The Greek always strove for mastery and control over people and things, lest his own limits, his own weakness, his own vulnerability to luck, become apparent to himself and others. As we saw earlier in this chapter, this is precisely the orientation that makes ancient Greece a culture of narcissism (though it should not be overlooked that in many respects this orientation is more mature than one that seeks mastery by drastically reducing the sphere over which it may be exercised—the strategy of the minimal self). Adorno writes of "idealism as rage" at a world too sparse to be dominated.[46] Nietzsche put it a little more generously when he said: "To imagine another, more valuable world is an expression of hatred for a world that makes one suffer; the *ressentiment* of metaphysicians is here creative."[47] Our considerations of the origins of philosophical eros in poverty, need, and cunning support this interpretation of the origins of idealist philosophy.

The agonal orientation gives rise to a philosophical program that attempts to achieve absolute self-sufficiency by denying human dependence (or at least the dependence of human reason) on anything transitory, finite, or mortal. One seeks the Good in order to transcend one's own limits, one's own finiteness, by participating in the Good, identifying with it, sharing in its perfection (*Republic* 500c–d). "Limits are always narcissistic injuries," says Rothstein.[48] The quest for transcendence in Plato's program is driven by narcissistic injury but not bound by it. Were it bound by narcissistic injury, it would seek the quickest route to fulfillment, as Agathon does (*Symposium* 175c–d). But Plato stresses the lifetime of hard work necessary to share in the universal Good (*Republic*, book 7).

He also emphasizes that we seek the Good not merely to fill a lack in ourselves, but also because there is something in us that seeks transcendence (*Republic* 583b–587b). We are not Nietzsche's "last man." There is something in human nature—what has here been called "progressive narcissism"—that desires to associate with something transcendent, something better and more beautiful than we are, in order to give our finite lives a meaning touched by the infinite. Plato's insight is a fine expression of the duality of narcissism. For, while all individuals experience narcissistic injury and the consequent feeling of deficiency or lack, some are able to draw on their earlier experience of narcissistic perfection not merely as reparation, but as a kind of signpost to the genuinely transcendent. That Plato may have something like this in mind is suggested by his claim in the

Phaedrus that the soul knows the way to the transcendent because it has been there before, prior to birth (247c–249d).

In her discussion of Socrates' (Diotima's) speech in the *Symposium*, Nussbaum stresses not the rootedness of philosophical eros in the body, but the goal of eros to transcend the body. Whereas I have stressed the location of the bottom rungs of the ladder of love in the needs of the body, Nussbaum stresses the distance between top and bottom, how the uppermost rungs are in the clouds, as it were.[49] This perspective leads to a tendency to equate the active, creative character of philosophical eros in the *Symposium* with the mimetic character of reason in the *Republic*.[50] Even if this is not quite true to some of the differences between the dialogues, it nevertheless leads to an important insight: that once one has reached the top of the ladder, one cannot go back. One must blind oneself to earthly beauty in order to seek its heavenly counterpart. This is the source of Socrates' hubris. Alcibiades, flawed as he is, appreciates this. He recognizes that Socrates has made a tragic choice, tragic in that he has sacrificed one good for another, since he cannot have both.

What is it that allows Alcibiades such great insight into the character of Socrates, an insight that has no equal in any of the other dialogues? Nussbaum argues that it stems from Alcibiades' genuine love for the unique individual that is Socrates. Through this love for an individual, Alcibiades gains insight into the particular and the unique. Because Socrates is free of this love for particular individuals, he "goes about his business with all the equanimity of a rational stone."[51] Alcibiades' speech seems to reflect a recognition on Plato's part that this equanimity, this total control, this almost complete transcendence of worldly contingency, has costs associated with it, epistemological as well as personal. Just as Alcibiades cannot reach the truth at the top of the ladder, because he is too undisciplined, so Socrates can no longer recall the truth at the bottom, the truth associated with the unique and the particular (*Republic* 517c–518b). Each has made a tragic choice.

Nussbaum explores the truth of the bottom rungs in an intri-

guing fashion. She recalls Plutarch's account of the death of
Alcibiades, in which Plutarch states that shortly before his death
Alcibiades dreamed that he was dressed in the clothes of his
mistress and that she was holding his head in her arms and
painting his face with makeup, as though he were a woman
(Plutarch, "Alcibiades," Lives 39). She sees the dream as expressing the wish for unmixed passivity, the wish to abandon
the agonal struggle for mastery over others.[52] It was suggested
above that this cultural agon is carried over into Plato's philosophy in the form of a quest to identify with the permanent and the
perfect and so partake of its attributes. What would the lesson of
Alcibiades dream be, were it, too, carried over into philosophy?
Perhaps that knowledge is not all of a piece; that unless we love
the imperfect and mutable, we cannot know it. Does Socrates
blind himself to that part of knowledge which is not gained by
intellectual mastery of the whole—that is, knowledge of the
unique and the particular—because in some way the struggle for
mastery of the whole is easier than the acceptance of worldly
contingency and human finitude? Perhaps it is easier to hold
onto one's primitive narcissism by transforming it into philosophy than to abandon it so as to come to know the variegated rich-
ness of this world. We shall see below, as well as in chapter 7,
that Socrates comes to appreciate the truth of Alcibiades' dream,
the truth of the bottom rungs of the ladder. However, unlike
Adorno, whose fascination with the partial and the particular is
discussed in the next chapter, Socrates is frequently able to
integrate part and whole. He is not incapable of descending the
ladder.

The Phaedrus

Nussbaum argues that it is only in the *Phaedrus* that Alcibiades' insights come to be reflected in the arguments of Plato's
Socrates. "What the *Phaedrus* will be saying, in effect, is that it
was over-simple and unfair to use Alcibiades to stand for all mad
people: that a lover can deliberate in a mad way without being

bad and disorderly in life and choice."[53] In the *Phaedrus* physical eros is no longer represented solely by the bottom rungs of
the ladder. It is also present at the top. Or rather, physical and
philosophical eros are bound together all the way up and down
the ladder. One sees this in the fact that eros itself comes to serve
a cognitive function, by pointing the way to the beautiful and
the good, by giving a person information—experienced as a
heightening of desire—as to what goodness and beauty truly are
(249e–250e). Marcuse draws on Plato to make a similar point,
stating that pleasure, properly educated, has an ethical function.
Good and evil, beautiful and ugly, are differentiated on the basis
of what gratifies and what does not.[54]

Unlike the purified soul that Diotima praises in the *Symposium*, the developing soul in the *Phaedrus* grows only because it
is watered by the springs of physical eros, understood as the love
of a particular person. It is love for a particular boy's beauty, not
beauty in general, that is required for the growth of the soul's
wings, by which the soul becomes capable of associating with
the transcendent (251a–253c). The view of the good life in the
Phaedrus is correspondingly different. Unlike the purified ideal
life of the *Symposium* or the *Republic*—Nussbaum is correct in
stressing the continuity of these dialogues in this regard—the
good life in the *Phaedrus* involves ongoing devotion to another
individual (255a–256d). It involves not only shared intellectual
activity, but also shared erotic desire, even if—ideally—this desire does not culminate in physical relations. The lovers' erotic
madness is tempered, not transcended. The lovers "do not move
from the body to the soul to institutions to sciences. They pursue
science or politics in the context of a deep love for a particular
human being of similar commitments."[55] That this is the mes-
sage of the *Phaedrus* is seen clearly in Socrates' concluding ad-
vice to Phaedrus, in which he states that only the friendship of a
lover enables one to approach true beauty and goodness, to transcend one's finitude. Love of philosophy is not sufficient. Only a
person in love with another human being can offer anything of
lasting value (256e–257a). From this perspective it is Alci-

biades, not Socrates, who has the most to offer. Only now it is Socrates who has taken the lesson to heart.

For our purposes the lesson of this story is that the best life is one that abandons the quest for total mastery and total control and accepts that happiness, as well as wisdom, may in some measure depend on another and on worldly contingency. If one is not fortunate enough to find a lover or one's lover leaves for another or perishes, then one will be less happy, less fulfilled, and perhaps less wise. There are ways of avoiding this outcome, but all, in one way or another, involve the invocation of narcissistic omnipotence: making oneself tantamount to the entire world; depending only on objects that can never leave, never disappoint—that is, internal, fantasied objects, rather than actual people. In invoking this strategy, however, one guarantees that there are certain things that one will never know and will certainly never feel. The *Symposium* suggested that these are the things at the bottom of the ladder. The *Phaedrus* suggests that they are also the things at the top. In terms of the philosophical moral of Alcibiades' dream, it is the unique, the particular, and the individual that we shall fail to know if we invoke the strategy of philosophical narcissism. Otherwise expressed, there are some things we can know only if we approach them with an open, receptive, "feminine" attitude and abandon the attempt for total control. One sees this too, perhaps, in the way in which Plato utilizes what can only be the imagery of female sexuality (or perhaps passive male homosexuality) to express the way in which beauty affects the soul (251b–c).

We shall pursue this general line of inquiry in chapter 7. Here it is appropriate to turn to the philosophical program of Adorno; for Adorno rejects every expression of philosophical mastery, the desire to know the whole.

• Chapter 4   Adorno and the Retreat from Eros

Our consideration of Theodor Adorno in this chapter will be divided into three parts. First, we will look at Horkheimer and Adorno's *Dialectic of Enlightenment*, in order to set the stage, then Adorno's philosophical program, often called "negative dialectics," and finally, his psychological studies, also undertaken with Horkheimer. It is only in his psychological studies that Adorno addresses the theory of narcissism per se. Yet it would be a mistake to think that the theory of narcissism can illuminate only this aspect of his work. In our discussion of Adorno's philosophy, we will be examining the issues raised by our consideration of Socrates, especially eros and wholeness, and will contrast the theory of narcissism expressed in Socratic philosophy with Adorno's philosophical program. Because Adorno's philosophy is terribly abstract, the link between it and the theory of narcissism must be established indirectly. In the section on Adorno's and Horkheimer's psychological studies, however, we will apply the theory of narcissism directly. Then, in the conclusion to the chapter, we will see how Adorno's philosophy and psychology are united by similar concerns, concerns that are illuminated by the theory of narcissism.

Habermas argues that the "promise, familiar in Jewish and Protestant mysticism, of the 'resurrection of fallen nature' . . . directs the most secret hopes of Walter Benjamin, Max Horkheimer, and Theodor Adorno. It is also present in Marcuse's

thought."[1] These authors are commonly called "nature roman-
tics," a term that connotes a certain irrationality. I will argue below, however, that Adorno is neither irrational nor romantic,
that his alternative to instrumental reason is neither mystical nor
irrational, unless one equates rationality solely with instrumental reason. Nor is Adorno a romantic. Quite the contrary. Adorno
seems to reject eros, and for many of the same reasons that Socrates embraces it: eros is hubristic, wanting to know and possess the whole.

Adorno rejects the whole in both philosophy and psychology, and for much the same reasons: because today any philosophy that claims to know the whole and any individual who
claims to be psychologically whole must be instances of false
wholes. Wholeness today is inseparable from reification.
Adorno's claims are worthy of serious study, for he is probably
the most brilliant of all the Frankfurt theorists. Yet his rejection
of the whole fills his project with difficulties and ironies and almost leads him to reject philosophy, not because he is a nature
romantic, but rather because in an important sense he is not romantic enough. He rejects eros because he rightly intuits that
eros is not entirely separable from instrumental reason (recall
Socrates on the lineage of Eros). But in rejecting eros, he also rejects the motive force behind philosophy: the quest to know the
whole. It is this—not his so-called nature romanticism—that
leads to a certain stasis in his project. Adorno's rejection of the
ideal of psychological wholeness also influences his project,
leading him, as Jessica Benjamin has shown, to embrace a developmental process—the oedipal conflict in the patriarchal bourgeois family—that seems to reproduce instrumental reason.
Adorno's critics are correct in sensing that his project terminates
in a certain stasis; but it is important to see why this is the case
so that the wrong lessons are not applied to other thinkers, especially Marcuse. What we shall find is that Adorno's project could
profit from a greater infusion of Socratic eros, not less.

As regards the strictly philosophical issues considered here,
Horkheimer's views will be considered primarily as they illumi-

nate Adorno's, since I assume that Adorno was the more original, stringent thinker of the two. With regard to psychological
issues, however, Horkheimer's work will be taken as virtually
inseparable from Adorno's. Before turning to Adorno's concept
of reconciling reason, which would take the place of instrumental reason, it may be fruitful to consider Horkheimer and
Adorno's critique of what they called the "dialectic of Enlightenment," in which reason comes to be an instrument of domination
and control. For it is only as an alternative to instrumental
reason that Adorno's concepts of mimesis and reconciling reason can be understood. Indeed, much of what is radical about
Adorno's views is radical only because of, and in contrast to,
what he calls "instrumental reason."

Dialectic of Enlightenment

Dialectic of Enlightenment was written during World War II and
published in 1947. It seeks to explain how fascism could develop within a nation that was apparently the embodiment of the
Enlightenment. There must be something terribly shallow and
vulnerable about Enlightenment ideals, Horkheimer and Adorno
suggest, if they could be displaced so easily by the myths of
national socialism. Horkheimer and Adorno trace this vulnerability back to a flaw at the core of Western reason itself[2] The flaw
is that Western reason is unable to carve out a midpoint between
idealism and materialism. Reason and its objects are divided
into two spheres. Ideals, values, ethics, and so forth are removed
to the abstract realm of the intellect and the spirit, where, like religion, which is an instance of these ideals, they are applauded
in the abstract. However, precisely because they come to be seen
as an expression of our higher selves, they are split off from everyday life, which is then given over to a crass materialism that
tolerates no opposition to the merely given.[3] The term "dialectic
of Enlightenment" refers to this division of reason into abstract
idealism and crass materialism.

  In order to wrest human existence from nature, it has been

necessary, according to the dialectic of Enlightenment, to ignore idealistic reason. In practice, reason is equated with instrumental reason. Science epitomizes this equation, according to which the laws of nature are learned only by slavishly imitating the lawfulness of nature itself. This is the real story behind Homer's *Odyssey*, according to Horkheimer and Adorno.[4] Odysseus outwits nature and returns home safely, but only by denying aspects of his own nature, particularly the Dionysian aspects. Thus, he must have himself tied to the ship's mast, because he knows that he lacks the strength to resist the Sirens' call—a call that represents the desire to abandon the self for the sake of fusion with the All. Odysseus is rational enough to think ahead, to make plans to outwit his own nature, his own archaic needs. But his sailors, like most men, must have their ears stopped with wax, lest they cease their laborious rowing altogether. This episode, says David Held, "symbolizes the mode in which crews, servants and labourers produce their oppressor's life together with their own. . . . Their master neither labours nor succumbs to the temptation of immediate gratification. He indulges in the beauty of the song. But the Sirens' voices become 'mere objects of contemplation' —mere art."[5]

The *Odyssey* portrays the transformation of comprehensive reason into mimesis as the price of survival. Man was once weak and ignorant, whereas nature was powerful and mysterious. Man came to master nature, but only by imitating her most rigid, routinized aspects. One sees this in experiments in science, in which the researcher subjects his every action to the stringent discipline of experimental controls. Reason comes to be defined in terms of a single task: prediction and control of the given. Thus man gradually learns to dominate nature, but at the price of renunciation. He must subject himself to a terrible discipline, under which he is forced to reject those facets of human nature that are incompatible with the controls of the scientific experiment. These are the same facets that are denied by the order and regularity imposed by the factory. Horkheimer and Adorno see the discipline imposed by the industrial system as merely the latest stage in the scientific conquest of nature. The outcome is the diminution of the concept of reason itself. Inasmuch as it is concerned with the potential of things to become more than they are, reason is split off as idealism, where it comes to symbolize little more than "an imaginary *temps perdu*" in the history of mankind. A reason powerful enough to ensure human survival and comfort in a hostile world is purchased at the price of Reason itself. Originating in human weakness, instrumental reason overcomes nature only by renouncing the Dionysian aspects of human nature, as well as the potential of reason itself. Thus it becomes powerful only by becoming an instrument.[6]

Horkheimer and Adorno's study is not merely philosophical; it is an explanation of modern history. As reason becomes an instrument of the cunning thinker, rather than an objective principle, it becomes solely a human attribute. But this attribute does little to make the individual more secure, because it cannot speak to his need for meaning and purpose, as objective reason once could. The result is an individual susceptible to mass movements that speak to his needs for security via unity with a power greater than himself. In times of economic and social crisis, such an isolated, powerless individual is all too likely to respond to a demagogue like Hitler, who panders to the most regressive narcissistic needs for fusion. This, too, is the dialectic of Enlightenment.[7]

Almost every aspect of Adorno's project of reconciliation with nature can be understood as an attempt to formulate an alternative to instrumental reason that does not simply recur to an older concept of objective reason like Plato's. For in today's world, Horkheimer and Adorno both believe, Neoplatonism can be only ideology.[8]

Before going on to clarify further what reconciliation with nature means in Adorno's works, it may be useful to state what it is not. It is not man's mimetic identification with mere nature. As Adorno put it in one of his later essays "The picture of a temporal or extratemporal original state of happy identity between subject and object is romantic, however—a wishful project at times, but today no more than a lie. The undifferentiated state before the subject's formation was the dread of the blind web of nature, of myth; it was in protest against it that the great religions had their truth content."[9] Martin Jay interprets this passage as demonstrating that Adorno held that "for all the costs of leaving behind man's primal unity with nature, his departure was ultimately a progressive one."[10] Reconciliation with nature is fundamentally about the reformation of reason, reformation of nature being quite secondary. Or rather, the reformation of nature is to be achieved only indirectly, via the reformation of reason.

Adorno's Philosophical Program: Reconciling Reason

One of Adorno's most famous aphorisms—"dwarf fruit" as he calls them—is "The whole is the false," an inversion of Hegel's famous dictum "The whole is the true."[11] How Adorno differs from Marcuse is succinctly captured by Marcuse's aphorism "'The whole is the truth,' and the whole is false."[12] This difference will be taken up later in this chapter. As far as Adorno is concerned, it is apparent that although reconciliation—with nature, man, and divided reason—is the goal, it has little to do with the recovery of a lost wholeness. Quite the contrary, for Adorno tends to equate wholeness with reification, and as Gillian Rose points out, Adorno sees reification in terms of identity theory, the nondialectical claim that concepts are perfectly adequate to the things they represent.[13] Identity theory is an especially aggressive form of categorization, which denies that reality can be anything more than the concepts we apply to it. Adorno writes of "idealism as rage" at a world too sparse to be dominated.[14] Identity theory is also rage; it forces reality into strictly human categories and denies the possibility that anything important could be left out if reality is considered under the horizon of human purposes. "The name of dialectics," states Adorno "says no more, to begin with, than that objects do not go into their concepts without leaving a remainder, that they come to contradict the traditional norm of adequacy. . . . It indicates the untruth of identity, the fact that the concept does not exhaust the thing. . . . Dialectics is the consistent sense of nonidentity."[15]

In important respects Adorno is anti-Platonic. He denies the importance of definitions in capturing the essence of reality. For him, definitions are tantamount to an aggressive act against reality, whereas for Plato, they are knowledge, since it is not possible to know something until one has defined it (Republic 354b, 490b). (It would be most mistaken to see Adorno as a nominalist, however; the point of his antisystem is to avoid forcing thought into categories such as this.) Horkheimer equates eros with dialectics, in that both seek to know an objective order, a view that comes close to Plato's. Adorno's view is almost the opposite: dialectics, unlike eros, avoids attempting to grasp an objective order directly; it says only what reality is not, and then only tentatively. It makes little sense, therefore, to talk in terms of the "Frankfurt school's position" on reason or reconciliation. Adorno also denies that the goal of philosophical knowledge is the whole, in contrast to Plato, for whom philosophy is love for and knowledge of the whole (Republic 475b, 485b; Symposium 205d). In this respect, too, Adorno differs from Horkheimer, or at least from one of the poles of Horkheimer's thought. As both Susan Buck-Morss and Martin Jay point out, Adorno's "The Actuality of Philosophy" (1931) implicitly criticizes Horkheimer's embrace of a loosely structured totality composed of research and theoretical synthesis.[16]

In his inaugural address as director of the Institute for Social Research (1931), Horkheimer stated that "the problems of empirical research and theoretical synthesis can only be solved by a philosophy which, concerned with the general, the 'essential,' provides the respective research areas with stimulating impulses, while itself remaining open enough to be impressed and modified by the progress of concrete studies."[17] Many have understood this to be the heart of the program of the Frankfurt school, a program that has proved enormously fruitful. One might call this position a commitment to a mutable whole. The goal of critical philosophy is to know the whole, while recognizing that the claim to do so is hubristic; thus, one's vision of the whole must be open to revision under the impact of empirical research, without surrendering to this research. In fact, this is precisely what Marcuse seems to mean with his statement that "'the whole is the truth,' and the whole is false." No method can be authentic that fails to recognize that both of these statements are meaningful descriptions of our situation, says Marcuse. The power of facts is an oppressive power. Against this power philosophy continues to protest with its claim to know the truth, which Marcuse, in the great philosophical tradition, equates with the whole.[18] Yet philosophy cannot claim a monopoly on cognition either. The facts are part of the true whole, as well as of the false whole. Marcuse is the member of the Frankfurt school with the greatest affinity for the classical concept of reason. But this must not blind us to how far Adorno stands from Marcuse on this point. Apparently responding to Horkheimer, Adorno stated that "whoever chooses philosophy as a profession today must first reject the illusion that earlier philosophical enterprises began with: that the power of thought is sufficient to grasp the totality of the real. . . . Only polemically does reason present itself to the knower as total reality, while only in traces and ruins is it prepared to hope that it will ever come across correct and just reality."[19]

Adorno sees reconciling reason as nonhubristic. Unlike science, it does not impose its categories on reality, as though nothing meaningful could be left over. Unlike totalizing philosophy, it does not seek to know the whole. Indeed, it appears that for Adorno the search for the whole is simply identity thinking at a higher, more abstract level. This does not mean that he rejects the existence of objective reality. It is rather that aggressive, domineering reason, in both its instrumental and idealistic guises, has virtually destroyed it, putting human self-assertion in its place. To know reality today, one must pick one's way through its traces and ruins, focusing on these fragments as though they are all that exists. Jean-François Lyotard, as Jay points out, sees a Hegelian "nostalgia" for totality latent in *Negative Dialectics*,[20] perhaps because Adorno sometimes writes as if it were human subjective reason that has fragmented reality, an argument that seems to imply a lost whole. However, as we have seen, Adorno also recognizes that nostalgia for a lost, mythic whole must be tempered by the recognition that this whole often exacted human subjectivity as its price.

Adorno, it appears, will go neither forward with affirmative reason nor backward into a false (because it sacrifices human subjectivity) whole. This is seen in his method—or rather, antimethod—of negative dialectics, which is content to pick through the ruins. It is not difficult to see why so many philosophers, including Habermas, have thrown up their hands and asked in effect "What's left of reason?" For Habermas, nothing is left: Adorno's alternative to reason is a nonrational, mimetic, highly sympathetic, snuggling (*anschmiegen*) relationship to nature. Such a relationship, says Habermas, while expressing genuine human needs, lacks intellectual content. It is the "pure opposite" (*bare Gegenteil*) of reason, pure impulse.[21] Elsewhere Habermas states that Adorno practiced "ad hoc determinant negation."[22]

Although Habermas's frustration with Adorno is quite understandable, it may be that he gives up too quickly. Adorno's concept of reconciling reason actually possesses considerable intellectual content. "The cognitive utopia," says Adorno in *Negative Dialectics*, would be to use concepts to unseal the nonconceptual with concepts, without making it their equal."[23] Somewhat cryptic, this statement nevertheless lends itself to a relatively straightforward interpretation—albeit at the cost of modest violence to Adorno's subtlety. Reconciling reason, Adorno seems to be saying, takes the reality and the separateness of the things of the world seriously, without falling on its face in front of these things. As he puts it elsewhere in *Negative Dialectics*, "It is not the purpose of critical thought to place the object on the orphaned royal throne once occupied by the subject. On that throne the object would be nothing but an idol. The purpose of critical thought is to abolish the hierarchy."[24]

From this perspective it may be useful to consider Adorno's brief, but complex, reference to Plato's *Phaedrus*, which shows aspects of Plato's thought to be a model for reconciling reason. The context is Adorno's criticism of the tendency of "enlightened" thought to equate rationality with quantification. Rationality, says Adorno, is not merely a matter of categorizing phenomena according to their species; it should involve great sensitivity to the phenomena themselves, so that they are not forced to lie in Procrustean beds. Procrustes should not be the patron saint of reason. Adorno calls this rationality that respects the integrity of phenomena "qualitative rationality" and says that it was introduced by Plato "as a corrective for the violence of unleashed quantification. A parable from *Phaedrus* leaves no doubt of it; there, organizing thought and nonviolence strike a balance. The principle, reversing the conceptual motion of synthesis, is that of 'division into species according to the natural formation, where the joints are, not breaking any part as a bad carver might.' "[25]

The quotation from *Phaedrus* is drawn from a particularly important section of the dialogue (265e). Serving as a transition to Socrates' concluding discussion of rhetoric (266d–279c), the example to which the quote applies is the divine madness of eros. What are to be properly distinguished are the different types of erotic madness. Some, indeed, lead to a passionate frenzy that disrupts society; but others are gifts from the gods, which lead man to the divine. It would be a crude thinker, a clumsy carver, who would lump all forms of eros together, as though they were a single species without joints. Yet, in one respect Adorno is himself a clumsy carver regarding eros, for he seems unable to separate it from the cunning of instrumental reason, a point that will be taken up shortly.

It is this ability to discriminate carefully regarding the subtlety and integrity of reality that is the foundation of mimesis. According to Adorno, the capacity to discriminate "provides a haven for the mimetic element of knowledge, for the element of elective affinity between the knower and the known."[26] Habermas is certainly correct that mimesis is Adorno's alternative to enlightened—categorizing—reason. But why Habermas sees mimesis as tantamount to snuggling with nature, whatever that might mean, is puzzling. He states:

> As the placeholder for this primordial reason that was diverted from the intention of truth, Horkheimer and Adorno nominate a capacity, *mimesis*, about which they can speak only as they would about a piece of uncomprehended nature. They characterize the mimetic capacity, in which an instrumentalized nature makes its speechless accusations, as an "impulse." The paradox in which the critique of instrumental reason is entangled, and which stubbornly resists even the most supple dialectic, consists then in this: Horkheimer and Adorno would have to put forward a *theory* of mimesis, which, according to their own ideas, is impossible.[27]

Our interpretation of mimesis as an orientation toward reality that actively seeks to avoid forcing things into *inappropriate* categories fails to support this view. What Adorno says, in effect, is that the things of this world have their own order and purpose, which human thought and practice should respect. This is how the mimesis of reconciling reason differs from the mimesis of instrumental reason that Horkheimer and Adorno write of in *Dialectic of Enlightenment*. The mimesis of instrumental reason imitates only the most rigid, routine, and routinized aspects of nature, those most subject to technical control, whereas the mimesis of reconciling reason respects the integrity and uniqueness of the object, which is not, however, tantamount to slavish conformity to it. This is reconciliation with nature. It does not involve passive acceptance; indeed, it may be quite active. One sees the active dimension of mimesis most clearly in what Adorno calls "exact fantasy." This is "fantasy which abides strictly within the material which the sciences present to it, and reaches beyond them only in the smallest aspects of their arrangement: aspects, granted, which fantasy itself must originally generate."[28] As Buck-Morss points out, exact fantasy is mimetic in that it lets the object—the facts presented by science in this

case—take the lead. Although the subject's imagination inter-
venes to create something new, it is at the same time guided and
constrained by the object.[29] Literary translation and musical
performance are similarly mimetic. They do not merely copy the
original; they maintain the "aura"—the presence—of the original by transforming it in the very process of reproduction. Such
an active, transforming process, while perhaps not lending itself
to a strictly theoretical account, is hardly a mere "impulse" either. That it is subject to rational elaboration has, I hope, been
demonstrated.

For Adorno, mimesis has very little to do with a direct,
unmediated encounter with nature. Such an encounter, were it
even possible, would amount to a fetishization of nature. Ab-
stracted from the whole, which includes its social context, the
natural object "congeals . . . into a fetish which merely encloses
itself all the more deeply within its existence."[30] In fact, our experience of nature is always mediated by history, culture, and
science. The primacy of the particular that mimesis involves
does not refer to the object per se, but rather to the constellation
of mediating factors that Adorno substitutes for the intellectu-
ally lazy practice of apprehending an object simply by subsum-
ing it under some familiar category. Perhaps the most dramatic
way in which Adorno sought to abolish conceptual hierarchy is
his own paratactic literary style, which places elements in opposition, rather than arguing from the general to the particular or
vice versa.

Mimesis is reconciliation with nature, including human nature, for it would hardly force human nature into fixed categories (such as defining it strictly in opposition to external nature).
"While doing violence to the object of its syntheses, our thinking
heeds a potential that waits in the object, and it unconsciously
obeys the idea of making amends to the pieces for what it has
done."[31] Adorno's statement calls to mind the stereotype of a
primitive people asking the forgiveness of the soul of an animal
before killing it. But kill it they do, in order to survive. One does
not find this attitude in Plato. Platonic thought, while allowing

itself to be guided by reality, seeks to know it all. Yet this hubris is tempered by the recognition that there exists an objective order to which human thought must conform if it is to be called knowledge. It is this objective order that instrumental reason abandons, and with it the moderating influence on the tendency of human thought to impose itself everywhere.[32] Because instrumental reason does not recognize that the animal has a soul, as it were, nothing stands between reason and world domination.

Why Adorno Spurns Eros

While Adorno's style is often cryptic, occasionally abstruse, this should not be allowed to obscure his concept of reconciling reason, which seems quite straightforward and not the least irrational, unless one equates reason with the subsumption of unique events under universal categories. But this does not mean that reconciling reason is unproblematic. At its worst, it leads to philosophical and practical stasis. It is as if the philosophical hunter can neither kill his prey nor let it be, but continues to circle around it forever. On this point Habermas, Buck-Morss, and Jay agree, that negative dialectics seem to lead to a philosophical and certainly a practical cul-de-sac.[33] Theirs is a familiar argument and need not be pursued here. Just one example will suffice. As Buck-Morss points out, the substance of Adorno's work on anti-Semitism was not original, but relied heavily on the work of Erich Fromm. Their differences had to do not merely with Fromm's notorious optimism, but with the more fundamental fact that for Fromm the goal of knowledge was to make something—a theory, an account, or a hypothesis—whereas for Adorno even this was suspect, in that it risked reifying reality.[34] Adorno's cautions are well taken, his goal to keep criticism alive. Yet if this becomes the only goal, is there any hope that the future can be made better than the past?

We have seen that the power of Platonic philosophy stems in large measure from its ability to draw on the narcissistic quest for wholeness, transforming it into the philosophical desire to apprehend the whole. In *Marxism and Totality*, Martin Jay makes the interesting point that the perennial appeal of the philosophical concept of totality "cannot be attributed solely to its intellectual content."[35] To be sure, Jay notes that psychological explanations of philosophical concepts are sometimes reductive and debunking in intent. Nevertheless, the possible relationship between Freud's speculation on "'the oceanic feeling,' an infantile state of oneness with the mother," and the appeal of the concept of totality should not be ignored.[36] These considerations hint at an interesting possibility: that it is Adorno's abandonment of the quest for the whole that contributes to the stasis of his project. For in abandoning the quest for the whole, Adorno abandons eros, which seeks to know and possess the whole; and in abandoning eros, he abandons the force responsible for the renewal of life itself.

Before proceeding further with this argument, a possible objection must be addressed: that different senses of totality and whole are being conflated here. After all, not only Adorno, but most Western philosophers, including Aristotle (N. *Ethics* 1096a6–1097a14), reject Plato's understanding of philosophy as a quest for an undifferentiated whole. Furthermore, not only Adorno, but thinkers of the stature of Kant and Nietzsche have questioned the power of reason to know the whole. Thus, Adorno's rejection of the whole can be seen as part of a philosophical tradition, not merely as a personal choice. However, the thoroughness with which Adorno rejects every sense of the whole is not required by this tradition. This is best seen by turning to Jay's *Marxism and Totality*, in which a number of different senses of the words *totality* and *whole* are employed. Among these the following can be distinguished:

1. A relational totality: the preservation of relational integrity, in which the whole makes sense of the parts. This is the view found in Lukács's *History and Class Consciousness*.
2. A longitudinal totality: grasping the whole by seeing where history is coming from and where it is going. Hegel and Marx are exemplary here.

3. The whole as something bad or negative, because it is forced on individuals by a totalitarian or one-dimensional society and state.

4. The normative totality of a totally integrated and harmonious society. Plato's ideal republic is exemplary.

5. A latitudinal whole: a set of related or partial wholes—for example, various societies and cultures.

6. A whole comprised of research (*Forschung*) and representation (*Darstellung*), in which a sense of the whole guides research but can also be modified by it. Horkheimer's inaugural address is exemplary, as is much of Marx's project.

7. An expressive/humanistic whole which emphasizes that it is made by man, perhaps by a transcendental subject.

8. A decentered whole, the opposite of an expressive/humanistic whole.

9. A personal totality: the achievement of individual wholeness. For Hegel this depends on global totalization; but for others, such as Plato, it is possible as an individual act in a corrupt world.

Other senses are also mentioned by Jay: the whole as organic and opposed to the individual; the whole as teleological in nature and prior to its parts (Aristotle); and the undifferentiated whole (Plato).[37] Jay makes no systematic distinction between wholeness and totality; nor shall I. However, he does cite psychoanalyst Erik Erikson's interesting claim that the quest for totality stems from a need for absolute boundaries between inside and outside, good and bad—that is, the demand for totality stems from the breakdown of wholeness, a more fluid integration of discrete parts.[38]

The key point, of course, is that Adorno rejects every sense of the whole and totality discussed above except for the third (the whole as bad). While one might think that Adorno would accept the possibility of personal totality in a corrupt world, we shall see that he praises Freud precisely because Freud rejects this possibility. Against totality Adorno asserts negativity. To be sure, he occasionally makes assertions such as the following:

The only philosophy which can be responsibly practiced in the face of despair is the attempt to contemplate all things as they would present themselves from the standpoint of redemption. Knowledge has no light but that shed on the world by redemption:

all else is reconstruction, mere technique. . . . But beside the demand thus placed on thought, the question of the reality or unreality of redemption itself hardly matters.[39]

It is remarks such as these that support Lyotard's claim that
Adorno evinces a nostalgia for the whole—in this case what
might be called, following Jay, a "redemptive latitudinal whole."
Yet, even here the emphasis is almost totally on the negative.
The perspective of redemption is valued because "perspectives
must be fashioned that displace and estrange the world, reveal it
to be, with its rifts and crevices, as indigent and distorted as it
will appear one day in the messianic light."[40] The whole is
valued by Adorno not for itself, but almost entirely for how it
heightens by contrast the negativity and fragmented character of
the world. The whole is a useful imaginary construct to the degree that it reveals reality to be lacking in wholeness. That this is
not backhanded praise of the whole is revealed by Adorno's
statement elsewhere that "totality is not an affirmative but rather
a critical category. Dialectical critique seeks to salvage or help to
establish what does not obey totality."[41]

If it is true that it is eros—understood ultimately as the narcissistic quest to recapture a lost unity—that energizes the quest
for wholeness, then it is apparent why Adorno's project seems to
end in stasis: in abandoning the quest for the whole, Adorno
abandons eros itself. In abandoning eros, Adorno abandons the
source of life, the force which brings change and renewal—
something new—into the world. One sees this, for example, in
Adorno's difference with Fromm over the goal of knowledge. For
Adorno, even the construction of a positive theory is suspect, because it must always risk reification—a false whole. Adorno's
famous statement that "To write poetry after Auschwitz is bar-
baric" captures the spirit of his abandonment of eros.[42] Adorno
calls his a "melancholy science."[43] Melancholia, says Freud, is
characterized by a withdrawal of erotic interest from the world.
It is for this reason that he classifies melancholia as a narcissistic
disorder.[44]

One might expect that Adorno would embrace eros as an

alternative to instrumental reason, as Horkheimer and Marcuse do. That he does not is perhaps because he recognizes how closely eros is related to instrumental reason. Eros seeks to own and possess all that is beautiful and good and will employ cunning and trickery to do so. In this sense it is not only instrumental reason, but also eros that is the opposite of mimesis. Although Socrates' distinction between common madness and divine eros, a distinction to which Adorno alludes, would mitigate the greed of eros, that greed is hardly eliminated in the sublimation of physical into philosophical eros. Socrates remains hubristic, not in spite of, but because of, his divine eros.

In a world in which the whole was an objective order, this hubris was tempered, as we have seen. Human reason would possess the divine only by copying it, assimilating itself to it, and thus becoming like it, at least insofar as it is possible for humans to do so (Republic 500c–d). Similarly, eros can create virtue and beauty (and thereby achieve its goal of a certain immortality) only by becoming virtuous. There are no shortcuts. Mimesis—the principle of elective affinity between knower and known, as Adorno puts it—is as central to Plato's work as it is to Adorno's. Indeed, it may be even more important for Plato, since he still believes in an objective order worth copying. For Plato, mimesis educates and sublimates eros, requiring it to become like the good in order to truly know the good. Mimesis thus serves the goal of progressive narcissism: it demands that eros abandon polymorphous perversity, seeking satisfaction everywhere, and focus on the truly beautiful and truly virtuous. In so doing, eros will receive even greater pleasure.

Adorno's position appears to be that in an "enlightened" world such an objective order is no longer compelling. Released from the constraints of classical cosmology, allowed to be merely subjective, the madness of eros loses its divinity. Nothing then stands between eros and its mythological father, Cunning. Eros is cunning because it shares with its mythological mother that aspect of the world revealed under the perspective of redemption: it is indigent, in need. In its need and cunning, eros expresses precisely the orientation that led instrumental reason to become a form of wild self-assertion (*verwilderte Selbstbehauptung*) in a scarce, threatening world.

Perhaps Adorno is right. Certainly his work serves as an important and necessary corrective to the hubris of human reason. The importance of Adorno's project in this regard is revealed by how readily his program is misinterpretated as romantic irrationalism. Only a perspective that cannot imagine reason as anything other than a hierarchical, totalizing, synthesizing force could see Adorno's project as either irrational or romantic. In fact, our considerations suggest that Adorno's view of reason is quite the opposite. If eros and romance are related, as they are (for Freud, as for Plato, eros encompasses every expression of love, from the most direct to the most highly sublimated), then Adorno's program is, if anything, not romantic enough. Rather, it is too self-denying, too demanding of what reason should and should not do—like Odysseus having himself tied to the mast, so that he cannot heed the Sirens' call. For to heed this call is to heed the most primitive, polymorphous demands of eros, which in its need and its selfishness might devour the world. Adorno, on the other hand, writes of approaching the world "without velleity (Willkür) or violence, entirely from felt contact with its objects—this alone is the task of thought."[45] But velleity is the weakest kind of desire, one that does not lead to the slightest action. The term seems an excellent rendering of Adorno's intent.[46]

Far from being a romantic, Adorno is like a spinster, fearful of the divine madness of eros, yet seeing it everywhere without its romantic guise, as instrumental reason. To see him as a nature romantic is entirely to miss the point. If one were to label his philosophy, it would probably be more accurate to call it "depressive," as in Melanie Klein's depressive position. Consider, for example, his statement that idealism is rage at a world too sparse to be dominated, a statement that recalls Klein's remarks on the sources of rage in greed and frustrated omnipotence. Indeed, one could read much of Adorno's philosophical program in Kleinian terms: as a depressive attempt to make amends to and help heal a world almost destroyed by human greed, aggression, and anxiety. Certainly Adorno's concern for the integrity and autonomy of the object recalls Klein's work.

The "End of Internalization": Horkheimer and Adorno's Psychological Studies

Before turning to a genuine nature romantic, Marcuse, it may be useful to speculate a little further as to why Adorno (and Horkheimer to a somewhat lesser degree) fails to move beyond the *critique* of instrumental reason—that is, beyond negation. Such speculation will set the stage for the discussion of Marcuse, who moves from negation to utopia. The context is the Frankfurt school's assimilation of Freud, generally regarded as one of its most brilliant achievements.

Psychoanalysis or Philosophy?

Adorno, Horkheimer, and Marcuse held fast to Freud's libido theory as a source of resistance to and nonidentity with an increasingly intrusive, rationalized world. Indeed, adherence to libido theory and to Freud's drive theory in general became the standard by which these thinkers measured the revisionism of Erich Fromm, Karen Horney, and Harry Stack Sullivan, among others, who promoted a premature reconciliation between man and world. This is not to say that Horkheimer, Adorno, and Marcuse all believed that Freud's theory of drives, particularly the death drive, was literally and universally true. But, as Horkheimer put it in a letter to Leo Lowenthal, "even when we do not agree with Freud's interpretation and use of them [the drives, particularly the *Todestrieb*], we find their objective intention is deeply right and that they betray Freud's great flair for the situation"[47]—"deeply right," because Freud's drive theory expresses the unalterable opposition between actual human needs and a historical world that demands the suppression of these needs as the apparent price of civilization.

The greatness of Freud, stated Adorno in "Die revidierte

Psychoanalyse," consisted in his letting contradictions such as that between human nature and the needs of society remain unresolved. He refused "to pretend a systematic harmony when the subject itself is rent."[48] Whereas Marcuse sought to transcend this unalterable opposition between man and world by transforming the world to meet every human need, Adorno and Horkheimer embraced Freud's discovery of the mind as in conflict with itself, because this discovery stands opposed to false psychic wholeness, just as negative dialectics stands opposed to false philosophical wholeness.

Yet, in an important sense Horkheimer and Adorno see an end to contradiction where Freud and many of his psychoanalytic followers see a profound contradiction. They reject Freud on an issue on which they should have stuck to him closely: the contradiction between fantasies of world domination and the reality of human finitude. In "Totem and Taboo" (1912), Freud distinguishes three phases in the evolution of humanity's view of the universe: animistic, religious, and scientific. "At the animistic stage men ascribe omnipotence to *themselves*. At the religious stage they transfer it to the gods but do not seriously abandon it themselves, for they reserve the power of influencing the gods in a variety of ways. The scientific view of the universe no longer affords any room for human omnipotence; men have acknowledged their smallness and submitted resignedly to death."[49] Horkheimer and Adorno see Freud as mistaken in his assertion that group fantasies of collective omnipotence over the natural world are but a collective version of narcissism, appropriate only to primitive tribes. They maintain that there can be "'no over-evaluation of mental processes against reality' [the phrase Freud used to characterize narcissistic and primitive thought] where there is no radical distinction between thought and reality."[50] Thus modern science, by virtue of its ability to turn the world into an idea, a scientific theory, is capable, through its technical application, of turning virtually any thought of world domination into actual domination. In the modern era, primitive narcissistic fantasies of world domination have become scientific and technological realities, which the "reality-adjusted ego" cannot help but recognize. To be sure, Horkheimer and Adorno loathe this development, for it leads to a conception of the world as prey;—but the tone of irony in their discussion relates solely to their assessment of the desirability of this development,[51]—not to any doubt that fantasy has become reality.

However, Horkheimer and Adorno have made a fateful error. Far from being the realization of narcissistic fantasies of omnipotence, modern science and technology frequently serve to deny human dependence. Indeed, several theorists of narcissism, including Grunberger, Chasseguet-Smirgel, Andreas-Salomé, and Lasch, have interpreted the cultural role of science and technology in terms of how these enterprises abet the denial of human separateness and mortality. At the unconscious level, says Chasseguet-Smirgel, science is experienced "as magic itself."[52] As such, it promises to meet our deepest needs in an effortless fashion. Deepest of all needs, according to the theorists of narcissism, is the need to deny one's separateness and mortality. In fact, several of Marcuse's comments in *Eros and Civilization* to the effect that death is "perhaps even an ultimate necessity" (i.e., perhaps it is not!) and that it should not be converted from a biological fact into an ontological essence suggest that Marcuse is not immune to this tendency to denial.[53] Marcuse apparently hopes that scientific and technological progress may one day culminate in victory over the ultimate natural constraint.

Horkheimer and Adorno become revisionists at precisely the point at which a strict reading of Freud would have been more fruitful, for, unlike Freud, they fail to distinguish narcissistic fantasies of world domination from reality. The reality is that science can ease the material conditions of human existence. Under the best of circumstances it can also help heal the narcissistic wound, by promoting mastery of certain aspects of nature. The fantasy is that science can effortlessly restore narcissistic omnipotence and perhaps conquer even death itself. The reason why Horkheimer and Adorno confuse scientific reality and narcissistic fantasy seems to be related to their critique of the dialectic of Enlightenment. They believe that philosophy, which is an act of thought, seeks to devour an entire world: "idealism as rage." They see science as fundamentally idealistic (not materialistic, as one might expect), insofar as its theories, or acts of thought, seek to restructure the world in their own image.[54] They are also tremendously impressed by the results of science. From there it is but a short step to the conclusion, false to be sure, that scientific theories, like philosophical idealism, can restructure the world any way the theorist chooses. Had they stuck more closely to Freud on this issue, they might have seen that the program of world domination which they deplore is better understood as a narcissistic fantasy. This makes this program no less dangerous, perhaps; its pursuit could conceivably destroy the world in its wake. Nevertheless, in order to understand the so-called domination of nature, it is necessary to understand its psychological, not merely its philosophical, sources, and Horkheimer and Adorno tend to confuse them.

One reason why Adorno and Horkheimer did not apply psychoanalytic categories to humanity's relationship with nature more insightfully may well have been that several of the psychoanalytic categories most appropriate to this relationship had not yet been developed, or at least, that they were not aware of them (Melanie Klein's first major work, "A Contribution to the Psychogenesis of Manic-Depressive States," was published in 1935). These categories concern how fantasies of world domination help to compensate the child, and later the adult, for his fear of separation and death, a fear that strongly evokes narcissistic injury. The Frankfurt school, however, tended to see almost all modifications of Freud's system as trivializing revisions. Thus, they saw psychoanalysis almost exclusively in terms of the oedipal conflict, whereas the theory of narcissism is concerned almost exclusively with pre-oedipal issues.

The oedipal conflict is central to the Frankfurt school, because it is the link back to Marx. It is the father's deflection of the son's libido from the mother that prepares the son for a lifetime of labor, by teaching the son that libidinal pleasure must be postponed, and later confined to the genitals, so that the rest of the body may become an instrument of labor. Marcuse goes further, drawing the parallel between Marx and Freud so tight that Marx's socially necessary and surplus labor become basic and surplus repression. In such a tendentious interpretation of psychoanalysis there is no place for the insights associated with the theory of narcissism. These insights—which members of the Frankfurt school were far too smart to ignore altogether—were left to philosophy, with the result that philosophy and psychology were sometimes confused, as we have just seen.

The "End of the Individual"

But there is another—albeit closely related—reason why Horkheimer and Adorno see psychoanalysis almost exclusively in terms of the oedipal conflict. They see the process by which the oedipal conflict is resolved as a source of potential opposition to a false harmony. The son's internalization of the father's authority provides a basis from which that authority may later be challenged. They argue, roughly following Freud, that the son at about four or five years of age comes to fear that his father will castrate him in revenge for his desire for his mother, as well as his murderous fantasies against his father. As a defense against this anxiety, the son internalizes the father's authority, taking over the father's values and attitudes as his own. It is this process, according to their interpretation of Freud, that is the foundation of the superego.[55] Society's values, embodied in the father, are internalized in the son. As Horkheimer puts it, "the self-control of the individual, the disposition for work and discipline, the ability to hold firmly to certain ideas, constancy in practical life, application of reason," are all developed through the child's relationship with the father's authority.[56]

There is, as Jessica Benjamin has argued so insightfully, something very puzzling about this argument.[57] Horkheimer recognizes that society's values are esteemed by the son in large measure simply because they are the values associated with power and authority. He writes: "When the child respects in his father's strength a moral relationship and thus learns to love what his reason recognizes to be a fact, he is experiencing his first training for the bourgeois authority relationship."[58] But why would Horkheimer and Adorno embrace a process by which the son, in response to the fantasied threat of dismemberment, internalizes the values of society? Part of the reason seems to have to do with their recognition that in the best of circumstances the authority of the bourgeois father is combined with love, and that it is through internalization of the values of a feared and loved father that a strong ego is fashioned. As Horkheimer puts it, "In earlier times a loving imitation of the self-reliant prudent man, devoted to his duty, was the source of moral autonomy in the individual."[59] Similarly, Adorno sees the oedipus conflict as a source of adult spontaneity and non-conformity, apparently because the conflict can take such idiosyncratic forms, among which Adorno seems to include neurotic protest against society, which is better than no protest at all.[60]

Horkheimer and Adorno's position would seem to be that if the process of building a strong ego via authority and love requires the internalization of society's values, so be it. Such individuals at least have the potential to challenge authority someday, in that they possess what Horkheimer calls "moral autonomy." By contrast, individuals who have failed to internalize the father's authority lack even this potential. Their argument recalls Freud's observation that women, precisely because they have not internalized the father's authority to the degree that men have (in part because girls do not face the same threat of castration as boys), tend to be more corruptible morally. Their superegos will always be less thoroughly internalized, which means weaker.[61]

It has not been overlooked, by Jessica Benjamin and others, that Horkheimer and Adorno are doing more than idealizing the patriarchal bourgeois family. They are also explaining why they

themselves were able to transcend their upper middle-class origins and produce critical theory. Benjamin also points out the
irony involved in their resting their hopes on a psychological
process which, in effect, transmits instrumental reason from one
generation to another. What one learns from the father, says
Horkheimer, is that "one travels the paths to power in the bourgeois world not by putting into practice judgments of moral
value but by clever adaptation to actual conditions."[62] This *is*
instrumental reason. Benjamin argues that they have confused
the process which produces a strong (primarily in the sense of
harsh, demanding, and punitive) superego with the process
which produces a strong ego. Internalization produces the
former, but not the latter, for it fosters fearful compliance— cunning (which may be directed at tricking the superego as
well)—but not criticism. Horkheimer and Adorno make this
mistake because they confuse the oedipal conflict, in which the
son's sexual identity is consolidated, with an earlier process,
separation from the mother, in which the basis of individuality
and autonomy is established.

In making her case, Benjamin turns to the object relations
theory of Fairbairn and Guntrip, arguing that the issues of separation from the mother and the building of a strong ego should
not be confused with the later oedipal conflict. From this perspective, it is the quality of the relationship with the mother, not
the oedipal conflict, that is central to the development of a strong
ego and individual autonomy. The theory of narcissism and the
psychological theory associated with it support the general outlines of Benjamin's analysis, including her argument that it is the
quality of the child's earliest, pre-oedipal relationships to the
parents that is the foundation of genuine autonomy. The key issue is thus not the internalization of the father's authority, but
whether the young child's relationships with its parents are sufficiently satisfying emotionally, that the child need not retreat
into a world of compensatory internal objects. For as Fairbairn
and Guntrip argue, this retreat is accompanied by ego splitting,
which generally renders the individual less autonomous and

more dependent. How later relationships with parents, which are also not fully explicable in terms of the oedipal conflict, reinforce this early pattern will be discussed shortly.

Horkheimer and Adorno and their associate Marcuse all reach the same conclusion. Horkheimer writes: "The socially conditioned weakness of the father prevents the child's real identification with him. . . . Today the growing child, who . . . has received only the abstract idea of arbitrary power, looks for a stronger, more powerful father."[63] Often he finds this more powerful father in the state. Marcuse writes of a similar process, characterizing it by phrases such as the "obsolescence of the Freudian concept of man."[64] The process that all three describe in such similar terms has come to be known as the "end of the individual" or the "end of internalization." What is meant here is that the (male) individual no longer develops his ego in a protracted struggle with the father within the confines of the bourgeois family, a process which at least held out the possibility of various idiosyncratic accommodations, all resting on the process of internalization. Rather, as the family has become weaker as a result of social and economic changes, the child has come to be pre-socialized, as it were, by the administrative agencies of the state—for example, the schools. Thus, new generations are far more likely to be drawn into and corrupted by a false social whole. Not only is this social whole more powerful than ever before, but fewer individuals have the psychic resources to stand up to it. As usual, Adorno captures the process in the fewest words, stating that "the pre-bourgeois order does not yet know psychology, the over-socialized society knows it no longer."[65]

It is in the context of his analysis of the oversocialized society that Adorno writes:

> The introduction of the concept of narcissism counts among Freud's most magnificent discoveries, although psychoanalytic theory has still not proved quite equal to it. In narcissism the self-preserving function of the ego is, on the surface at least, retained, but, at the same time, split off from that of consciousness and thus lost to rationality. All defence-mechanisms bear the imprint of nar-

cissism: the ego experiences its frailty in relation to the instincts as well as its powerlessness in the world as 'narcissistic injury.'[66]

Adorno's point seems to be that individuals today cannot rationally confront their own all-too-real feelings of powerlessness vis-à-vis the industrial state, because these feelings are joined with primitive feelings of narcissistic injury, and both are split off from consciousness. Narcissism operates as a defense mechanism, but a clumsy one, for it conflates present and past, what might be changed—for example, political powerlessness—with what never can be—for example, infantile helplessness. In this sense it undergirds false consciousness and stands as a barrier to rational social change.

In the chapter on Marcuse this issue will be taken up in considerable detail. It is important, for it bears upon how radical social change might help to heal the narcissistic wound. For now we will conclude by saying that it is not only psychoanalytic theory "that has still not proved equal to" Freud's theory of narcissism, but Horkheimer and Adorno as well. To be sure, Adorno brilliantly intuits that narcissism is more about ego weakness than self-love.[67] However, it has been argued that neither he nor Horkheimer fully distinguish socially sanctioned narcissistic fantasies of omnipotence—for example, science as magic—from reality. Nor are they fully prepared to integrate the psychoanalytic focus on the first years of life into their accounts. That this leads to certain ambiguities in their psychological, as well as their philosophical, studies has been demonstrated.

Lasch's Criticism

Lasch also detects an ambiguity in the Frankfurt school's treatment of authority and the family. He argues that the Frankfurt school, by which he means Horkheimer and Adorno, never fully confronts the discrepancy between its argument in *The Authoritarian Personality* that authoritarian families produce authoritarian personalities and the argument we have been considering, that it is not strong families, but weak ones, which promote authoritarianism. To be sure, Lasch recognizes that in commenting on *The Authoritarian Personality* Horkheimer makes statements such as "What they [authoritarian types] seem to suffer from is probably not too strong and sound a family but rather a lack of family."[68] However, Lasch is probably correct in seeing this as a discrepancy that the Frankfurt school noted but did not pursue. The real contribution of the Frankfurt school was its recognition that the decline of patriarchal domination under capitalism simply freed the individual for domination by new forces that would mold the ego more directly than ever before.[69]—"patriarchy without a father," as it has been called. Though our primary concern is the impact of narcissism on philosophy, not the psychological study of the family, it may be useful to consider briefly *why* the decline of the family makes personality structure less autonomous. This is especially important if, following Benjamin, we reject the centrality of the oedipal conflict in building strong egos. If we agree that the contemporary modal personality structure is more compliant than the modal personality of several generations ago, but reject the Frankfurt school's explanation that this has to do with the decline of the oedipus conflict, then it is seemly to offer an alternative explanation.

Lasch argues that one result of the "socialization of reproduction"—the expropriation of parental functions by agencies outside the family—is to allow the child's earliest images of his parents to remain uncorrected and unmodified by later experiences of them. These earliest images, it will be recalled, can be characterized in Kleinian terms as split-off persecutors, avenging figures who represent the child's own split-off rage and anxiety. When the parents remain a strong presence in his life as he grows older, the child ideally has an opportunity to integrate his more mature experience of his parents as frequently helpful and loving, albeit often frustrating, with his more primitive images of them. In other words, the active presence and involvement of parents in the child's life allow him to continue to work through the depressive position, in which good and bad experiences of parents—and hence different aspects of the self (recall the assumption of object relations theory that the ego is always "twinned" with its objects—are integrated. It is this integrative process that is forestalled by the socialization of reproduction.[70]

The outcome, says Lasch, is the externalization of dangerous impulses. Unintegrated and split-off images of parents as persecutors are projected onto the outside world, reinforcing the—unfortunately not totally unrealistic—perception that the world is an incredibly dangerous place, beyond human control. This leads to a tendency to withdraw from this world altogether, leaving it to various elites, which often pander to the public's desire for an avenging force strong enough to counter the forces of evil and chaos. This is, of course, the ground of the minimal self, the withdrawal of the self into a world small enough that it can exert almost total control over it. This withdrawal, coupled with a willingness to hand over to others the burdensome responsibilities of public life, is the process behind what the Frankfurt School identifies as an increase in compliance or a decline in autonomy. A better description of this process might be that it is a decline in the belief that the world is subject to human mastery. Lasch puts it this way:

> The sense of man's isolation and loneliness reflects the collapse of public order and the loss of religion; but the waning of public order and of religion itself reflects the waning of parental authority and guidance. Without this guidance, according to Alexander Mitscherlich, the world becomes 'totally inaccessible and incalculable, continually changing shape and producing sinister surprises.'[71]

The preceding analysis is drawn almost entirely from Lasch's *Haven in a Heartless World* (1977). In this book, Lasch focuses on the way in which society, family, and individual psyche interact to make it more difficult for the child to integrate his nascent self. He also deals with the consequences of this process for public life. In this, he employs a model that is consonant with the psychoanalytic theory associated with the theory of narcissism, which also sees the experiences of the early oral stage and their subsequent integration as the key to the integrity of the self. As stated above, it is the Frankfurt school's unfamiliarity with this theory, coupled with its consequent reliance on Freud's account of the oedipal conflict to explain more than it can, that largely accounts for the limits of, and contradictions in, the Frankfurt school's account of authority and the family.

The Convergence of Internalization and Negative Dialectics

Theoretical differences between the Frankfurt school and the theory of narcissism, while relevant, are not fundamental to our concerns as long as they are confined strictly to the realm of psychoanalytic theory. Our primary concern here is the way in which the theory of narcissism illuminates traditional philosophical issues. In fact, there is a relationship between Adorno's philosophy of negative dialectics and his account of the "end of internalization." Adorno and Horkheimer accept oedipal internalization because what in their eyes is the only available alternative, the end of internalization, is worse. For the product of internalization, instrumental reason, at least sets the individual against the world: man against nature, man against man, man against society (as described by Freud in *Civilization and its Discontents*). In so doing, instrumental reason, the source of so much conflict, misery, and despoliation, stands as a barrier to something even worse: a false totality of man and world. The unpleasant truth is better than the hypocrisy of false harmony. Though internalization reproduces instrumental reason, it also serves as a barrier to a society in which every contradiction is smoothed over in an administered whole. Internalization protects against such a society not in spite of, but because of, its association with instrumental reason: both set a cunning individual against the world. Internalization is thus the psychological correlate of negative dialectics. Both embrace fragmentation, opposition, and lack of harmony, not as goods in themselves perhaps, but because the only historically viable alternative is false unity.

One sees an expression of this viewpoint in Adorno's attraction to Freud's supposed coldness and misanthropy. After praising Freud for "refusing to pretend a systematic harmony when the subject itself is rent," Adorno goes on to argue that only resignation and pessimism regarding human nature and civilization allow genuine criticism of society, since almost any expression of optimism can be co-opted as a justification for a repressive order. Only a "cold," "misanthropic," pessimistic thinker like Freud can maintain a "negative" perspective consistently. Critics who accuse Freud of lacking love for humanity fail to understand that only a thinker steeled against his own sentimentality can be truly radical and truly critical. Jessica Benjamin points out the parallel between these assertions and Adorno's viewpoint that "only the hard, judging father can make the child fit for struggle in the world, teach the child to abandon the illusory hope of an easy life."[72] Adorno's praise of coldness and misanthropy as defenses against a love that might—even for just a moment—consider the possibility of harmony and wholeness in a less than perfect world, tells us about more than his view of Freud. It demonstrates how the principle of negative dialectics links Adorno's psychological and philosophical work, both of which stand opposed to the false promises of eros and wholeness, choosing coldness over love, because love is too easily blinded to the flaws of the beloved.

There appears to be another reason why Adorno rejects the whole, however, a reason that goes beyond his fear that the false whole will be mistaken for the true. Adorno may recognize that something of the cunning and strength that Odysseus needed to return home safely is also needed to navigate around the harms and dangers that stand in the way of the successful completion of everyday life, understood as what MacIntyre calls a narrative quest. For everyday life also seeks wholeness and unity, what Jay might have called a "biographical latitudinal" (that is, having a meaningful direction) whole. From this perspective it appears that the wild self-assertion of instrumental reason can be tempered but not fully transcended, because it is needed to overcome the Sirens of regressive narcissism, whose attractions are the principal danger to the successful completion of the narrative quest.

Why this is so, at least for Adorno, was revealed in our discussion of the psychological process that reproduces instrumental reason—namely, the young boy's internalization of the reality principle during the oedipus conflict, which leads the boy away from union with the mother, and hence away from the regressive solution to narcissistic injury, toward mastery of himself and the environment. It is this object mastery that will eventually help heal the narcissistic wound. It thus appears that instrumental reason is necessary to avoid the temptations of false and regressive wholeness. Because Adorno does not idealize a regressive wholeness that would sacrifice individual subjectivity, he sometimes seems, particularly in his philosophy, to retreat from the quest for wholeness altogether, as though the self-assertion associated with this quest will never be anything but wild. The conclusion is clear: without the accompaniment of instrumental reason, the quest for wholeness risks regression and false wholeness. However, with the accompaniment of instrumental reason, it risks domination of man and nature. This, of course, is a source of great tension in Adorno's work, for the psychological theory rejects the philosophical ideal of transcending instrumental reason.

In not fully coming to terms with these tensions in his work, Adorno's project remains incomplete, flawed, and filled with contradictions. Adorno appears to have recognized the power of the forces associated with eros and narcissism and to have been frightened by them. This is preferable, however, to simply assuming that these forces do not exist or assuming that their power can be neutralized and transcended by language, as though they could become merely an object of discussion. In his epigrammatic, paratactic literary style, one sees what is perhaps his fundamental strategy for dealing with these forces. His style represents an attempt to sneak up on these powers, to catch them unawares, and thereby reveal their true magnitude. Although this strategy only heightens the contradictions in his project, it is superior to assuming that these forces need only be called by their right names to be fully subject to the power of reason.

• Chapter 5: Narcissism and Civilization: Marcuse

It has been over thirty years since the publication of *Eros and Civilization*, the book that Herbert Marcuse, as well as many of his critics, regarded as his most significant work.[1] It is based almost entirely on a reinterpretation of Freudian psychology. Yet, even as it sharply attacks revisionists who would deviate from this psychology, it introduces a theme that Marcuse would develop more fully in subsequent writings, such as "The Obsolescence of the Freudian Concept of Man" (1963). There Marcuse argues, as we saw in the previous chapter, that key Freudian categories such as the oedipus complex fail to capture the experience of growing up in a one-dimensional society. Today the child is socialized by the capitalist state before he has had an opportunity to develop his own ego. Marcuse and the Frankfurt school in general have been sharply criticized for idealizing the partriarchal bourgeois family. Yet, at the same time, a number of scholars, while not necessarily following Marcuse's exact line of analysis, have agreed that the character of psychopathology has indeed changed since Freud's era as a result of social changes, one facet of this transformation being the apparent rise in the number of narcissistic personality disorders.[2] Moreover, the very idea of a "culture of narcissism" draws heavily on Marcuse's analysis of the way in which a one-dimensional society gives rise to a new personality type: outwardly adaptive and compliant, but inwardly filled with rage. Lasch has discussed at

136

some length the relationship between Marcuse's analysis and his own.[3] His criticism of Marcuse will be taken up later.

It would be misleading, however, to view Marcuse merely as one of the first critics of the culture of narcissism. *Eros and Civilization* contains a wide-ranging reevaluation of narcissism, which shows it to be a potentially emancipatory force, not merely a regressive one, as Stanley Aronowitz has pointed out.[4] Indeed, Marcuse is perhaps the only social theorist to have labeled this progressive force "narcissism." In this respect Marcuse is in tune with the theory of narcissism, which emphasizes its dual orientation. In some respects he is also in tune with Plato, for, like Plato, he sees a transformed eros—transformed in ways that are explicable in terms of the theory of narcissism—as the means by which a higher state of being is realized. Unlike Plato, however, Marcuse values the physical expression of eros over its spiritual expression. The theory of narcissism reveals why Plato's view possesses certain advantages over Marcuse's.

Since the publication of *Eros and Civilization* in 1954, the theory of narcissism has undergone rapid development. While Marcuse anticipates aspects of this development, recent theories of narcissism can help clarify Marcuse's attempt to make narcissism the core of a new reality principle. Like Horkheimer and Adorno, Marcuse seems not to have been conversant with the work of Melanie Klein or the British object relations school. He framed the issue almost exclusively in terms of Freud versus social-psychological revisionists who would trivialize Freud. Two aspects of *Eros and Civilization* are especially controversial. First, Marcuse's reinterpretation of Freud on the process of sublimation seems to involve a fundamental misrepresentation of Freudian theory. Second, and more troubling, aspects of Marcuse's erotic utopia seem terribly regressive, even infantile, in character. The goal seems to be instinctual gratification for its own sake. "Higher values" reflect not only a deflection from genuine gratification; they are nothing more than this. It is the virtue of the theory of narcissism that it can help distinguish between the progressive and regressive moments in Marcuse's ideal. Fur-

thermore, because narcissism is not readily socialized or co-
opted (recall Chasseguet-Smirgel on the demanding character of
the ego ideal), a reinterpretation of Marcuse's erotic utopia in the
light of narcissism is not likely to lead to accommodationist or
revisionist conclusions. We will sometimes have to search hard
for the progressive moment in Marcuse's work, because it is not
always apparent. The search should prove rewarding, though, as
it will allow us to move beyond the debate over whether *Eros
and Civilization* is flawed because Marcuse sticks too closely to
Freud or because he does not stick closely enough.[5]

Marcuse and Narcissism

Marcuse argues that Freud's discovery of primary narcissism
signified more than just another stage in the development of the
libido. Narcissism reflects another orientation toward reality,
one that engulfs its environment, rather than simply standing in
opposition to it. It is in this vein that Marcuse quotes from *Civilization and its Discontents*: "Originally the ego includes everything, later it detaches itself from the external world. The ego-
feeling we are aware of now is only a shrunken vestige of a far
more extensive feeling—a feeling which *embraced the universe*
and expressed an *inseparable connection of the ego with the external world*."[6] Freud, as is well known, goes on to say that he
has never experienced such an oceanic feeling and finds it difficult "to work with these almost intangible quantities." Marcuse
is less circumspect, arguing that the fundamental relatedness to
reality expressed in narcissism might, under the proper social
conditions, "generate a comprehensive existential order. In
other words, *narcissism may contain the germ of a different reality principle:* the libidinal cathexis of the ego (one's own body)
may become the source and reservoir for a new libidinal cathexis
of the object world."[7]

This view holds out the possibility of an entirely different
mode of sublimation, one that derives from an extension rather

than a "constraining deflection of the libido."[8] Much of the rest of *Eros and Civilization* is speculation about how such a nonrepressive sublimation might become the basis of an entirely new order resting on the pleasure principle. It should not be overlooked that in framing the issue in this way, Marcuse must to some extent misrepresent Freud. For Freud allows the possibility that sublimation may heighten pleasure by finding more reliable, realistic, and ego-syntonic (where erotic cathexes are in accordance with ego tendencies) means to its realization.[9] Such a view is alien to Marcuse. For him, repression and Freudian sublimation hang together, because both deflect eros from its ultimate aim, which is the sole issue for Marcuse.

In formulating the possibility of nonrepressive sublimation, Marcuse turns to "The Ego and the Id," where Freud asks "whether all sublimation does not take place through the agency of the ego, which begins by changing sexual object-libido into narcissistic libido, and then, perhaps, goes on to give it another aim."[10] If this is the case, says Marcuse, then perhaps "all sublimation would begin with the reactivation of narcissistic libido, which somehow overflows and extends to objects. The hypothesis all but revolutionizes the idea of sublimation: it hints at a non-repressive mode of sublimation."[11] However, as many critics, including Schoolman, Berndt, and Reiche have pointed out, there is virtually no evidence in Freud for such a concept of nonrepressive sublimation.[12] Even in the passage that Marcuse quotes in support of his claim that "sublimation would begin with the reactivation of narcissistic libido, which somehow overflows and extends to objects," Freud suggests that the ego is the agency (mediator) involved. Marcuse's "somehow" process if it refers to Freud at all, can refer only to the discussion that follows the passage cited by Marcuse, where the ego is said to be the agency (mediator) involved. Marcuse's "somehow" process, if his mother, by encouraging his confrontation with the reality principle as represented by his father.[13]

Marcuse misses this point because he sees repression as a social, rather than a biological, category. He takes the confrontation with the reality principle, as enforced by the father during the oedipal conflict, to be the cause of both repression and the freezing of the instincts at the genital level, so that the body is prepared (that is, desexualized) for labor. In fact, according to Freud it is not the oedipal encounter with the father, but the genital stage of libidinal development itself, that focuses the instincts at the genital level, thereby creating the need for repression in the first place.[14] Repression is an effect, not the cause, of the localization of the sexual instincts. If this is the case, then Marcuse can hardly employ Freud in support of his claim that a reactivation of primary narcissism could provide a means of nonrepressive sublimation, as Sidney Lipshires argues so clearly.[15] Furthermore, Freud's mention of narcissism in the passage quoted by Marcuse refers only to the way in which the ego abandons its libidinal attachment to objects, such as its mother. It says nothing about the way in which libido is redirected or generalized, what Marcuse refers to as the "transformation of sexuality into eros"—that is, sublimation, repressive or otherwise.[16]

Marcuse's goal is clear: that the entire body become libidinally cathected as it was before the localization of the sexual instincts in the genitals (polymorphous perversity), so that it is no longer an object of labor and the subject of political manipulation. Instead, the erotic body would come to make the whole world in its image. Our considerations suggest that this is hardly likely, or at least that there is very little support for such speculation in Freud. Nevertheless, when all these quite reasonable criticisms are said and done, there remains in Marcuse's employment of narcissism as "the germ of a different reality principle" a fascinating idea. Indeed, it is probably more fruitful to approach the whole issue of a "different reality principle" from the perspective of narcissism than from that of drive theory. A new reality principle based on a highly sublimated narcissism would not require the theoretical contortions that Marcuse must perform in order to transform Freud's drive theory into the foundation of a utopia.

Narcissism and Civilization

Marcuse claims that the "images of Orpheus and Narcissus reconcile Eros and Thanatos." He characterizes this reconciliation in terms of the "halt of time, the absorption of death; silence, sleep, night, paradise—the Nirvana principle not as death but as life."[17] Surely the reconciliation Marcuse writes of here is tantamount to a return to the womb, the paradigm of the most regressive moment of narcissistic gratification. It involves no misrepresentation to conclude that Marcuse comes close to equating eros and narcissism. Indeed, he provides the missing term in this equation. In a society governed by the pleasure principle, says Marcuse, eros and thanatos would cease their constant struggle and together be transformed into the nirvana principle, which seeks eternal freedom from pain, stimulation, and anxiety.[18] It is the nirvana principle, in which eros and thanatos are *aufgehoben*, that is tantamount to narcissism. Like nirvana, regressive narcissism seeks a state of primitive gratification so complete that the distinction between self and other and hence (as Grunberger, among many other theorists of narcissism, has pointed out) between life and death is blurred.[19] It is for this reason that several theorists of narcissism have characterized narcissism in terms of its indifference to death. Further, pathological narcissism, in which later psychological development remains under the thrall of primary narcissism, is often characterized by insomnia, which some theorists see as deriving from an unconscious failure to distinguish between sleep and death.[20] As Marcuse puts it in discussing the autoeroticism of Narcissus, "If his erotic attitude is akin to death and brings death, then rest and sleep and death are not painfully separated and distinguished: the Nirvana principle rules throughout all these stages."[21] It is precisely this aspect of narcissism, of course, that accounts for its regressive potential, particularly its inability to distinguish freedom from fusion with the power of another, life from death.[22]

Marcuse's analysis epitomizes the duality of narcissism. In particular, it exemplifies how close progressive narcissism stands to its regressive counterpart. Sometimes the difference seems to be only a matter of emphasis. The problem is that Marcuse's emphasis is almost always on the regressive form. One sees this even in his elevation of Orpheus and Narcissus as culture heroes. Marcuse is surely correct when he states that the dominant mythic culture heroes are Apollonian figures such as Odysseus and Prometheus, clever tricksters who create culture at the price of perpetual sacrifice of the Dionysian aspects of the self. The dialectic of Enlightenment is about precisely this process, of course. Marcuse is also correct in saying that figures representing the Dionysian aspect, such as Orpheus and Narcissus, can usefully be employed to represent the aspect of the self sacrificed in the struggle for existence. "They have not become the culture-heros of the Western world: theirs is the image of joy and fulfillment; the voice which does not command but sings; the gesture which offers and receives; the deed which is peace and ends the labor of conquest; the liberation from time which unites man with god, man with nature."[23]

Still, it is revealing that Marcuse neglects to tell us the full story of his heroes. Narcissus, it will be recalled, rejects the erotic charms of Echo for the autoeroticism of his own image. He finds his image so attractive that he pines away and dies while admiring it in the still water. Orpheus, Marcuse's other antihero, could charm wild beasts with his lyre. However, after striking a deal with Pluto to recover his wife Eurydice from Hades, he could not control his own desire and anxiety sufficiently to lead her back to this world. Instead, he seeks a reassuring glance of her, and she is snatched away from him forever. Thereafter Orpheus held himself apart from women, dwelling on his lost opportunity. Thracian maidens sought to capitvate him, but he resisted their erotic charms, until one day they became so incensed that they drowned out the music of his lyre with their screams and tore him to pieces.[24] That Marcuse chooses Orpheus and Narcissus as his heroes, while virtually ignoring the fate of each, is revealing vis-à-vis the psychological dynamics of his vision of liberation.[25] Is an erotic hero fixated on himself unto death really an image of fulfillment? Is someone who cannot control his own anxiety and longing sufficiently to reach safety and spends the rest of his life in mourning, rejecting eros utterly, an ideal? Surely the balance can be better struck than this.

The insight that by *eros* Marcuse means *nirvana*—that is, the reconciliation of eros and thanatos—and that the nirvana principle can be interpreted in terms of narcissism allows us to bring the theory of narcissism to bear on Marcuse's project. Doing so allows us to forge a better compromise between the Apollonian and Dionysian elements in Marcuse's work. From the perspective of the theory of narcissism the most problematic aspect of Marcuse's work is its utter separation of object mastery and gratification. Marcuse overlooks the way in which mastery can also serve to recover something of the lost omnipotence of primary narcissism, by fostering reconciliation between ego and ego ideal. This too can be a source of gratification, if gratification is not reduced simply to instinctual relief, as it frequently is by Marcuse.

Narcissistic injury stems from the infant's inability either to meet his instinctual urges or to recapture narcissistic satisfaction. Object mastery can provide some degree of compensation for narcissistic injury, however, by demonstrating to the individual that he can meet his needs in a satisfactory manner. Chasseguet-Smirgel interprets object mastery in terms of reconciliation between ego and ego ideal. In the course of normal development the ideal is projected before the individual as a hope, guide, and promise. The content of this promise is that in growing up the individual will be able to recapture something of the lost perfection of the world that he experienced in the state of primary fusion, by acquiring capacities to influence the world, by integrating libidinal needs with the demands of the superego, and above all, by moving closer to the ideal.

To be sure, much of what passes for object mastery should be called by its right name: alienated labor. Marcuse is quite correct in rejecting Ives Hendrick's "Work and the Pleasure Principle," which posits a separate mastery instinct that is fulfilled in labor but makes no adequate distinction between alienated and nonalienated labor.[26] Instead, Marcuse embraces Barbara Lantos's "Work and the Instincts," which argues that play is dominated by polymorphous sexuality, whereas labor serves only the purpose of self-preservation.[27] Yet, Marcuse misinterprets Lantos on a key point. For Lantos, the child's play represents more than just autoerotic gratification; it may also provide gratification by promoting a sense of mastery and control. It is thus quite misleading for Marcuse to suggest that Lantos provides support for his claim that eros and mastery belong to two entirely different realms of experience. Lantos's point is precisely that eros and mastery are thoroughly blended in play. She writes: "We may say that the pregenital organization of the sexual instincts has its parallel in the play organization of the ego-activities."[28] Marcuse writes of "erotic labor," which might seem to suggest that he believes that eros and mastery can be blended. However, erotic labor turns out to have little in common with labor as ordinarily understood. In particular, any activity performed under the constraint of necessity, however remote, cannot qualify as erotic labor. To be sure, Marcuse calls eros a "prop" for "work relations." But by work relations, he means primarily the social relations of building culture and only secondarily social relations among workers. In neither case does he refer to the actual act of laboring itself.[29] Marcuse states that it is the purpose, not the content of an activity that marks it as work or play,[30] which implies that under erotic social relations even such activities as ditch digging could be pleasurable. But ditch digging could be pleasurable only if it were a hobby done entirely for its own sake. The issue for Marcuse is only whether the work is necessary. It is the necessity of work that marks it as a constraint on human freedom, thereby showing it to be labor.[31] It appears that only hobbies, performed entirely for their own sake, in utter contempt of necessity, qualify as erotic labor.

There are two reasons why Marcuse separates eros and labor so sharply. The first and most fundamental has to do with the regressive, Dionysian character of Marcuse's utopia, in which it is

neither pleasurable activity nor mastery, but oceanic contentment, that is idealized. This contrasts sharply with Plato's ideal
in the *Symposium,* in which the creative act of making virtue
and beauty is the goal. The second reason concerns the internal
theoretical structure of his argument, and here we see the cost of
Marcuse's failure to recognize any distinction between repression and sublimation.[32]

Nonrepressive Sublimation Reconsidered

The "dialectic of civilization," according to Marcuse's interpretation of Freud, works as follows. Culture demands the sublimation of eros, so that the psychic energy that would otherwise
be directed toward immediate gratification can be channeled
into work. However, such repression enhances aggression, because the desire for pleasure is frustrated and because repression
leads to guilt regarding desires to transgress social sanctions, and
resentment at feeling guilty expresses itself as aggression. The
outcome is that erotic impulses which have the capacity to
"bind" aggression by directing potentially aggressive energy toward social tasks are themselves weakened, thereby requiring
even higher levels of repression to control aggression, which
weakens eros still further, and so on.

> Culture demands continuous sublimation; it thereby weakens Eros,
> the builder of culture. And desexualization, by weakening Eros, un-
> binds the destructive impulses. Civilization is thus threatened by
> an instinctual de-fusion, in which the death instinct strives to gain
> ascendency over the life instincts. Originating in renunciation . . .
> civilization tends toward self-destruction.[33]

Though Marcuse employs terms such as "stabilization" or
"binding" of aggression by eros, he does not elaborate on the
process designated. Although he does not say so explicitly,
Marcuse appears to have drawn these terms from Freud's distinction between bound nervous processes, which do not press
for discharge, and mobile processes, which do.[34] In any case,
Marcuse's understanding of binding is unique. Because he no-

where else explains the binding mechanism, it appears that he understands it in terms of the previously discussed process of nonrepressive sublimation, in which object-oriented libido is transformed into narcissistic libido, "which somehow [!] overflows and extends to objects," thus neutralizing aggression by transforming the world into an expression of narcissistic libido. This interpretation is supported by Marcuse's reference, immediately prior to his summary of the "dialectic of civilization," to Freud's claim that after sublimation (a process initiated during the oedipal stage), eros no longer has the power to bind the destructive elements previously combined with it.[35]

We have already examined the problems associated with Marcuse's theory of nonrepressive sublimation. But let us assume for a moment that it is Marcuse, not Freud, who is correct —that is, that it is the necessity of labor, not the process of psychosexual development itself, that causes repression. If this is so, nonrepressive (narcissistic) sublimation requires that labor be virtually eliminated, not merely rendered more humane. Nonrepressive sublimation is based on an overflow of narcissistic eros to the entire body and world, thereby restoring a state akin to polymorphous perversity. Since, according to Marcuse, it is the father, as representative of the reality principle, who puts an end to this state, it presumably requires the elimination of the reality principle itself to restore it. This in turn requires the elimination, or utter transformation, of labor. For it is nature's scarcity, which requires man to labor, that is the ground of the reality principle in Marcuse's view.[36]

Marcuse does not shrink from this radical conclusion. In fact, it is precisely what he has in mind. He states that in a social order governed (bound) by eros, humanity's alienation from labor would be complete, for the automation of labor would so reduce labor time that individuals would no longer need to find satisfaction in their work. They could devote themselves fulltime to seeking gratification elsewhere. Marcuse puts it baldly: "The more complete the alienation of labor, the greater the potential of freedom: total automation would be the optimum."[37]

Marcuse's erotic utopia thus comes to depend heavily—perhaps more heavily than that of any theorist since Francis Bacon—on scientific and technological progress. Only such progress can create the conditions of nonrepressive sublimation: the elimination of labor, under whose constraint eros is localized in the genitals, rather than remaining free to overflow to other elements of the psyche, thus binding both aggression and eros itself. Science and technology thus become terribly important in Marcuse's project. Transformed by industry, they become the vehicles by which Marcuse's erotic utopia is to be realized.

But, as Chasseguet-Smirgel points out, while scientific and technological progress requires secondary process thinking, in that it demands highly sophisticated versions of reality testing, such progress is nonetheless experienced at a deep psychological level as magic—that is, as primary process, in which wish and fulfillment are one. It seems to her

> legitimate to take into account the external activating factors (which nonetheless have their roots in the individual psyche of every human being) of this ancient wish for reunification of ego and ideal, by the shortest possible route, namely Illusion. The development of the pathology I have attempted to outline is to be set to the account of those factors which take progress made by science as confirmation of the possibility of an immediate reunification of ego and ideal.[38]

Nowhere is this illusion more clearly expressed by Marcuse than in his vision of science and technology, guided by eros, leading to a world which "could (in a literal sense!) embody, incorporate, the human faculties and desires to such an extent that they appear as part of the objective determinism of nature."[39] Such a vision is profoundly narcissistic, reflecting themes of grandiosity, omnipotence, and oceanic fusion with an entire universe. Andreas-Salomé interprets the myth of Narcissus in a way that captures this aspect particularly well. She writes: "Bear in mind that the Narcissus of legend gazed, not in a man-made mirror, but at the mirror of Nature. Perhaps it was not just himself that he beheld in the mirror, but himself as if he were still All."[40]

Progressive Aspects of a Regressive Ideal, and Vice Versa

Marcuse might see the charge that his ideal is terribly regressive as a compliment, given the prevailing reality principle, which sees maturity in terms of repression, sacrifice, renunciation, and control. There would be some truth in such a response. Some progressive consequences of Marcuse's regressive ideal are suggested by Martin Jay in "Anamnestic Totalization: Reflections on Marcuse's Theory of Remembrance." According to Marcuse, it is because we once knew a surfeit of gratification— "oceanic contentment"—that we continue to demand (even if this demand is generally repressed and confined to the unconscious) happiness. It is this memory, often ineffable, that is a primary source of revolutionary activity if it can be tapped.[41] We saw in chapter 3 that Plato seems to make a similar claim about the source of the soul's quest for transcendence (*Phaedrus* 248c–249d). The memory of primitive gratification thus serves not merely as a Siren call toward passivity and withdrawal; it also has the potential to spur the self to action. Jay notes an additional aspect of Marcuse's account that raises an issue not frequently addressed in psychoanalysis, at least until recently. Marcuse considers the possibility that the "memory" of primitive gratification could, at least in some measure, be the memory not of an actual experience but of an ideal, a "return to an imaginary *temps perdu* in the real life of mankind."[42] However, even if it were the case that the ego ideal derives from a longing for something that never was, this would not fundamentally alter my argument. For the latter depends only on the demanding character of the ego ideal, not its sources, as was pointed out in the introduction in response to Stern's *The Interpersonal World of the Infant.*

Marcuse's observation reminds us once again of the subtlety of his analysis. This subtlety is confirmed by the way in which he frequently approaches the ideal of primitive gratification: as an aesthetic experience. It is Orpheus and Narcissus as they are mediated by the aesthetic experience of their stories that Marcuse values so highly. He values this experience because he believes, following Kant, that the aesthetic experience is the realm in which the senses and the intellect meet. This suggests that he does not always intend his erotic utopia to be seen as a place. Rather, it is a realm, an aesthetic dimension, of truths as valid and timeless as the truths of reason and intellect. It is the purpose of *Eros and Civilization* to champion this realm, which, of course, is not the same thing as championing regressive gratification per se. The details of an actual world in which the rational and the sensuous (the original meaning of aesthetics, according to Marcuse[43]) would meet as equals remain unclear in Marcuse's work. The guiding principle of such a world, however, is definite. The performance principle and the domination of nature would give way to play and joy as principles of civilization.[44]

It might seem that the emphasis on object mastery and control associated with the theory of narcissism is incompatible with Marcuse's insight into the truths of the aesthetic dimension. Were this so, the theory of narcissism would be incompatible with Marcuse's project and could hardly serve as the source of an immanent critique. But in fact, the theory of narcissism sharply challenges the unbounded quest for mastery that is so closely associated with the prevailing reality principle, particularly as expressed in the project that the Frankfort school called the domination of nature. Narcissism originates in the infant's symbiotic fusion with its mother, a state in which the distinction between dependence and independence is not yet meaningful. The theory of narcissism sees in the unmitigated scientific and technological quest to control nature a denial not merely of infantile dependence, but of any dependence at all, including that of humanity on nature itself.[45] The denial of genuine, realistic dependence and relatedness is as characteristic of narcissism as is the quest for fusion. Indeed, it is the paradoxical coexistence of these two orientations that is one of the leading themes associated with the theory of narcissism.

Eros and Civilization is a striking expression of narcissism precisely because both orientations are expressed dramatically in virtually a single breath. In Marcuse's utopian vision, science, technology, and total automation are to achieve humanity's utter independence from the constraints of the natural world, so that humanity can achieve an erotic fusion with this world so extensive that human desires "appear as part of the objective determinism of nature." Narcissism, according to Grunberger, represents a time when the infant lived in a "cosmos filled solely with his own being, which is both megalomaniacal and intangible, merging with his own bliss."[46] It is this state that Marcuse's utopia seems designed to recapture, and if the theory of narcissism is correct, this is precisely what utopia should—indeed, must —recapture. The only question is whether Marcuse's utopia does not confuse progressive and regressive means to its realization, in part because he sees mastery and gratification as implacably opposed no matter how society might be organized. This, in turn, is because he sees the pleasure principle as the only alternative to the reality principle. Although he introduces the narcissism principle in order to theorize the possibility of nonrepressive sublimation, he never truly captures the complexity of narcissism. It remains a somewhat less socially disruptive— in large measure because its aims are pre-genital—version of the pleasure principle.

Lasch's Critique

Lasch's powerful criticism of Marcuse in effect radicalizes the preceding argument. Were Lasch entirely correct, there would be little point in using the theory of narcissism to distinguish the progressive and regressive aspects of Marcuse's ideal, for he suggests that there is little to work with in Marcuse's account. He summarizes Marcuse's argument as follows: repression originates in the subjection of the pleasure principle to the patriarchal compulsion to labor; thus, if one could abandon labor, repression could be eliminated.[47] Lasch concludes: "The achievement of 'libidinal work relations,' it appears, requires the organization of society into a vast industrial army."[48] However, our considerations point to the opposite conclusion. Machines are to do the soldering required to master scarcity, so that men can be entirely free of labor's constraint and hence of repression. Lasch is unclear on this point, perhaps because he fails to recognize how central the problem of aggression is to Marcuse.[49] It is aggression, not merely the socially disruptive character of eros itself, which requires that nonrepressive sublimation be seen as a "binding" process, a process that is incompatible with any limitations on the overflow of eros, according to Marcuse, and hence incompatible with labor.

Lasch argues that Norman O. Brown comes closer to the mark in *Life Against Death* (in his well-known article on Brown, Marcuse addresses only Brown's later, and truly mystical, *Love's Body*).[50] Brown, says Lasch, confronts the problem of scarcity in a spirit closer to that of Freud, seeing psychic conflict as a response not merely to the demands of work, but to separation anxiety and, ultimately, the fear of death. For Marcuse, the "struggle for existence necessitates the repressive modification of the instincts chiefly because of the lack of sufficient means and resources for integral, painless and toilless gratification of instinctual needs."[51] For Brown, on the other hand, scarcity stems not from a lack of sufficient means and resources, but from the very intensity and urgency of the instinctual demands themselves. For Brown, says Lasch,

> 'scarcity' is experienced first of all as a shortage of undivided mother love. (From this point of view, the Oedipus complex merely reinforces a lesson the child learns much earlier.) 'It is because the child loves the mother so much that it feels separation from the mother as death.' The fear of separation contaminates the 'narcissistic project of loving union with the world with the unreal project of becoming oneself one's whole world.' It not only 'activates a regressive death wish' but directs it outwards in the form of aggression.[52]

Brown's reading of Freud is superior to Marcuse's in several respects, says Lasch. It takes seriously Freud's later works, which emphasize separation anxiety as the prototype of all later anxiety, including castration anxiety.[53] Marcuse takes Freud's most speculative metapsychological assumptions regarding the primal horde and makes them the basis of an "economic" account in which it is the father's authority, as representative of the world of work, that causes repression. Brown, on the other hand, sees the sources of repression as running deeper, into that Minoan-Mycenean stage of mental development that precedes the oedipal stage, at which the issues are separation, the anxiety associated therewith, rage and depression as characterized by Klein, and individuation.[54] Thus it is Brown who is the more profound critic of neo-Freudian revisionism. For the problem with such revisionism is not only that it glorifies adjustment, promoting conformity of the individual with a repressive civilization, but that it frequently employs simplistic theories of psychological conflict, according to which unhappiness and repression stem merely from frustrated desires. Because Marcuse basically shares this perspective, his work is not as well placed as Brown's to generate criticism of such revisionist accounts.[55]

Lasch's criticism is trenchant. Its most powerful aspect is perhaps the way in which it reveals that, despite Marcuse's praise of Freud's depth psychology, as well as his criticism of neo-Freudian revisionism, it is Marcuse's account that is in many respects one-dimensional, seeing all psychic conflict as centering on the repression of eros. Not unlike Horkheimer and Adorno, Marcuse turns from psychology to sociology and economics at precisely the point at which psychology might have been most useful: in studying the sources of human anxiety and unhappiness in utterly nonmaterial modes of scarcity. Nevertheless, there is a complexity to Marcuse's account which Lasch ignores. One sees this just where one might have expected Lasch to look most closely, in Marcuse's account of narcissism. As Lasch notes, Freud conceptualizes narcissism in two different ways: first, as a withdrawal of libidinal interest from the outside world into the self, and second, as a state of primary perfection and wholeness, characterized by an oceanic merging with the All.

Lasch sees Freud's concern with this second aspect of narcissism as what led him to speculate, in *Beyond the Pleasure Principle* and elsewhere, that part of the mind seeks not merely gratification of instinctual desire, but primordial oceanic contentment beyond desire. Indeed, what turns the individual from this "backward path" is the experience of narcissistic injury: the insight, forced on the child by experience, that he is neither perfect nor omnipotent.[56]

Marcuse does not ignore that aspect of narcissism which Lasch finds so fruitful theoretically: narcissism as an archaic quest for merger with the All, understood as an oceanic feeling beyond all desire. Indeed, the problem is that sometimes he pursues this quest all too directly (regressively), seeking to eliminate all forces—that is, the reality principle, which inflicts narcissistic injury—that would turn the individual from this "backward path." To be sure, he often writes of eros as though the issue were simply one of inadequate instinctual satisfaction, as in his account of nonrepressive sublimation, into which his discussion of narcissism is admittedly drawn. At other times, however, he writes of eros as though it were the precursor of the narcissism principle. It has been my approach to distinguish these two aspects of Marcuse's work, suggesting that the latter is more illuminating. Lasch is surely correct that Marcuse's analysis suffers as a consequence of his simplistic analysis of the sources of repression in material scarcity and labor. However, there are other themes in Marcuse's work that penetrate more deeply, themes that deserve to be sorted out, so that we may separate insight (narcissism as an alternative reality principle) from confusion (narcissism as a basis of nonrepressive sublimation). It is to this task that we now turn, via a reconsideration of Marcuse's utopian ideal.

Mastery and Gratification

Marcuse's erotic utopia grasps the social implications of what is ordinarily a private, indeed unconscious, quest: the pursuit of narcissistic perfection—what Marcuse calls nirvana. In so doing Marcuse reveals the incompleteness of Grunberger's claim that "one could regard all the manifestations of civilization as a kaleidoscope of different attempts by man to restore narcissistic omnipotence." *Eros and Civilization* suggests that this claim might better read: "One could regard all the manifestations of civilization as a kaleidoscope of different attempts by some men to restore their narcissistic omnipotence by perpetuating the narcissistic humiliation of others, in the form of differential opportunities to exercise mastery and control." That such a statement could readily have been written by Marcuse reminds us that he is also a great realist. Indeed, this is why Freud's *Civilization and its Discontents* so attracted him. It states uncompromisingly that society requires far more instinctual renunciation than it ever compensates for via opportunities for secure gratification.[57] Not socialist revolution, but only an erotic utopia could ever eliminate this discomfort. Or, as Marcuse puts it in responding to Erich Fromm and other revisionists who are too easily satisfied, "socialism cannot liberate Eros from Thanatos."[58] Yet this remains the goal.

However, our considerations suggest that Marcuse's embrace of Freud regarding the burden of civilization could be misleading, at least insofar as it neglects to explain why instinctual renunciation is so painful. It is not merely a matter of lost opportunities for satisfaction, but rather, as Grunberger puts it, "the instinctual sacrifices that man must make to become civilized are painful in large part because they have the nature of narcissistic injury, which is compensated for in only small measure by the cathexis of civilization as a value in itself."[59] In other words the cost of civilization is not so much absence of gratification per se, but that lost gratification is coupled with narcissistic humiliation, rather than being compensated for by mastery.

Such a perspective suggests that mundane—albeit thoroughly revolutionary—social changes could help to heal the narcissistic wound, by promoting reconciliation between ego and ego ideal. Indeed, mature forms of mastery may not only compensate for lost gratification, but may themselves become a form of gratification. Why this is so is suggested by Chasseguet-Smirgel. She notes that the ego ideal follows directly from Freud's observation that nothing is harder to give up than a pleasure once experienced. Indeed, we never give up a pleasure; we only exchange one pleasure for another. Freud suggests that the ego ideal is a substitute for the greatest pleasure of all: narcissistic perfection.[60] Reconciliation between ego and ideal, fostered by mastery, thus brings genuine pleasure, not merely satisfaction in a job well done; or to adapt a phrase of Chasseguet-Smirgel's, mastery is not merely bread, but roses.

In this regard it is well to recall Chasseguet-Smirgel's analysis of the origins of the ego ideal in the most primitive narcissistic desires for wholeness and perfection. Though later integrated with the superego, the ego ideal, like eros, continues to demand genuine, not manipulated, satisfaction. Both are driven by a fantasy that is not easily civilized: eros by the incest fantasy, the ego ideal by the fantasy of fusion with the mother as representative of the All. The ego ideal is thus driven by Dionysian, rather than Apollonian, themes, even as, ideally, it is subsequently integrated with Apollonian strivings. While the mature ego ideal accepts compromise, its archaic, uncivilized beginnings suggest that it will not be readily sold out. This means that if lessening the distance between the ego and its ideal is made the standard of political, social, and economic change, the changes will be radical indeed.

But these changes need not be utterly utopian. They do not require the abolition of labor via total automation. Not Francis Bacon's *New Atlantis*, but E. F. Schumacher's *Small Is Beautiful* comes closer to the mark in this regard. The goal is to maximize self-determination in every aspect of life, which probably requires that political and economic units be made smaller, even if this involves a certain sacrifice in the sheer quantity of material goods and services available. Against the objection that this might involve an increase in social labor, it should be recalled that the theory of narcissism, unlike Marcuse's theory, suggests that labor undertaken to overcome natural scarcity can be pleasurable if it promotes mastery. Put simply, the goal is not to reduce labor, but to reduce the narcissistic humiliation so often associated with it. This begins to sound somewhat like Marx's critique of alienated labor in the "Economic and Philosophic Manuscripts of 1844," in which labor is described in terms of how it alienates man from his own essential nature (menschlichen Wesen).[61] There are differences in emphasis, however. The theory of narcissism requires that the control exercised by workers be real, immediate, and concrete, and that it concern actual working and living conditions. Formal theoretical control of the means of production is not enough.

The precise character of the necessary reforms cannot be addressed here; nor is this necessary. The list of reforms, from self-determination in the work-place to political empowerment of local groups, is familiar and has been addressed by a wide variety of authors: Karl Marx, John Stuart Mill (On Liberty), Carole Pateman (Participation and Democratic Theory), Rudolf Bahro (The Alternative), Benjamin Barber (Strong Democracy), and Philip Green (Retrieving Democracy), to mention just a few. Indeed, in his last published work, Marcuse enthusiastically embraces Bahro's book.[62] The key point, of course, is that neither bureaucratic socialism nor the welfare state will suffice. Whatever the exact outlines of a society in which genuine mastery was fostered, it would have to be highly participatory and genuinely democratic in every aspect of collective life. Unlike abstract theories of the good life, the theory of narcissism directs our attention to the actual humiliation suffered by real individuals in daily life. It thus leads us to focus on mundane, concrete measures that might enhance an individual's mastery over his own life. But if the means are mundane, the goal is not. It remains that of healing the narcissistic wound and thus restoring something of the original experience of narcissistic wholeness and perfection.

Narcissistic injury stems from the discrepancy between the ego's abilities and the ego ideal. A society that fostered genuine mastery for every citizen, by creating real—not merely formal—opportunities for self-determination in politics and in the workplace, would foster reconciliation between ego and ego ideal by reducing the distance between them. Self-determination, such a familiar cliche, would take on a new meaning: it would refer to opportunities for each citizen to exert greater mastery over his environment (the mature object world) by taking on increasingly more sophisticated responsibilities at work and in the community. A society so organized would encourage the individual to project his ego ideal forward into the possibility of his own development, rather than backward into more regressive modes of satisfaction. The path of mature narcissism should not be confused, however, with that of repression and denial. The path to mastery may be long and arduous, but it is nonetheless the path of pleasure, because it connects the most primitive narcissistic desires (particularly for the perfection of the self) with the greatest achievements of individuals and groups, those that make the world a more humane place in which to live. This last statement assumes, of course, that decent, humane values are practiced, as well as praised, in society, so that there is a real chance of their being internalized within the ego ideal in the first place. In general this is a counterfactual assumption. However, our considerations suggest that the attempt to promote, as well as realize, such values can itself be a form of mastery and hence gratification. The theory of narcissism thus does more than characterize utopia; it connects utopia with efforts to realize it. That Marcuse is unable to make this connection has been noted repeatedly.

Although my account of narcissism connects utopia with efforts to realize it, it is nonetheless incomplete. Utopian political thought, says William Galston in *Justice and the Human Good*, "attempts to specify and justify the principles of a comprehensively good political order."[63] Among these principles will be justice. A complete account of justice will have two components: one focusing on the human good, the other on how this good and the means to its realization are to be distributed. My

account has focused almost exclusively on the first aspect; it has
sought to characterize the human good in terms of healing the
narcissistic wound, achieving narcissistic wholeness, and so
forth. I have simply assumed that it is just that this good be distributed as equally as possible. But it is more complicated than
this. What if equal distribution violates Pareto-optimality? What
if the "least advantaged man" would actually have greater
chances for narcissistic fulfillment in a society of considerable
inequality? These questions cannot be answered here; they will
be elaborated on in chapter 7, but the conclusion there is the
conclusion here as well. My account of narcissism is an account
of the human good, not an outline of utopia. Nevertheless, my
account does tell us something crucial about utopia: that it will
be both incomplete and inadequate if it does not seriously confront the quest for narcissistic perfection, by whatever name it is
called.

Another more practical objection might be raised at this
point: that the object mastery achieved by adults, even if substantial, will not adequately compensate for the narcissistic
injury they suffered as infants and young children (especially
since so many idiosyncratic factors, such as tolerance of frustration, come into play). Hence, even if society were able to foster
mature narcissism on a large scale, it might be a poor substitute
for genuine narcissistic gratification. Even if realized, the revolutionary social changes proposed would not extend very far beyond the socialist ideals promoted by Erich Fromm and other
easily satisfied neo-Freudian revisionists. This objection may or
may not be valid. Since a society that fosters genuine and wide-
spread self-determination in almost every aspect of collective
life has never been realized, there is no evidence one way or the
other. Needless to say, socialist revolution as currently practiced
hardly promotes mastery for most individuals; instead, it promotes new forms of bureaucratic dependence, even as it may
make life easier materially.

There are theoretical reasons to believe, however, that revolutionary changes promoting genuine mastery might reach
deeply into the individual psyche. In particular, such changes

might heighten, rather than simply deflect, instinctual gratification. Reinterpreting the discontent produced by civilization in terms that emphasize humiliation—that is, lack of mastery—as much as lost opportunities for instinctual gratification suggests that mastery is not merely compensation for lost gratification, but itself a form of gratification. From the perspective of the theory of narcissism, lost opportunities for gratification are painful not only because of the absence of pleasure, but also because they highlight the ego's vulnerability and inadequacy. Gratification and mastery are inseparable. Or rather, mastery is the highest form of gratification, for it meets the narcissistic needs of the self for wholeness and perfection. It will be recalled that it is none other than Freud who suggests that it is the fulfillment of these needs that is the greatest pleasure of all, because it recalls the satisfaction associated with primitive narcissistic gratification.[64]

Conclusion

It is now apparent that Marcuse's misrepresentation of Freud is not a key issue. The key issue is whether doing so leads Marcuse in a fruitful direction. The proper answer would seem to be yes, but. . . . Yes, because as the theory of narcissism reveals, the narcissism principle is as fundamental as the pleasure and reality principles; indeed, it bridges the gap between them, by emphasizing the depth of pleasure possible from mastering aspects of reality. No, because Marcuse does not take this insight as far as he might. Narcissism is not merely the helpmate of eros, as Marcuse would have it; it is also the vehicle by which mature autonomy itself becomes a source of gratification, a view that leads to a quite different vision of utopia, as we have seen.

This, perhaps, is the most important point. The theory of narcissism supports a view of the utopian goal—the achievement of narcissistic wholeness and perfection—at least as radical and demanding as Marcuse's. But, unlike Marcuse's theory, the theory of narcissism does not idealize the most primitive expression of this utopia, in large measure because it views mature narcissism not merely as a detour from regressive narcissistic satisfaction, but in terms akin to the Platonic theory of sublimation, in which it is the higher pleasures that offer the greatest satisfaction, because they draw on a wider variety of human capabilities and talents, thereby promoting the perfection of the whole self. It is for this reason too that the theory of narcissism better connects utopia with efforts to realize it—namely, these talents can also be brought to bear in the discussion and creation of utopia.

Aristophanes argues that his account of eros is necessary because physical pleasure alone could never account for the things that men and women do in the name of eros, such as sacrificing their fortunes, reputations, future happiness, even life itself. This speech, as we saw, opens the door to Socrates' discussion of the something more behind eros. According to Diotima, this something more is what lies ahead of eros, what it aims at: the creation of virtue and beauty. In the contemporary discussion of eros, this insight that eros might best be understood by considering the larger purposes that it serves, rather than by reducing it to its most primitive expression, is often forgotten. Marion Oliner has the emphasis wrong when she states that "the role of the narcissistic factor within psychosexual development rests in its bestowing a sense of worth on strivings that have a foundation in biology.[65]

Though it obviously works this way too, the emphasis should be on the fact that strivings that have their foundation in biology become important because of how they serve narcissistic needs. In other words, the emphasis should be on the primacy of narcissism and its teleological character. Narcissism, understood as the quest for wholeness and perfection, can be viewed as the telos served by eros, as well as the ego. In this way narcissism gives meaning and direction—what MacIntyre calls "narrative unity"—to human life, by connecting the mature quest for fusion with the ego ideal with the primitive quest for fusion with the All, without reducing the former to the latter or suggesting that primitive gratification is somehow more satisfying if only it were possible. Chasseguet-Smirgel's claim that it is the primitive quest (that is, fantasy) that first energizes the mature quest merely connects these two pursuits, much as the "ladder of love" connects immature with mature eros. Neither Plato nor Chasseguet-Smirgel thereby implies that the immature is more satisfying. To the contrary, both define the immature version in terms of its developmental potential for making something new: virtue and beauty in Plato's case, an ego truly worthy of its mature ideal in Chasseguet-Smirgel's.

Why does Marcuse idealize the most regressive aspects of eros and narcissism? In part because he views so-called higher and more mature pleasures as little more than expressions of humanity's alienation from itself. For Marcuse, "higher pleasures" are frequently repression by another name: at best a euphemism, but more frequently a case of self-deception and false consciousness. A related reason why Marcuse embraces the most primitive expression of eros is because, like the rest of the Frankfurt school, he is looking for a hidden potential in humanity, a potential demand for genuine freedom and happiness that cannot be totally eliminated or manipulated by a one-dimensional society. Eros, the enemy of civilization, seems to fill this bill. Indeed, its primitive character, so hostile to society's norms, recommends it.

From this perspective, it is apparent that eros theoretically fulfills expectations that the proletariat fails to fulfill: it continues to demand total freedom, total happiness. While eros may be exploited—in a process that he describes as "repressive desublimation"—its demands will not be silenced by the welfare state compromise of a merely comfortable existence. Eros remains a revolutionary force. To find in eros what was lacking in the proletariat is an extremely clever theoretical strategy. But it is also risky. In choosing what is most primitive as the key to understanding society, as well as the key to building a new society, Marcuse turns to an aspect of human experience less susceptible than most to total social control. But in turning to the most primitive, Marcuse is never truly able to transcend it, as is seen in his regressive view of pleasure and of utopia itself.

Whether this aspect of Marcuse's project is adequately tempered by the theory of narcissism might be questioned. Narcissism may be a useful category for analyzing certain philosophical issues, but is it an adequate basis for social theory? Evidently a decent society will be built on the grounds of mutuality and sharing, and such a society may require considerable self-sacrifice. How can narcissism, even mature narcissism, generate this? Can even the mature narcissist come to recognize that others have narcissistic needs as valid as his own? If the answer is no, then narcissism can never be the basis for progressive social theory. Even mature narcissism may be more compatible with the institutionalized selfishness of liberal individualism. Indeed, how can a philosophy of selfishness, no matter how refined and enlightened, ever get beyond this point? Isn't this problem—that the good society requires mutuality, even self-sacrifice—the ultimate limit to the theory of narcissism as social theory? These questions are addressed in the concluding chapter because they concern not only Marcuse's program, but the overall desirability of placing the theory of narcissism at the center of progressive social theory.

• Chapter 6 Habermas and the End of the Individual

Jürgen Habermas, a student of Adorno, is by far the best-known successor to the Frankfurt school. Indeed, he is often credited with leading critical theory out of the cul-de-sac into which it was led by Adorno, through his fixation on the fragments and ruins of reason, and Marcuse, through his pessimistic retreat into the aesthetic dimension, by restoring its status as a rational, interdisciplinary research program. Certainly the brilliant scope of his project, coupled with his great responsiveness to criticism, renders his de facto status as the leading critical theorist of the day well deserved. Perhaps his greatest contribution has been his defense of the progressive aspects of the Enlightenment against those who would abandon its legacy altogether.

Yet, from the perspective of the theory of narcissism, Habermas's project is deeply flawed, because the concept of the self that it implies resembles the detached, ghostly self described by MacIntyre as the outcome of emotivism. This is most ironical, because Habermas's entire project is aimed at overcoming emotivism, as indeed it does. However, the way in which it overcomes emotivism gives rise to a view of the self as abstract, insubstantial, and detached. The theory of narcissism and, more generally, the psychoanalytic theory associated therewith reveal that Habermas lacks a robust concept of the self and also suggests the direction that philosophical social theory should take. A philosophy concerned with the good for man should be concerned with the needs of the self, the way in which society influences these needs, and how the self fares under different social arrangements. While the theory of narcissism does not support the thesis of the "end of internalization" per se, it does support the concerns that Horkheimer, Adorno, and Marcuse express in terms of this thesis. Habermas, however, rejects not only the details of this thesis, but also its thrust.

The theory of narcissism draws our attention to the quest for narcissistic perfection as perhaps the most profound human striving. It suggests that a critical philosophy should question how society acts to foster or retard progressive solutions to this quest and, in particular, how progressive narcissism can be encouraged. Of course, a philosophy adequate to this task need not use the language of narcissism. MacIntyre never mentions the term. For Marcuse, narcissism is often but a version of *eros*. Yet, in very different ways—the intensely conservative implications of *After Virtue* have been commented on frequently—each captures the issues with which the theory of narcissism is concerned. So does Plato. Habermas, as we shall see, abstracts excessively from these considerations.

It will not be possible to do full justice here to the breadth and depth of Habermas's work. Instead, we will focus on his treatment of psychoanalysis, not only because this is the way in which the issues with which we are concerned are studied, but also because in Habermas's work psychoanalysis serves as a model of emancipation in almost every aspect of life. In particular, it is a model for the ideal speech situation,[1] and ideal speech, in turn, is a model for Habermas's ideal society, or at least for how the ideal society would be realized. After seeing how Habbermas goes wrong, we shall be in a position, in the next chapter, to conclude with a number of general comments on the relevance of the theory of narcissism to critical philosophy and social theory. In general these comments will implicitly contrast the abstraction from self and family seen in Habermas's project with the centrality of these issues in approaches—such as those of MacIntyre, Socrates, and the Frankfurt school—that seem to

capture better the intensity of the pursuit for narcissistic fulfillment, by whatever name it is called.

In this chapter, we will focus not on narcissistic themes per
se, as we did in earlier chapters, but on the psychoanalytic theory associated with the theory of narcissism. The reason for this
shift in approach is simply that Habermas ignores the narcissistic quest for wholeness and perfection almost entirely, perhaps
because he disregards the earliest stages of human development
from which it stems. He neither embraces this quest, as Marcuse
does, nor seeks to transform it, as Socrates does; nor is he actively ambivalent toward it, like Adorno. This disregard has consequences for Habermas's project, even if they are not immediately apparent. Indeed, it is Habermas's neglect of the power of
the quest for narcissistic integrity and fulfillment that largely accounts for his pale view of the individual.

Relevance to the Postmodernism Debate

It is, to be sure, becoming less and less common to evaluate
Habermas's work from this perspective, one which faults Habermas for being insufficiently concerned with the foundations of
autonomous selfhood. Indeed, much of the current debate over
Habermas's work seems headed in the opposite direction, being
concerned with the relationship between Habermas's project
and so-called postmodernism, the view that it is self-deception
to see Western modernity in terms of a historical "meta-narra-
tive" concerned with the struggle of humanistically conceived
individuals to construct free institutions.[2] From the perspective
of postmodernism the question is not whether Habermas is sufficiently concerned with the conditions of autonomous selfhood,
but whether autunomous selfhood is a desirable ideal. Perhaps
the ideal of autonomous selfhood (*Mündigkeit*) is itself an ideological veil, a guise for repression on the one hand and the will
to power on the other. It is not possible to address this issue
here, unfortunately, but it may be worthwhile to outline the rele-

vance of my argument to this debate. The relationship is more complex than one might suspect.

Jacques Lacan might well be called a postmodern psychoanalyst, for reasons that will become apparent shortly. Habermas mentions him a number of times, almost always in association with Michel Foucault.[3] In key respects Habermas's view of psychoanalysis resembles that of Lacan. Both see it as hermeneutics. Lacan's concept of the signified "sliding" under a chain of Signifiers is similar to Habermas's view of neurotic symptoms as an expression of a private language, unknown even to the individual. Although Habermas holds to the concept of an instinctual unconscious in a way that Lacan does not (for Lacan, desire is not an expression of libido), in the end this theoretical difference turns out not to be central. Both see analysis as achieving a cure by reversing the linguistic process by which symbol was split off from meaning.[4]

Yet the views of Lacan and Habermas are hardly identical. Indeed, what is so striking is how sharply they differ given their agreement regarding how analysis cures. For Habermas, the goal of analysis—and its society-wide correlate, discourse—is the reestablishment of the autonomous individual on a new basis, grounded in the mutual recognition of self and other. The goal is to reconstruct (as Habermas uses the term in Zur Rekonstruktion des Historischen Materialismus, to signify the transformation of a still valid perspective, in order to give it new life) rational individuality on a new basis. For Lacan, the goal is to show that the very idea of rational individuality is a veil, concealing repression on the one hand and the will to power on the other. In a nutshell, Habermas seeks to recenter the subject, Lacan to decenter him.

The psychoanalytic theory associated with the theory of narcissism stands in an interesting and complex relationship to this dynamic. In general, it holds to a modern view of the individual as potentially autonomous. It stresses the importance of pre-verbal modes of experience in grounding individuality, in contrast to both Habermas, who ignores this stage altogether; and

Lacan, who treats the largely pre-verbal "mirror stage" as the source of a false ego.[5] From this perspective, one could formulate the issue as the psychoanalytic theory associated with the theory of narcissism versus Habermas's and Lacan's hermeneutic interpretations of psychoanalysis and individuality. However, from another perspective, the psychoanalytic theory associated with the theory of narcissism supports Habermas against Lacan, for both Habermas and the theory of narcissism see mature, autonomous individuality as rooted in and maintained by the mutual recognition of others. One sees this especially in the work of Kohut, for whom the coherence of even the mature, adult self depends on the recognition of others—so-called selfobjects. It seems fair to conclude that the psychoanalytic theory associated with the theory of narcissism generates an immanent critique of Habermas. Both share the modern project of fostering mature autonomy.

Taking the theory of narcissism seriously means rejecting key aspects of Habermas's project, but not his goal. Indeed, the psychoanalytic theory associated with the theory of narcissism reveals an element of pathos in Habermas's project; for he seeks fervently to restore autonomous individuality on a new basis and thereby reestablish the validity of the Enlightenment project against authors such as Lacan and Foucault, and yet, as the theory of narcissism reveals, it is precisely what he shares with Lacan—a hermeneutic view of psychoanalysis and the individual generally—that prevents him from doing so.

The relationship of my critique to the debate over postmodernism would seem to be straightforward: my criticism of Habermas's view of psychoanalysis and individuality goes double for Lacan and the postmodern view of the individual generally. Yet, it is not this simple. Habermas and the theory of narcissism share the same universe of discourse. To say that the psychoanalytic theory associated with the theory of narcissism shows Habermas to hold a pale, insubstantial view of the individual is a genuine criticism, given that Habermas values mature individuality. But to criticize Lacan for holding a view of the individual as constituted totally by culture and society is really no criticism at all, but only a compliment, since Lacan holds such a view of the individual to be liberating. To truly criticize Lacan, one would have to show why autonomous individuality is good and not merely one more form of false consciousness.

While this issue cannot be taken up here, it might be helpful to outline what an answer to Lacan would have to include. In many respects Lacan's view of narcissism is similar to that distilled in chapter 2, since it sees narcissism not merely as a stage to be superseded by object love, but as persisting throughout a lifetime. Not unlike other theorists we have considered, Lacan sees pathological narcissism as the result of the child's failure to separate psychically from the mother. The result is an inability to submit to what Lacan calls the "Law of the Name-of-the-Father," which resembles the reality principle as enforced by the father during the oedipal conflict.[6] But for Lacan, primary narcissism is not just about fusion with the mother as world and the associated feelings of grandiosity and wholeness. Rather, it is a process by which the infant internalizes an alien ego as a result of an inherent lack of being—the mother provides the constancy and continuity that the infant lacks in itself—coupled with the infant's erotic captivation by the image of the mother. It has been noted that Lacan's account of this internalization process can be seen as an elaboration of the work of Melanie Klein.[7]

In "The Ego and the Id," Freud describes the ego as "a precipitate of abandoned object-cathexes . . . [which] contains the history of those object choices."[8] Freud argues, however, that a mature ego will not be bound by these precipitates. Lacan responds that Freud is mistaken on this score, perhaps because Freud lacked our current knowledge about the role of mimesis in animal behavior. In fact, says Lacan, narcissistic identification, the process to which the above quotation refers, is the way in which the ego is formed and maintained. Indeed, Lacan sees the ego as ultimately little more than a series of identifications, and maturity as a matter of substituting a series of more abstract identifications for the primary identification with the mother.

Against mature autonomy, Lacan praises a subject with the courage to confront the ultimate vacuity of his own identity.[9]

How such a view leads Lacan to challenge the possibility of an autonomous ego—at least as this possibility has been understood in the tradition of the Enlightenment as *Mündigkeit*[10]—is apparent. Why such a view also leads Lacan to question the desirability of autonomy is complex and cannot be dealt with here. Suffice it to note that the answer to this question depends in large part on whether Lacan's psychoanalytic account of the premirror and mirror stages is correct, on whether the ego is capable of transcending its identifications. If it is not, then the ideal of ego autonomy is a false goal. We are faced here with a situation similar to that encountered in considering MacIntyre's *After Virtue*. Lacan and MacIntyre both raise interdependent empirical and normative issues which must nonetheless be distinguished. Although it would take us too far afield to try to sort out the various issues raised by Lacan, the relevance of issues raised by postmodernism will be highlighted at several points in our discussion of Habermas.

In the next section, Habermas's view of psychoanalysis will be contrasted with the psychoanalytic theory associated with the theory of narcissism. In the section after that, it will be shown how Habermas's view of psychoanalysis leads him to render the individual in terms excessively abstract, in the apparent hope that individuals so conceived might be more responsive to the emancipatory power of language. In the final section, it will be concluded that in many respects the first generation of Frankfurt theorists was on the right track in focusing on the relationship between authority and the family.

Habermas and the Hermeneutic Interpretation of Psychoanalysis

The two essays on psychoanalysis in *Knowledge and Human Interests* remain central to Habermas's interpretation of the psychoanalytic enterprise. His observations on psychoanalysis in

Theorie des kommunikativen Handelns suggest that his ideas on the subject have changed very little,[11] and his brief remarks on Freud in several pieces collected in his recent *Der philosophische Diskurs der Moderne* confirm this impression.[12] Habermas calls psychoanalysis a "depth hermeneutics."[13] By this he means not merely that it interprets those who would deceive themselves, but also that virtually all psychopathology can be viewed as a suppression of communication. However, for psychoanalysis to be plausibly construed as depth hermeneutics, the phenomena with which it deals must be shown to be essentially linguistic or at least pre-linguistic in character. This is what Habermas sets out to demonstrate in the two essays on Freud in *Knowledge and Human Interests*. It is a far more crucial, difficult project than simply demonstrating that Freud "scientistically" misunderstood himself. For even if Freud were mistaken about the scientific status of analysis, this by itself would not demonstrate that psychoanalysis is properly construed as depth hermeneutics. Indeed, this is precisely what the psychoanalytic theory associated with the theory of narcissism suggests.

Habermas argues that psychopathology originates when a traumatic event causes a *"deviation from the model of the language game of communicative action, in which motives of action and linguistically expressed intentions coincide."*[14] The outcome, which may not become apparent until much later, is the development of symptoms. For Habermas, symptoms are an expression of a private language unknown to the conscious self. Hence the individual is unable to communicate freely not only with others, but also with himself. "Because the symbols that interpret suppressed needs are excluded from public communication, the speaking and acting subject's *communication with himself is interrupted.* The privatized language of unconscious motives is rendered inaccessible to the ego."[15] From this perspective the goal of analysis, as well as its practice, is straightforward: to reverse the process of symptom (private symbol) formation by translating the alienated private language into public language, thereby bringing the analysand back into the public world, in which intentions and actions coincide, and there are no secret codes and hidden meanings. As Habermas puts it: "The ego's flight from itself is an operation that is carried out in and with language. Otherwise it would not be possible to reverse the defensive process hermeneutically, via the analysis of language [that is, psychoanalysis]."[16]

But this assertion, as is quite apparent, begs the question. It is hardly given that psychoanalysis is best understood as achieving its results by depth hermeneutics. Arguments along these lines have been leveled against Habermas frequently. Most point out that Habermas misinterprets Freud in suggesting that it is insight that cures the patient and that insight has the potential of being almost total. Henning Ottmann, for example, argues that Habermas overintellectualizes the process of psychoanalytic reflection.

> It seems exaggerated to elevate the patient's "self-reflection" to a means of liberation. In psychotherapy, liberation is more the result of the "emotional acting-out of the conflict," of repetition, resistance, and emotional upset. . . . In Habermas' intellectualised interpretation, reflection is attributed to what is actually accomplished by the working out of the conflict.[17]

In similar fashion Russell Keat argues that Habermas is quite mistaken in equating id with alienated ego.

> Having (mis)-understood the concept of the id as the alienated ego, he [Habermas] presents in effect a literal and unqualified reading of this dictum ["Where Id was there Ego shall be"], so that the abolition of the id is seen as a possible and desirable outcome of the therapeutic process. Likewise, the instincts are regarded as the sources only of pathological neurotic activity; and indeed the same is true of all unconscious determinants.[18]

Ottmann exaggerates perhaps; certainly Keat does. As early as 1968, in an appendix to *Knowledge and Human Interests*, Habermas suggested that emancipation—in psychoanalysis and discourse—depends on the interaction of understanding and catharsis. It is the latter that removes emotional barriers standing in the way of admitting needs to consciousness and hence to rational understanding.[19] Nevertheless, there does seem to be a certain alienation from aspects of human nature implicit in Habermas's concept of psychoanalysis, since there is little room for aspects that cannot be made transparent in discourse.[20]

Kohut argues that analysis cures not by means of increased insight and understanding, but rather by a largely unconscious process, "transmuting internalization," in which the analyst's presence and empathic responsiveness are internalized by the analysand.[21] Interestingly, one finds a hint of this idea of how analysis cures in Habermas's work, not in his discussion of psychoanalysis, to be sure, but in his reinterpretation of Horkheimer and Adorno's ideal of reconciliation with nature. Habermas quotes from Adorno's interpretation of Eichendorff's concept of "beautiful otherness" (Schönen Fremde) in order to capture the concept of reconciliation as applied strictly to human relations. "The situation of reconciliation does not annex the foreign as a form of philosophical imperialism; its happiness stems from its protected nearness to the distant and different, on the other side of the heterogeneous as well as individual."[22] Though he did not intend to, says Habermas, Adorno described reconciliation in terms of an unimpaired intersubjectivity that is established and maintained in discourse.[23] To understand the power of discourse in this fashion—that it is based not so much on bracketing all that keeps language from its telos of truth, but rather on heightened empathy that has unconditional regard for the subjectivity of the other person—is to come close indeed to Kohut's concept of how analysis cures. It is unfortunate that Habermas did not develop this point. It remains confined to his encounter with the most utopian moments of Horkheimer and Adorno's work. We shall see that this is part of a pattern in Habermas's work, that he recognizes the importance of needs not readily expressed in language, but cannot integrate them into his system because he has no categories for them.

From the perspective of the psychoanalytic theory associated with the theory of narcissism, the most striking aspect of

Habermas's treatment of psychoanalysis is his utter neglect of the earliest stages of life. In his "Historical Materialism and the Development of Normative Structures" (originally published in 1976), Habermas devotes three sentences to the first year of life.[24] This is in a long section on the stages of ego development according to psychoanalytic and cognitive developmental psychology. That Habermas does not consider what he calls the "symbiotic" stage theoretically significant may be because it is prior to the full differentiation of subjects: mother and child. At this stage it is not conceptually meaningful, he suggests, to speak of intersubjective communication, intersubjective interaction, and the like. Once again, the assumption that development is to be understood in terms of language renders stages and events that cannot be so explained theoretically vapid.

One is reminded here of Rousseau's criticism of previous state-of-nature theorists: that they take as man's nature what is in reality the outcome of a long process of civilization, and that to apprehend man's true nature, it is necessary to go further back.[25] Similarly, the theory of narcissism suggests that Habermas presumes what should no longer be taken for granted: namely, that psychologically informed social theory begins— and should begin—with a fully differentiated self. That he does so is not too surprising. Object relations theorists sometimes argue that Freud took the existence of the self for granted, which may have been because the types of neuroses with which he was primarily concerned are characterized by a relatively intact, albeit generally repressed, ego.[26] Habermas's hermeneutic interpretation of Freud cannot draw out what is not there in the first place. If a robust vision of the self is not found elsewhere in Habermas's project, then it will not be found at all.

The Seventh Stage

Why a concern with the self is so important has already been suggested in chapters 4 and 5. If one abandons Freudian drive theory, especially libido theory, then one lacks a powerful, virtually untouchable source of opposition to repressive socialization. The self is left vulnerable to manipulation. Habermas's hermeneutic interpretation of Freud in effect abandons the force of libido theory and the drives generally. In its place, as a source of opposition to totalitarian socialization by parents and state, Habermas puts language, especially discourse. However, it is most problematic whether language can fulfill this function. Even more problematic is whether it should. For language to fulfill this function, the individual must be rendered in more abstract, shadowy terms than would otherwise be necessary. In other words, Habermas's neglect of the first, least individuated stage of development leads to a certain neglect of aspects of adult individuality as well.

One sees this neglect most clearly in Habermas's reinterpretation of Lawrence Kohlberg's stages of moral development. Habermas argues that Kohlberg's account of the stages of moral development, culminating in the sixth stage (the stage of universal ethical principles), while a most valuable perspective, stops short. In his reinterpretation of Kohlberg's stages in light of the general structures of communicative action, Habermas demonstrates the possibility of a seventh stage. But, as Joel Whitebook points out, this seventh stage reflects a shift in Habermas's thinking. It represents his recognition of the validity of the claim not only to justice, but also to happiness, a recognition that has otherwise not played as important a role in Habermas's work as it has in the work of the first generation of critical theorists.[27]

Habermas argues that Kohlberg's sixth stage takes as given the conflict between reason and needs, that it expresses a Kantian view of morality, insofar as it conceives of morality as the subordination of needs to universal rational principles. Habermas's seventh stage seeks to transcend this hierarchy so that "need interpretations are no longer assumed as given, but are drawn into the discursive formation of will." At this stage, says Habermas, inner nature is no longer regarded as fixed or given. Rather, needs are "released from their paleosymbolic prelinguisticality" and themselves become subject to discourse. "But this means that internal nature is not subjected, in the cultural preformation met with at any given time, to the demands of ego autonomy; rather, through a dependent ego it obtains free access to the interpretive possibilities of the cultural tradition."[28]

More recently, Habermas has written about this process in terms of a radicalized aesthetic consciousness. He suggests that the radical decoupling of aesthetics from science and tradition characteristic of the modern world ("autonomous art") allows the possibility that an aesthetic sensibility might generate a purer insight into needs, bypassing the way in which these needs are deformed by society and culture.[29] This appears to be what Habermas has in mind when, in the otherwise puzzling quotation above, he refers to an ego, released from the demands of autonomy, able to gain free access to the cultural tradition. How these considerations address the issues raised by postmodern critics such as Lacan and Foucault is obvious. Indeed, Habermas refers to this aesthetic experience in the language of postmodernism, using terms such as "decentered, unbound subjectivity."[30] This concern with a reality revealed by aesthetics is not entirely new to Habermas's work. In a piece originally published in 1972, Habermas expressed sympathy for Walter Benjamin's idea of a mimetic, nonpurposively rational, spontaneous attitude toward nature, especially as this attitude is expressed in "post-auratic" (that is, exoteric) art.[31] Habermas found such an attitude attractive because he recognized that it represents a genuine human need for communion with nature, a need not adequately fulfulled by either technical or practical cognitive interests (what he now calls, following Max Weber, the cultural value spheres of science and technology, and law and morality).[32]

Habermas thus recognizes the significance of experiences and needs that are not essentially linguistic.[33] The difficulty, as many critics, such as Martin Jay and Stephen White, point out, is that while Habermas insists that "autonomous art" cannot and should not become a social force by itself, he seems to have no very clear idea of how the needs and experiences it reveals might be rendered in language.[34] These needs and experiences remain at the edge of Habermas's program, recognized as significant, but not theoretically integrated into his system. This is quite unlike Habermas's earlier "emancipatory cognitive interest," which he took great pains to derive from the practical cognitive interest in language.[35]

Yet, at points in Habermas's work where the utopian impulse is strongest, the ideal of theoretically integrating the elements that Habermas calls aesthetic is a powerful presence. Indeed, this is precisely what Habermas's stage seven is about. What Whitebook calls the "implicit linguistic idealism" of Habermas's interpretation of Freud is nothing else but the suggestion that the needs and experiences that Habermas now deals with under the rubric "aesthetics" might become totally transparent in language.[36] Jay, Whitebook, and White have shown how sketchy Habermas's conception of this ideal truly is. It may be more useful here to consider its desirability than its content. Thus we will examine, in terms of Habermas's understanding of psychoanalysis and discourse, whether the integration of pre- and non-linguistic needs and experiences into discourse would foster mature autonomy.

Why the integration of these needs and experiences into Habermas's larger project might not be desirable is suggested by the relationship of individual and society implicit in stage seven. For at this stage there is almost no difference between individual and social needs. Which individual needs are to be met seems to depend entirely on cultural consensus, such needs being evaluated solely in terms of "the interpretive possibilities of the cultural tradition" as interpreted in discourse.[37] There seems to be no place for an understanding of individual needs as valuable precisely because they challenge, by their very privacy and intensity, even a discursively achieved cultural consensus and so emphasize the separateness and hence the potential autonomy of the individual. Needs themselves, understood strictly as an expression of primary (unconscious) psychological processes, brook no compromise and hence no consensus: there is no such thing as too much satisfaction of needs. Indeed, it is precisely this aspect of eros that the Frankfurt school found so valuable as a source of opposition to a false totality. Needless to say, the uncompromising character of individual needs is not an unalloyed value. The goal is rather to strike a balance between individual and social needs. The problem is that the balance which Habermas strikes is weighted too much to the social side. Or rather, that sometimes he seems to see no difference between the two sides.

The implicit goal of stage seven is to restore happiness as the goal of the good society. However, in "On Hedonism," Marcuse reminds us that happiness has rarely been a principle of social organization, both because its unfettered pursuit is socially disruptive and because happiness is such an individual, private matter.[38] By contrast, Habermas writes of happiness as though it were almost solely a matter of groups discursively determining which needs are to be met. Happiness, traditionally such a private matter, becomes primarily a public affair. It becomes strictly a matter for discourse. For Habermas, group discourse is psychoanalysis writ large. Both seek to make the private public and thereby overcome the individual's alienation from himself. The result, however, is the totally socialized man, for whom social integration (nonalienation from society) is identical with personal integration (nonalienation from self).

One might respond that Habermas's stage seven characterizes utopia. For only in utopia is it acceptable to eliminate the tension between individual and group. As a theoretical observation about the role of negative—that is, nonaffirmative—thinking in critical social theory, such a response may be correct. However, we have seen the origins of this loss of tension between individual and group in Habermas's view of psychoanalysis, in which the therapeutic goal is to render the private totally public. From this perspective Habermas's utopian stage seven is continuous with his reinterpretation of contemporary psychoanalytic practice. In both, the thesis of the linguistic mediation of needs becomes a thesis of the linguistically mediated character of individuality. Such a thesis is partially correct, of course. However, in Habermas's system, and especially within stage seven, individuality becomes so thoroughly mediated by language that the individual's access to himself is —ideally— identical with the access of others to him in discourse. The unique, substantial individual is lost to the group.

In "A Reply to my Critics" (1982), Habermas writes: "I do not regard the fully transparent society as an ideal, nor do I wish to suggest any other ideal."[39] However, in "Moral Development and Ego Identity" (originally published in 1974), Habermas stated that in the seventh stage, "internal nature is thereby moved into a utopian perspective. . . . Inner nature is rendered communicatively fluid and transparent to the extent that needs can . . . be kept articulable (sprachfähig)."[40] How is this difference in tone regarding the ideal of transparency to be explained? Has Habermas changed his mind? He now appears to make a distinction between transparency as means and transparency as end. It is through maximal individual and social transparency that we are assured that a discursively achieved consensus is, ceteris paribus, legitimate: that it does not repress or deny needs and experiences that would otherwise be addressed in discourse. As Habermas suggests in a recent article, transparency is a formal condition of utopia, but the content of utopia remains open, to be determined by communication communities themselves.[41] But Habermas's distinction—which seems correct as far as it goes—does not really address the problem raised here. Maximal transparency, as Habermas understands it, is a problem whether seen as means or end. It is the tendency to equate individual and social needs that is the problem, regardless of whether this equation is seen as the means to a contentless utopia or the utopia itself. Indeed, the equation may be even more problematic when seen as a means. For the discrepancy between means and ends reveals that Habermas questions as an ideal the process on which he relies so heavily as a means to its realization.

The "End of the Individual"?

Habermas explicitly rejects what he calls the "thesis of the end of the individual" promoted by Adorno and Marcuse.[42] Though stated in different ways at different times by each, the core of this thesis, as we saw in chapter 4, is the assertion that the subjection of hitherto private sectors of existence (such as child rearing, family planning, and education) to administrative direction and control has led to a generation of individuals no longer able to resist authority. This is because the development of an independent ego is a long, slow process that requires that the child be sheltered for some time from the outside world; but this is precisely what the administrative state's intrusion into family life does not allow. Habermas states that Adorno and Marcuse have been seduced by "an overly sensitive perception and an overly simplified interpretation of certain tendencies, into developing a left counterpart to the once popular theory of totalitarian domination. I mention these utterances only to draw attention to the fact that critical social theory still holds fast to the concept of the autonomous ego, even when it makes the gloomy prognosis that this ego is losing its basis."[43] This is one of Habermas's sharpest criticisms of the first generation of critical theorists. It is also not entirely clear. Are Adorno and Marcuse stating anything more than Habermas admits in the last sentence?

Elsewhere Habermas says that what would constitute the real end of the individual would be the separation of socialization from justification.[44] This would be tantamount to the total administration of meaning; for individuals would no longer demand that norms be discursively justified. Habermas's is a trenchant reconceptualization of the character of total administration. However, he goes too far in the other direction; for there is a sense in which Habermas's stage seven also threatens the individual. Culture is equated with the self to such a degree that the unique, concrete individual is diminished. In stage seven the individual is only the mirror of culture. One sees this most clearly in Habermas's treatment of happiness, as though its content were best determined by groups deciding which cultural values to realize. In another respect, though, culture is located too much outside the individual, as though it had no intrapsychic persistence. By treating culture in stage seven as though it were a catalog of alternatives to be sifted through in discourse, Habermas downplays the ways in which family and society may circumscribe these choices. His likely response that in stage seven such constraints are removed by adherence to the principles of free and open communication—the general symmetry conditions of discourse[45]—would not be compelling, in view of our consideration in chapter 4 of how such constraints may become part of the self.

The preceding discussion suggests that in Habermas's work the individual and his culture hover too freely above the real world. The individual is not bound by the developmental conditions that constitute the self, and culture becomes a catalog of opportunities, rather than a virtual extension of the self. Why Habermas sees the relationship between individual and culture in this fashion stems not only from his hermeneutic interpretation of Freud. There is another, albeit related, reason. Unlike Horkheimer, Adorno, and Marcuse, who see the end of the individual as an entirely negative affair, Habermas sees in it a potentially progressive development. For the transformation of a culturally given background into a politically administered foreground, while threatening individuality in new ways, also raises questions of justification and legitimation regarding practices previously taken for granted. Discourse over these practices thus becomes possible for the first time, as they are raised out of their apparent naturalness.

But such an argument assumes what can no longer be taken for granted: that individuals who can and will demand convincing justification and legitimation will continue to exist. Though Habermas recognizes the possibility that this questioning may not occur, at least as long as a legitimation deficit does not coincide with an economic crisis, he regards the emergence of demands for legitimation as likely.[46] Why? We have already seen the outline of the answer. From his view of psychoanalysis to his stage seven to his confidence in the potentially emancipatory aspects of the intrusion of politics into private life, Habermas sees individual autonomy as ultimately a reflection of the free use of language in groups. The thesis of the potential utter linguistic transparency of the psyche simply does not allow for the end of the individual, because in a certain sense there is no beginning of the individual. The source of the quest for freedom and autonomy rests far more in the transcendent structure of language than in the psyches of human beings. As Habermas put it in his inaugural lecture at the University of Frankfurt in 1965, "the human interest in autonomy and responsibility (*Mündigkeit*) is not mere fancy, for it can be apprehended a priori. What raises us out of nature is the only thing whose nature we can know: *language. Though its structure, autonomy and responsibility are posited for us.*"[47]

We can now see why the concerns of an earlier generation of critical theorists regarding the end of the individual do not weigh so heavily on Habermas, even if they have come due with interest. Habermas holds to what is really a quite different view of the individual, as one whose search for freedom and autonomy is in a certain sense derived not from assumptions about human nature, but from assumptions about the emancipatory character of language. It is for this reason that the private realms of individual and family are not central. This is not solely because Habermas's theory is abstract or merely because he emphasizes the public sphere. It is rather because in Habermas's model of the individual there is really no place for the private. Strivings that an earlier generation of critical theorists saw as emerging from man's innermost nature, as well as his most intimate relations, in Habermas's system reach down to him from the public sphere, and ultimately from the structure of language.

Conclusion

Our considerations suggest that Horkheimer, Adorno, and Marcuse were on the right track, that the critical study of society

182 HABERMAS AND THE END OF THE INDIVIDUAL

cannot ignore the way in which families reproduce the types of individuals that society requires. If families do not foster the growth of individuals with coherent selves, capable of utilizing culture while at the same time maintaining a critical distance from it, nothing else will. For the psychoanalytic theory associated with the theory of narcissism, there is no instinctual *deus ex machina*, in the form of an eros that longs to be free of social constraint and can substitute for the autonomy of the self. Nor is the discursive use of language capable of overcoming the effects of unresponsive and repressive socialization—at least, not without conceptualizing the individual in excessively abstract terms.

Were the critical study of society to focus on the family, it would be dealing with the conditions that produce or fail to produce those public individuals with whom political philosophy has traditionally been concerned. Political philosophy, of course, has not been concerned with the family for the most part. To the contrary, much Western political thought has sought to elevate the public realm, in the manner of ancient Greece, as against the modern world's fascination with another facet of the private: the realm of getting and spending. This is especially true of Habermas. Since the publication of his *Strukturwandel der Öffentlichkeit* (1962), he has sought to restore the realm of free public discussion to the center of political philosophy. Further, many feminists, otherwise so critical of much Western political thought, have directed their attention to expanding the public realm by opening it to women. However, the more acute insight would seem to be that of Nancy Chodorow and Dorothy Dinnerstein: that it is of equal importance to bring men into the private sphere, into the world of family and child rearing.[48] Were such a program successful, the private realm of child rearing and family would presumably come to be regarded as fundamental, important, and worthy of serious men's and women's attention as the public. It would seem to be an appropriate task for critical social philosophy to begin to weave this insight into its accounts, much as an earlier generation of critical theorists brought the insights of Freud to bear on its critique.

The first generation of critical theorists turned to Freud because he added depth to the concept of false consciousness so useful in explaining the failure of proletarian revolution. Freud also helped to explain the vast aggression that, while always a feature of world history, had recently become vastly more mechanized and rationalized. More important, perhaps, Freud's libido theory promised that a facet of human nature that loved freedom might survive the coming dark ages of fascism, as well as the totally administered state in both its Eastern and Western versions. Habermas also turns to Freud, but not the same Freud. Habermas turns to what he regards as the hermeneutic power of psychoanalysis, in order to explain and justify the emancipatory power of discourse. The psychoanalytic theory associated with the theory of narcissism presents a picture of the world without these trans-individual—indeed, transcendent—sources of autonomy and freedom. Yet, this does not lead the theory to reject these values as merely a chimera. Indeed, their mundane and fragile character makes these values even more precious, precisely because they are so rare. Such a perspective suggests new possibilities for good and evil that critical social philosophy would do well to come to terms with.

• Chapter 7 Narcissism and Philosophy

In reviewing the relationship between narcissism and philosophy in this final chapter, I will focus on aspects of the relationship that require further development. In particular, I will consider from a more systematic perspective what the theory of narcissism adds to our understanding of philosophy, including social philosophy. My account of narcissism, like the accounts of Freud and Marcuse, appreciates the origins of philosophy in the most archaic needs. However, it does not risk reducing philosophy to these needs, as Freud's and Marcuse's accounts do. We shall then take up the question of how the narcissistic pursuit of the whole may best avoid the greed and hubris to which it is so vulnerable. Next we will consider both formal and substantive limits to my account of narcissism, and finally, whether a philosophy of selfishness, no matter how mature and refined, can ever be the basis of a decent social theory. First, however, a reprise of my argument may be useful.

Reprise of the Argument

After showing that Lasch and MacIntyre are addressing similar problems and thus that a psychoanalytic perspective on narcissism might be philosophically fruitful, I defined narcissism in terms of four key themes: the persistence of narcissism throughout life, its inherent dualism, the way in which object mastery helps heal the narcissistic wound, and its quest for fusion and wholeness by means of reconciliation between ego and ego ideal. It is the content of the ego ideal and its relationship with the superego that largely determine whether this quest for wholeness is immature or mature. Mature reconciliation with the ego ideal will pass through object mastery. These four themes comprise what I call the theory of narcissism. I have also emphasized the psychoanalytic theory associated with the theory of narcissism, which stresses the importance of pre-oedipal issues, what Freud called the Minoan-Mycenean level of psychological development, to the development of mature autonomy. At this level it is issues associated with separation and individuation that are central.

Plato's Socrates, particularly in the *Symposium* and the *Phaedrus*, is revealed as having deep insight into the truths of narcissism. Indeed, the *Symposium* can be read as an argument designed to persuade Athenian gentlemen to abandon the temptations of immature narcissism for the satisfactions of mature narcissism. But it is not this that makes Socrates' program so rewarding for my reinterpretation of the program of the Frankfurt school. It is rather that the Platonic view of eros, which characterizes it in terms of its sublime aims rather than its mundane origins, is readily integrated with the theory of narcissism, enriching both our understanding of Plato and the theory itself. For, like Plato, the theory of narcissism defines eros in terms of the higher purposes that it may serve: the perfection of the whole self. Chapter 3 concluded with the caution that we should not let Socrates off the hook too easily, that there is an element of hubris even in the desire to *know* the whole.

Adorno's sensitivity to the arrogance and hubris of philosophy is almost preternatural. Indeed, much of Adorno's philosophical program can be read as a rejection of the attempt to know the whole. While a retreat from this attempt is characteristic of much modern philosophy, it is carried through by Adorno with an antisystematic rigor that is striking. Adorno's retreat from the whole has been interpreted as a retreat from eros itself.

This would seem to make his project the antithesis of Plato's. Yet this is not really the case. It is Adorno's respect for the power and intensity of eros that leads him to reject it. Such a response is vastly preferable to one which assumes that eros need only be called by its right name to be fully subject to the power of reason. Though Adorno's all-or-nothing view of eros is misleading—an erotically influenced philosophy need not devour the world in rage and *ressentiment*—it nevertheless leads us to appreciate the subtle and manifold ways in which eros is manifested in philosophy. Indeed, in rejecting every philosophical expression of eros, he must virtually reject philosophy itself, which is why his program is often seen as terminating in a cul-de-sac. After considering several contradictions in Horkheimer and Adorno's social psychology, we concluded that there are similarities between their psychological study of the "end of the individual" and Adorno's philosophical program of negative dialectics, both being characterized by a fear of false wholeness, of a false integration between man and world—false, ultimately, because the integration demands too great a sacrifice of the self.

It is Marcuse who best integrates the insights of the theory of narcissism. But his program is seriously flawed insofar as he idealizes the most regressive moments of eros and narcissism. This is precisely what the theory of narcissism corrects, by showing why mature gratification is even more satisfying—not merely more compatible with civilization—than its immature counterpart. This is also the point of the Platonic theory of sublimation. It is on the basis of the Platonic theory, as reinterpreted by the theory of narcissism, that we reformulated Marcuse's erotic utopia as what might be called "a utopia of mature narcissism." Our reformulation was sketchy, however, and it left important issues outstanding, not least, whether even mature narcissism is an adequate basis for social theory.

Both Adorno and Habermas fail to integrate the insights of the theory of narcissism into their accounts. However, it would be misleading to place them on a par in this respect. Adorno rejects eros and the quest for wholeness with reluctance, whereas

Habermas has no categories for them in the first place, in part because his psychological theory has no place for pre-verbal experience. One consequence of this is that Habermas's concept of the individual lacks roundness and depth, thereby coming to resemble the oversocialized man that Horkheimer, Adorno, and Marcuse fear may be the modal man of this generation. This does not seem to concern Habermas, in large measure because he holds that it is neither eros nor ego, but language, that is the font of genuine autonomy. But unless one assumes that language has a life of its own, Habermas's confidence is unwarranted, for it ignores the earliest, deepest effects of culture and child rearing on the inner lives of those who use language. As we have seen, the psychoanalytic theory associated with narcissism reveals new possibilities for good and evil that criticial social theory would do well to come to terms with. It shows the individual to be more vulnerable to manipulation than ever before, the narcissistic needs of the self to be more readily exploitable even than eros. At the same time, it reveals new sources of potential autonomy in the self's longing for perfection and control.

Narcissism, Sublimation, and Philosophy

Why would Freud put libido—eros in all its manifestations—at the center of his account of human motivation? A major reason is certainly that human nature is thereby linked with its biological basis and animal heritage. It makes sense to talk of an erotic drive (Trieb) in a way that it does not make sense to talk of a drive for self-esteem or a creative drive. The latter are, evidently, drives only in a metaphorical sense, whereas eros possesses a physical basis. Since Freud saw himself as founding a science of human nature, eros was an especially appropriate foundation for his account. The difficulty, as we have seen, is that he came to see the most primitive physical expression of eros as its most essential expression, toward which all eros would recur. The theory of narcissism turns this aspect of his thought around, while fully appreciating Freud's insight into the power and ubiquity of eros. Indeed, it is Freud's insight into the archaic sources of eros in self-love that explains why the narcissistic quest is so subject to regression.

The theory of narcissism conceptualizes eros in terms not so much of its origins as its telos: the wholeness and perfection of the self. The push toward this goal obviously has biological roots in the sex drive, which energizes the oedipus conflict, understood, in Grunberger's words, as a "displacement of the subject's narcissistic wound to his conflict with the father." However, we have seen that the narcissistic quest gains much of its impetus from an experience more primitive, more global, and more profound than the oedipus conflict: the experience of narcissistic injury, which destroys that blissful state of harmony that theorists of narcissism conceptualize in various, but similar, ways. It is the desire to restore this state and hence the perfection of the self that has the potential to push men and women forward or to entice them down a backward path. My account of narcissism brings together the aspect of narcissism stressed by Freud— narcissism as a vicissitude of the libido—and narcissism as a quest for mastery and control over self and world. In so doing, it shows why the narcissistic ideal is so compelling: it links pleasure and achievement, erotic passion and creative passion, ego satisfaction and id satisfaction, love and work.

This point is recognized by Freud, of course, particularly in his concept of the ego ideal. It is also recognized by Plato, especially in the Symposium. I have devoted a lot of attention to how Plato's account improves on Freud's. In particular, I have shown that Plato is quite justified, psychologically as well as philosophically and aesthetically, in seeing eros in terms of the higher, more abstract purposes that it may serve. The theory of narcissism explains why reconciliation between ego and ideal brings genuine pleasure, not just satisfaction in a job well done (though it brings this too). It does so because it recalls the most gratifying experience of all, narcissistic perfection. The theory of narcissism thus bridges the pleasure and reality principles, showing how mature object mastery satisfies both. It is on the basis of this

Platonic theory of sublimation, as revealed and systematized by the theory of narcissism, that I criticized and reformulated Marcuse's erotic utopia. It was also on this basis that I judged Marcuse's project to be more successful than that of either Adorno or Habermas.

Implicit in my argument is the contention that the account of human nature associated with the theory of narcissism enriches philosophy more than Freud's account does. To be sure, the theory of narcissism does not enrich every philosophy; it may be quite irrelevant to much analytic philosophy, for example. But it does enrich philosophies—such as Plato's, Aristotle's, and the Frankfurt school's—concerned with the good for man and how this good can be achieved. It does so by characterizing the good for man in terms of the pursuit of ideal values, while not forgetting the origins of this pursuit in the most primitive needs. It thereby connects the base with the sublime, the creation of beautiful philosophy with the potential for perversion. This is the key philosophical contribution of the theory of narcissism. It finds the sources of philosophy in the most primitive needs, without rendering these needs more fundamental than the philosophy they inspire.

Of course, one does not have to turn to the theory of narcissism to discover that men and women seek to perfect themselves by realizing ideal values. Plato certainly grasped this, and Aristotle's discussion of the good for man in terms of the complete development of the human excellences (N. Ethics 1097b22–1103a10) is also readily interpreted in these terms. What my account of narcissism contributes is an appreciation of the sheer intensity of the narcissistic quest. Plato seems to have recognized this intensity more fully than Aristotle, a claim that is supported by Nussbaum's assertion that Aristotle's writings exhibit "an almost complete lack of attention to the erotic relationships that Plato defended."[1] It is in these erotic relationships that narcissism is most intense, and hence most susceptible to regression. Indeed, this is the lesson of the Symposium.

Narcissism is subject to regression not only because of its intensity, but also because of its infantile origins. The pleasure that it recalls is purely Dionysian: a state in which there are no ego boundaries, a state of fusion of the self with the All.

I have devoted much of this book to demonstrating the usefulness of evaluating societies, cultures, and political arrangements in terms of whether they foster progressive or regressive solutions to the problem of narcissistic injury. This, of course, is what Lasch's *Culture of Narcissism* is about. It is certainly the concern of Plato's *Symposium*. However, the most interesting result of my study may be that it is Marcuse who comes closest to fully appreciating Plato's insights into the contribution of eros to the good life. Where Marcuse goes wrong is in seeing eros in Freudian terms, and in adopting the reductive focus of modern science generally, in which it is the most primitive expression of eros that is regarded as the most essential.

My account of narcissism allows us to strike a balance between Plato's exquisitely sublimated account (at least in the *Symposium*; in the *Phaedrus* eros is experienced more directly) and Marcuse's inadequately sublimated one. In other words, my account of narcissism allows us to see erotic satisfaction in terms of the larger purposes that it serves. Like Plato in the *Symposium*, the theory of narcissism sees these larger purposes in terms of the pursuit of ideal values. For Plato these values concern the creation of virtue and beauty. Not unlike Plato, the theory of narcissism sees the pursuit of these values as being in certain respects selfish, since it is the virtue and beauty of the soul (or self) that is the object of creation. That this project of creating a virtuous, beautiful soul (or self) is motivated by the narcissistic longing for perfection is apparent. Nor is it banal to liken self and soul. By *psuchē*, or soul, the Greek meant as much mind as spirit. (The German *Geist* is similar in this respect.) Kohut defines the self as an independent center of initiative and perception, integrated with our ambitions and ideals on the one hand, our bodies on the other.[2] Is this so different from the entity that Socrates sought to persuade his fellow citizens to care for?

Just as Plato suggests that people create virtue and beauty in order to win a certain immortality, so the theory of narcissism suggests that an individual may seek to become worthy of his ego ideal even at the expense of life itself—for example, in a heroic act that exemplifies one's highest values. For, in exemplifying these values, one lives on in them, as Kohut points out in a pair of interesting studies on martyrdom.[3] These parallels between the Platonic theory of sublimation and the theory of narcissism are not mere coincidences. Rather, they stem from the fact that both are concerned with the same thing: how and why people pursue, or fail to pursue, their highest values. It is to these values that the theory of narcissism "binds" eros and thus civilizes it, while still recognizing the validity of its demands for total satisfaction. But now, total satisfaction involves the demands of the total self.

"Transcendental Narcissism" or Minimal Philosophy?

Narcissism's demand for total satisfaction of the whole self may have troubling implications when transposed to philosophy, as we have seen. The desire to know and possess the whole may be so powerful that it rides roughshod over the unique and the particular. The appropriate philosophical lesson to draw, however, is not Adorno's, but Socrates' in the *Phaedrus*. It is from his study of eros that Socrates comes to recognize that there is value to the unique and the particular. Indeed, to truly know the whole, one must also come to know and value the individual. The unique and the particular, moreover, are not merely further instances of the whole. They must be appreciated for themselves, apart from the whole, even if at a more abstract level they partake of the whole, a loosely structured whole that has room for the individual. Is it the role of philosophy to pursue this loosely structured whole? Michel Foucault writes of "transcendental narcissism," the conceit—the hubris—that human knowledge might ever find a foundation outside the conventions of language and the flow of history.⁴ Surely the philosophical pursuit of the whole, even a loosely structured whole, betrays a similar conceit. Certainly it risks hubris.

My study of narcissism has stressed its duality: narcissism is evinced not only in grandiosity, but also in the retreat into the "minimal self." If this grandiosity finds its philosophical expression in transcendental narcissism, then perhaps the opposite pole is philosophically expressed in what might be called "minimal philosophy." The minimal self, it will be recalled, experiences the world as so dangerously out of control that it retreats into the self, in order to find something, anything, over which it can exert total mastery; diet, the body, any narrowly circumscribed activity that becomes a way of life, such as jogging, are all exemplary. Minimal philosophy is perhaps similarly motivated. It retreats to texts, narrowly framed analytic issues regarding language use, logical puzzles, and so forth, because the larger philosophical questions, the metaphysical questions with which philosophy has traditionally been concerned, now seem beyond human mastery. The cultural consensus that once allowed such mastery, as we now believe, seems gone forever.

The concerns expressed by minimal philosophy, like Foucault's concerns regarding transcendental narcissism, are real. Sometimes discretion really is the better part of valor. Nevertheless, it should not be overlooked that minimal philosophy is just as surely narcissistic as is its counterpart, transcendental narcissism. It is the search for total mastery and control, no matter what the scale, that marks an activity as narcissistic. What is needed, of course, is a balance, characterized not so much by a pulling back from the quest for mastery as by an appreciation that this quest must always tolerate vast amounts of contingency and imperfection: in one's self, in one's knowledge of the world, and in the world itself. In other words, this balance can be struck by continuing to pursue the whole, while recognizing that one can never know or possess it. Once again, Socrates shows us how.

Socrates and the Goal of Mature Narcissism

I will argue below that the pursuit of the whole, when en-
gaged in by a mature narcissist like Socrates, is characterized by
the type of internal limit that Marcuse would attribute to eman-
cipated eros. One could argue, following Marcuse, that this
means that mature narcissism is self-sublimating. But this would
not be quite correct. As Freud states, "a man who has exchanged
his narcissism for the worship of a high ego-ideal has not necessarily on that account succeeded in sublimating his libidinal instincts."[5] That is, the narcissistic pursuit of the highest values is
not identical with sublimation. What generates the internal limit
to the pursuit of narcissistic gratification is mature insight into
the nature of that gratification: that it is found in the *pursuit* of
wholeness and perfection, not in their possession. Knowledge is
virtue, as the Socratic adage has it. It is this mature insight that
underlies the balance referred to above, a balance that may help
us to tread a fine line between minimal philosophy and transcendental narcissism.

As Anne Carson points out in *Eros the Bittersweet*, Socrates
understands eros in terms that are in many respects typically
Greek. Eros yearns for that which is lacking; it reflects the fact
that something is missing, that the lover is incomplete.[6] This is
seen in Aristophanes' account, as well as in Socrates' mythic account of the parentage of eros. It is also reflected in Alcibiades'
longing to perfect himself, the intensity of which suggests that
for Alcibiades the goal of perfection is not merely to make the
good better, but to satisfy an inner longing and compensate for a
sense of incompleteness. What is it that allows us to say that
Socrates is successful in dealing with this longing in a way that
Alcibiades is not?

Recall the discussion, in chapter 4, of Socrates' argument in
the *Phaedrus*, that a principle of reason is to divide things along
proper lines, without forcing them into inappropriate categories
(265e). Socrates is discussing the divine madness of eros, but he

could be discussing knowledge of anything, as Adorno recognizes. But proper division is not the only task of reason. It is also necessary for reason to bring together scattered particulars, to collect and categorize, to synthesize (265d–e). It is both activities that constitute reason, activities that both complement each other and act as a check on each other. Synthesis can become a form of wild self-assertion, an instance of domineering reason, unless checked by proper division. Yet proper division alone is inadequate, since it cannot bring together things that are genuinely related but just happen to be separated conventionally.

It is at the intersection of division and synthesis that Socrates locates eros, as Carson points out. Socrates describes division and synthesis as the combined activity that allows him to speak and think (*Phaedrus* 266b). He states that he is in love with this activity. "The fact is, Phaedrus, I am myself a lover [*erastēs*] of these divisions and collections" (266b; see also idem, *Philebus* 16b). Socrates is in love with the process of learning. He loves to ask questions, pose riddles, construct arguments, tear them down, start over, make others uncomfortable with their knowledge, and make himself uncomfortable with his ignorance, but never at the expense of false certainty. Socrates and Alcibiades are different not only in the objects of their eros, but also in the way in which they approach their object: Socrates embraces the pursuit, whereas Alcibiades is interested only in the results, the capture. Socrates is "in love with the wooing itself," as Carson puts it.[7] This is the basis of the philosophical balance.

If physical eros is a model for its intellectual counterpart, the converse is also the case. Or rather, both expressions of eros are really one. This is the point of the "ladder of love" and certainly of the *Phaedrus* (249d–257a). From this perspective the goal of mature self-love is not merely to become worthy of one's mature ego ideal, but to find the meaning of life in the pursuit of this task. Yet, the phrase "meaning of life" may be a bit misleading, because it is so serious and ponderous. Socrates shows that this pursuit can have a light touch; it is serious, worthy of the devotion of a lifetime, but it is not deadly serious. For Socrates the meaning of life resides not in realizing abstract and demanding ideals of moral perfection, but rather in the pursuit of these ideals, a pursuit that may be joyous once it is freed of the burden of perfection, a burden that seems to stem, as in the case of Alcibiades, from the belief that one must achieve perfection in order to be cured of one's narcissistic injury.

At this point an objection suggests itself. Eros, particularly as it is expressed in the self-love of narcissism, has been characterized throughout in terms of its utterly demanding character. Narcissistic eros wants satisfaction now and forever. Indeed, narcissism is defined by Grunberger in terms of its quest to re-capture the experience of eternity. Furthermore, the eternity that narcissism seeks is the eternity of perfection: not the striving for wholeness but its perpetual realization, not the frustration of constant effort but the peace of permanent perfection. As Mar-cuse reminds us, "Joy wants eternity," a phrase that suggests to Marcuse the affinity of narcissism with the peace and cessation of stimulation that Freud writes of in *Beyond the Pleasure Prin-ciple*. How are these considerations compatible with Socrates' mature narcissism, which is characterized by a readiness to grasp the moment, to enjoy the pursuit, the wooing itself? The answer is that Socrates finds eternity in the moment of pursuit, and in so doing comes as close as is humanly possible to eternal perfection. This is the basis of the psychological balance.

Why this is so is suggested by Carson's analysis of eros. Eros is not only about unity; it is also about edges. It exists because certain boundaries do: between reach and grasp, desire and ful-fillment, one person and another, human finitude and perfec-tion, knowledge and ignorance.[8] Indeed, this is why eros is as relevant to the desire for knowledge as it is to the desire for an-other person. "Stationed at the edge of itself, or of its present knowledge, the thinking mind launches a suit for understanding into the unknown. So too the wooer stands at the edge of his value as a person and asserts a claim across the boundaries of an-other."[9] To look at eros this way reminds us that the edges are permanent. To try to obliterate them is bound to result in frustration and unhappiness. Alcibiades will never perfect himself—at least, not for more than a moment, and certainly not for eternity. Nor will Socrates. But Socrates recognizes this, which is why he embraces the pursuit, the wooing. It is the pursuit itself that connects what one once was, what one is, and what one could be, thereby giving continuity to what MacIntyre calls the narrative unity to a human life.

MacIntyre never suggests that this narrative unity depends on reaching a particular goal. Rather, it is the pursuit of noble goals that itself gives meaning, that connects one's past, present, and future, and in this limited sense realizes unity and wholeness. The boundaries, the edges—between self and world, self and other, self and ego ideal—are never effaced. Or rather, they are effaced only in an act of imagination, of longing, of desire, which projects what one is onto what one could be. This is why it is the desire, the longing, that must be embraced. It is through the desire, the wooing itself, that one catches a glimpse of perfection, a glimpse of what one would eternally be. But only a glimpse. It is because Socrates recognizes this that his pursuit of eros is tempered by lightness and irony. Unlike Alcibiades, he knows that the *effort* to achieve self-perfection is itself the goal. Socrates is already there. He no longer needs to struggle. He is free to be imperfect.

Reinterpreting Aristophanes

These considerations suggest that it is necessary to reinterpret slightly Aristophanes' account of the goal of love, an account that has served as a virtual motto for my account of narcissism. Aristophanes asks us to suppose that if Hephaestus were to stand over a pair of lovers and ask them what they want, their answer would be that they wish to be melded together, fused into one (*Symposium* 192d–e). My strategy has been to transform this expression of regressive narcissism into the progressive desire to fuse with the mature ego ideal and thereby achieve mature narcissistic wholeness. But Carson reminds us that neither Aristophanes nor Hephaestus can be considered very reliable commentators on love: Aristophanes is a poet of comic verse, and Hephaestus is the impotent cuckold of the Olympian pantheon.[10] Indeed, upon closer examination, aspects of Aristophanes' account are incoherent. If being whole is a source of complete satisfaction, why would the round beings of his fantasy challenge the gods? The conclusion would seem to be that not even actual fusion—with another, and perhaps even with the ego ideal—is a satisfactory goal. This is not "merely" because such a goal is unrealizable and bound to lead to frustration. Rather, the goal is too static; it would end the chase. If joy is in the wooing, then joy requires separation, edges, boundaries. Even Marcuse appreciates this point, stating that "all pleasure and all happiness and all humanity originate and live in and with these divisions and these boundaries [between individuals]."[11]

That Socrates recognizes this too is seen not only in his "location" of eros, as Carson calls it. Nor is it reflected only in the lightness and the irony with which he pursues eros. It is also seen in his recognition that the goal of eros is action: not the experience of virtue and beauty, not merely their acquisition, but their creation. But this seems but another way of saying that the narcissistic goal is to create for oneself a life that possesses a narrative unity, understood as the self-conscious pursuit of ideal values over time. The consequence of this perspective for the theory of narcissism is to heighten the importance of object mastery. Though fusion between ego and ego ideal remains the goal, it is best understood in terms of the means by which it is realized—mastery. The narcissistic ideal, which can be characterized in terms of the desire for undeserved, effortless, and perpetual wholeness via fusion with the All, is in fact realized by its antithesis: activity, creativity, effort that will inevitably fail to reach its goal, but that in failing succeeds. This too is the duality of narcissism.

Limits of the Theory of Narcissism,
Formal and Substantive

Today many thoughtful people agree that a philosophy which does not address the questions raised by what Habermas calls "the classical doctrine of politics"—the teachings of Plato and Aristotle—has in fact abandoned philosophy. My book is addressed to those who do not wish to abandon this tradition. It has been addressed to those who do not wish to practice minimal philosophy. MacIntyre argues that one does not fully understand a philosophy until one grasps the type of society within which it would be most perfectly embodied. In a related fashion I have argued that one does not fully understand a philosophy concerned with human good, and not merely analytic issues, until one understands how it deals with the narcissistic quest for wholeness and perfection. A fruitful way to begin this investigation might be to conceptualize a (possibly utopian) society which has as its goal the maximization of mature narcissistic satisfaction for its members and then, working in the reverse direction from MacIntyre, consider which philosophies are most compatible with and supportive of this ideal. This would not tell us which philosophies are good, obviously; but would tell us which philosophies take the power of the narcissistic quest seriously. Conversely, this exercise would act as a check on the ethic implicit in the theory of narcissism: that mature reconciliation between ego and ego ideal is good. One might conceivably discover, for example, that a philosophy esteemed on other grounds implies a quite different ethic. This would challenge the fruitfulness of much of my account, but it reveals an important point: namely, that the relevance of the theory of narcissism to philosophy is a hypothesis, not a tautology.

Formal Limits

As MacIntyre points out, epics such as the *Iliad* possess a narrative unity because the lives which they are about possess this unity. In the rationalized, relativistic modern world it is not so apparent that individual lives could possess this unity. However, the theory of narcissism, particularly as interpreted from a Socratic perspective, reminds us that even modern lives have the potential (generally unrealized) for narrative unity, understood as a lifelong quest for self-perfection via the pursuit of ideal values. What the theory of narcissism does not do is provide sufficient leverage by which to fully distinguish good from bad values, good from bad quests. It distinguishes only between progressive and regressive pursuits. In this, it allows us to reject shortcuts to narcissistic perfection as misguided, in the sense that, in the end, these shortcuts will result in less fulfillment than the pursuit of mature reconciliation between ego and ideal. To be sure, such a claim skirts the naturalistic fallacy. For one could argue quite rationally that regressive pursuits are morally good, even if they result in less happiness, because they affirm other higher values. Here I am making an antecedent moral decision. Because it is a decision, not a conclusion from factual premises, it avoids the naturalistic fallacy. The antecedent moral decision is simply that a life of mature gratification and happiness is, *ceteris paribus*, better than one without such fulfillment. The *ceteris paribus* proviso refers to such things as this fulfillment not depending on the gross exploitation of others and so forth. The difficulty is that this proviso cannot be derived from the theory of narcissism.

The theory does not allow us to fully distinguish good from bad goals, because it cannot exclude the possibility that some forms of mature reconciliation between ego and ego ideal might be morally repugnant. In a review of *After Virtue*, Philippa Foot suggests that a Nietzschean might well conceive of his life as a narrative quest, its telos being the aggrandizement of his own power.[12] Such a pursuit might well remove the Nietzschean from the community of the powerless, but it would not necessarily remove him from the community of other Nietzscheans, with whom he might share this quest. This Nietzschean community would presumably share a common ego ideal, characterized per-

200 NARCISSISM AND PHILOSOPHY

haps by the so-called aristocratic virtues of the great-souled man; and it is the sharing of a common ego ideal, Freud tells us, that binds a community.[13] It is not difficult to imagine that in such a community regressive shortcuts to reconciliation with this ego ideal would be regarded with great disdain. But would we really want to say that mature reconciliation with the community's ego ideal is ethically desirable? (To define an ethically repugnant ego ideal as, ipso facto, immature is, of course, no answer.) Just as Aristotle suggests that not every man, but only the good man, should love himself (*N. Ethics* 1169a10–15), so our considerations suggest that reconciliation between ego and ego ideal is good only when the content of the ego ideal is truly good.

The theory of narcissism provides no shortcut to the traditional philosophical analysis of what is right and good. The theory of narcissism is powerful philosophically only when combined with a comprehensive account of the good. It is this combination—which combines an analysis of the roots of human motivation with a justification of what it should aim at— that makes the accounts of Socrates and Marcuse so powerful. Another way of expressing the limits of my account of narcissism is in terms of Kant's distinction between intrinsic and extrinsic teleology.[14] Intrinsic teleology characterizes the internal relationships among the various parts and processes of an organized entity, such as a human being. Extrinsic teleology characterizes functional and hierarchical relationships among different kinds of entities.[15] My account of narcissism is an intrinsic teleology. It is about what people do to fulfill themselves, as well as what people should do if they wish to fulfill themselves more completely. What the role of narcissistic fulfillment is or should be in the larger scheme of things—from the perspective of extrinsic teleology—has not been addressed. Though this surely constitutes a deficit in my argument, I am consoled by the fact that two of the most profound, teleologically oriented books in recent years, Galston's *Justice and the Human Good* and MacIntyre's *After Virtue*, have also stopped short of trying to justify an intrinsic teleology in terms of an extrinsic one.

Substantive Limits: Selfishness or Individualism?

The considerations above concern the formal limits of my account of narcissism. However, there are also substantive objections, for it can be argued that narcissism, no matter how sublimated, is an inadequate basis for social theory, that a decent society can be based only on mutuality, and that narcissism, no matter how refined, is ultimately selfish. In "Beyond Drive Theory," Nancy Chodorow raises this objection to Marcuse's erotic utopia. But it is also applicable to my account of narcissism. Chodorow argues that Marcuse's view of narcissism in effect denies that the external world, including other people, possesses an independent existence. The narcissist's "'refusal to accept separation from the libidinous object (or subject),' [his] 'union with a whole world of love and pleasure,' denies the object or external world its own separateness and choice."[16] Chodorow concludes that the "higher values" that Marcuse would transcend must include respect and concern for the needs and autonomy of others. But the narcissist neither knows nor cares that others have needs as real and legitimate as his own, and a world composed solely of such individuals would seem to have more in common with Hobbes's state of nature than with an erotic utopia. As Chodorow puts it, the "narcissistic mode of relating and of drive gratification based on the pleasure principle precludes those very intersubjective relationships that should form the core of any social and political vision."[17]

Chodorow's criticism is trenchant. Though it has been countered from a number of different perspectives, it may be useful to review, from a slightly different angle, what all counter-arguments have in common. In *The Heresy of Self-Love*, Paul Zweig examines narcissistic themes in literature. Zweig's understanding of narcissism is not psychoanalytically informed, and he often seems to equate narcissism with withdrawal and a morbid concern with the self. Nevertheless, his main point is incisive and complements my approach here. It is that self-love is heretical because, as a source of subversive individualism, it chal-

lenges society and authority, in particular, all those forces that
alienate man from himself, that threaten his authentic wholeness and individuality. Paramount among these forces today are
industrialism, bureaucracy, and commerce (or rather, the transformation of all relationships into commercial ones).[18] Zweig's
heroes—Kierkegaard, Baudelaire, and Walt Whitman, among
others—all retreat into the self in order to resist these frag-
menting forces. However, Zweig is quick to distinguish between
heroes, neurotics, and madmen. His heroes are those who, after
withdrawing into the sanctuary of the inner self, are able to communicate to others the potential for authenticity and wholeness
that they find there. His heroes risk the madness of isolation and
are saved by their ability to reach out to others and touch them
with what they have found.

The role of narcissism in Marcuse's work should be seen in
a similar fashion. The roots of narcissism do indeed tap a level of
experience that cares only for the wholeness and fulfillment of
the self. But this is not a totally negative phenomenon, as Zweig
points out. For it is precisely because of these roots that narcissism is such a powerful source of opposition to all that would
fragment this wholeness. Indeed, Jay makes a similar point in his
analysis (discussed in chapter 5) of how Marcuse sees in the
memory of primitive gratification a source of revolutionary activity. What is necessary is that the profoundly selfish demands
of narcissism be socialized without being co-opted. What are
needed are men and women of the kind Zweig calls heroes, who
can communicate this experience to others and use its demands
to help build a better society. It has been my purpose to show
how this process is aided by the very duality of narcissism: its
potential for finding the most primitive narcissistic gratification
in the pursuit of the most mature values, including values that
recognize the autonomy and needs of others.

Although narcissism is not a source of mutuality per se, it is
compatible with mutuality and the recognition of the subjectivity of others. To ask more of narcissism would be to compromise
the source of its power, what Zweig calls the subversive individ-

ualism of self-love. Conversely, there is no reason to assume that narcissism is the only source of mature autonomy. Jessica Benjamin, for example, in studying the roots of autonomy in the child's earliest relations with others, has drawn on the object relations theory of Fairbairn and Guntrip, as we saw in chapter 4, to show how autonomy develops from relationships, not merely from the demands of drives. Nonetheless, though it is not the only source, narcissism remains a particularly deep and powerful font of genuine autonomy, which is why the theory of narcissism is so compatible with an immanent critique of Marcuse's project. Unlike the perspectives of Chodorow and Benjamin, the theory of narcissism supports Marcuse's subversive individualism. It also shows the individual to be capable of socialization in a way that Marcuse's perspective does not. Unlike Chodorow's theory, the theory of narcissism is sympathetic to the radical individualism that she correctly identifies as being at the root of *Eros and Civilization*. The theory of narcissism concerns how this individualism can be tempered, not how it can be overcome.

Mutuality, Individualism, or Harmony?

What degree of mutuality a society that sought to encourage mature narcissism could support remains an open question. Certainly there are no grounds for thinking that such a society could not move well beyond the competitive individualism of liberal democracy. An observation by Michael Balint supports this conclusion.

> It is taken for granted (by the infant) that the other partner, the object on the friendly expanse, will automatically have the same wishes, interests, and expectations. This explains why this is so often called the state of omnipotence. This description is somewhat out of tune; there is no feeling of power, in fact, no need for either power or effort, as all things are in harmony.[19]

To be sure, the expectation of harmony can readily degenerate into a struggle for control. Harmony on whose terms, regarding what needs, on the basis of whose compromises, are all questions especially subject to conflict. Nevertheless, there does seem to be a difference between understanding narcissism as the quest for omnipotence and control and understanding it as a quest for harmony, albeit on the narcissist's terms. For the latter way of putting it implies that narcissism contains within it the seeds of cooperation, mutuality, and intersubjectivity. From this perspective mature narcissism would involve recognition that harmony strictly on my terms is not harmony at all, but the ground of perpetual conflict. To realize my goal of harmony, which, if it is an expression of primary narcissism, is deeply rooted indeed, I must coordinate my narcissistic needs with the needs of others.

Nothing in my discussion of narcissism is incompatible with Balint's interpretation, once it is recognized that the harmony to which he refers is a harmony in which all things are in order and everything is perfect; for only in such a state is there "no need for either power or effort." From this perspective, the quest for mastery stems from narcissistic injury, understood as the loss of harmony, the loss of effortless equilibrium, the loss of nirvana. Perhaps this perspective renders narcissism less aggressive, less imperialistic. Nevertheless, there remains associated with the theory of narcissism an assertion of the value of individuality, even mastery and control, that is not associated with many visions of the good society. The harmony of primary narcissism must be disrupted, and only mastery—which is not the same as aggression or self-aggrandizement—can restore its simulacrum. However, to put it this way reveals more clearly than ever that to call ideal the society that fosters mature narcissism for all its citizens is not simply to call for all good things. The social theory associated with the theory of narcissism does not seek to decenter the individual or even to recenter him, in the manner of Habermas and Chodorow. Rather, it seeks to preserve and restore the individual in an era in which many of the most powerful economic, cultural, and social trends—as well as a surprising number of social philosophies—seem headed in the other direction.

Notes

Chapter 1: After Virtue, Narcissism

1. Most valuable to me has been Lasch's organization and assessment of the psychoanalytic literature, much of which does not refer to narcissism specifically. It is Lasch who points out its relevance. Useful, too, is Lasch's insight into the connection between seemingly disparate cultural phenomena and the theory of narcissism.

2. Alasdair MacIntyre, *After Virtue*, p. 22.

3. William Galston, "Aristotelian Morality and Liberal Society: A Critique of Alasdair MacIntyre's *After Virtue*," p. 1.

4. American Psychiatric Association, *Diagnostic and Statistical Manual of Mental Disorders*, 3d ed. (hereafter cited as *DSM-III*), pp. 315–17, esp. p. 316.

5. Ovid *Metamorphoses* 3. 464–68. Ovid's is by far the most complex and sophisticated version of the myth. It is he who introduces Echo. It is generally held that Ovid learned of the myth via the Alexandrian poetic tradition. Its ancient Greek origins are lost. Though Ovid's is the primary account, there are two major variants and many minor ones. One major variant is from a Greek author called Conon, roughly contemporary with Ovid (36B.C.–A.D.17). In this version, Narcissus invites a young man who has fallen in love with him to kill himself. He does, Narcissus then kills himself out of guilt and confusion (Felix Jacoby, ed., *Die Fragmente der griechischen Historiker*, pp. 197ff.). The other is by Pausanias. Writing in the second century, Pausanias asks how a grown man could fail to recognize his own image in a pond and goes on to offer what he regards as a more plausible version, according to which Narcissus is in love with his twin sister. When she dies, he finds some relief from his loneliness by looking at his own reflection, seeing in it her likeness (Pausanias 9. 31. 6–9). There is obviously a great deal of material here for psychoanalytic exploration! Yet

few psychoanalysts have taken it up. An exception is Hyman Spotnitz and Philip Resnikoff, "The Myths of Narcissus." I shall not analyze the myth, preferring instead to analyze more abstract philosophical expressions of narcissism.

6. *DSM-III*, pp. 315–17.

7. Daniel Stern, *The Interpersonal World of the Infant*, pp. 10, 46, 69–70.

8. See, e.g., the symposium on *The Interpersonal World of the Infant*, in *Contemporary Psychoanalysis* 23 (1987):6–59.

9. Ibid., pp. 34, 42; contribution by Louise J. Kaplan.

10. Herbert Marcuse, *An Essay on Liberation*, p. 90.

11. MacIntyre, *After Virtue*, p. 11.

12. Ibid., p. 27.

13. Christopher Lasch, *The Minimal Self*, p. 93.

14. MacIntyre, *After Virtue*, p. 32.

15. Ibid., p. 203.

16. Lasch, *Minimal Self*, p. 131.

17. Ibid., p. 165.

18. Lasch, *The Culture of Narcissism*, p. 391.

19. MacIntyre, *After Virtue*, p. 29.

20. Ibid., pp. 31–32.

21. Janine Chasseguet-Smirgel, *The Ego Ideal*, pp. 187–88.

22. MacIntyre does not entirely ignore these issues, however; see *After Virtue*, pp. 170–71.

23. See Galston, "Aristotelian Morality," p. 10.

24. Ibid., p. 13. I follow Galston closely here.

25. See May Brodbeck, "Methodological Individualisms: Definition and Reduction," and Ernest Nagel, *The Structure of Science*, chap. 11.

26. Colleen Clements, "Misusing Psychiatric Models," p. 284.

27. Ibid., pp. 293–94.

28. Max Black, *Models and Metaphors*, p. 242.

29. George Devereux, *Basic Problems of Ethnopsychiatry*, pp. 5–8.

30. Ibid., p. 6.

31. Ibid., p. 29.

32. Ibid., pp. 13–27; quote from p. 17.

33. Richard Sennett, *The Fall of Public Man*, esp. chap. 14.

34. Devereux, *Basic Problems*, pp. 214–36.

35. Ibid., pp. 235–36.

Chapter 2:   The Psychoanalytic Theory of Narcissism

1. Sigmund Freud, *Five Lectures on Psycho-Analysis*, p. 50.

2. Béla Grunberger, *Narcissism: Psychoanalytic Essays*, p. 78.

3. Considerable debate rages over whether narcissism has in fact become more common. Heinz Kohut, for example, believes that it has, as a result of large-scale social changes (see *The Restoration of the Self*, pp. 269ff.). However, Colleen Clements argues that the growing psychiatric attention to narcissism does not imply an actual increase in narcissistic personality orders ("Misusing Psychiatric Models: The Culture of Narcissism," pp. 288–91). This difficult issue will be addressed later in this chapter. It depends in some measure on how narcissism is defined.

4. Karl Popper, *Conjectures and Refutations*, pp. 34–39.

5. Popper, *The Logic of Scientific Discovery*, chap. 1.

6. Adolf Grünbaum, *The Foundations of Psychoanalysis*, pp. 4–6.

7. Freud, "On Narcissism," p. 88.

8. Freud, "Psychoanalytic Notes on an Autobiographical Account of a Case of Paranoia," p. 60.

9. Freud, "Group Psychology and the Analysis of the Ego," p. 90.

10. Freud, "On Narcissism," pp. 93–94.

11. Freud, "The Ego and the Id," pp. 28–39. Janine Chasseguet-Smirgel (Appendix to *The Ego Ideal*) traces the development of the concept of the ego ideal in Freud's work, from its first appearance in "On Narcissism" in 1914 through the *New Introductory Lectures on Psychoanalysis*" of 1932.

12. See Hanna Segal, *Melanie Klein*, p. 9.

13. Freud, "On Narcissism," pp. 101–02.

14. Freud, "Group Psychology and the Analysis of the Ego," pp. 115–16.

15. Theodor Adorno, "Sociology and Psychology," part 2, p. 88.

16. Christopher Lasch, *The Minimal Self*, pp. 281–82.

17. Freud, "Female Sexuality," p. 226. Immediately after this statement Freud adds that the universality of the thesis that the oedipal conflict is the basis of neurosis can be maintained by reinterpreting the conflict.

18. Freud, "The Ego and the Id," pp. 57–59.

19. Lasch, *Minimal Self*, pp. 281–82.

20. Segal, *Melanie Klein*, chap. 8. I find Segal very helpful and follow her closely at several points.

21. Melanie Klein, *The Writings of Melanie Klein*, vol. 2, *The Psycho-Analysis of Children*, pp. 3–8.

22. Klein, *Writings*, vol. 3, *Envy and Gratitude*, p. 190.

23. Freud, "The Ego and the Id," pp. 54–59.

24. Klein, *Writings*, vol. 3, pp. 178, 180.

25. Segal, *Melanie Klein*, p. 177.

26. Ibid., pp. 118–19.

27. Klein, *Writings*, vol. 1, *Love, Guilt and Reparation*, pp. 225–26. Segal, *Melanie Klein*, p. 128.

28. Klein, *Writings*, vol. 3, p. 176.

29. Ibid., p. 192.

30. Ibid., p. 189.

31. Segal, *Melanie Klein*, pp. 147–48.

32. Klein, *Writings*, vol. 3, pp. 217–21.

33. Segal, *Melanie Klein*, p. 153, mentions that narcissism can defend against envy but does not elaborate.

34. *DSM-III*, p. 316.

35. See Kohut, "Thoughts on Narcissism and Narcissistic Rage," pp. 383–85.

36. Klein, *Writings*, vol. 3, pp. 52–53.

37. Jay R. Greenberg and Stephen A. Mitchell, *Object Relations in Psychoanalytic Theory*, pp. 136–37.

38. Ibid., p. 137.

39. Ibid.

40. Freud, "On Narcissism," pp. 73–74.

41. Greenberg and Mitchell, *Object Relations*, p. 385. Lester Schwartz also suggests this ("Narcissistic Personality Disorders—A Clinical Discussion," p. 295).

42. Greenberg and Mitchell, *Object Relations*, p. 385.

43. Freud, *Three Essays on the Theory of Sexuality*, p. 34.

44. Greenberg and Mitchell, *Object Relations*, p. 146. These writers summarize the standard criticisms of Klein well (pp. 144–50).

45. Ibid., pp. 151–53.

46. Ernest Jones, Introduction to *An Object-Relations Theory of the Personality*, by W. R. D. Fairbairn, p. v.

47. Fairbairn, *An Object-Relations Theory of the Personality*, pp. 139–40; quoted by Greenberg and Mitchell, *Object Relations*, p. 157. I follow their discussion of Fairbairn quite closely at points.

48. Fairbairn, *An Object-Relations Theory of the Personality*, p. 48. Greenberg and Mitchell, *Object Relations*, p. 161.

49. Fairbairn, *An Object-Relations Theory of the Personality*, p. 42.

50. Harry Guntrip, *Personality Structure and Human Interaction*, p. 279; quoted in Greenberg and Mitchell, *Object Relations*, p. 163.

51. Greenberg and Mitchell, *Object Relations*, p. 165.

52. Fairbairn, *An Object-Relations Theory of the Personality*, p. 70.

53. Ibid., p. 99.

54. Freud, "The Ego and the Id," pp. 31–35.

55. Guntrip stresses this point in *Psychoanalytic Theory, Therapy, and the Self*, chap. 6–7. Greenberg and Mitchell criticize Guntrip for misrepresenting Fairbairn's position on this issue (*Object Relations*, pp. 215–17). Fortunately, this need not concern us here.

56. *Journal of the American Psychoanalytic Association* 22, no. 2 (1974). The volume includes pieces by Otto Kernberg, Arnold Goldberg, Vann Spruiell, Alan Eisnitz, Lester Schwartz, Martin Wangh, and Harold Wylie.

57. Otto Kernberg, "Contrasting Viewpoints Regarding the Nature and Treatment of Narcissistic Personality Disorders," p. 255. See Joan Riviere, "A Contribution to the Analysis of Negative Therapeutic Reaction"; Edith Jacobson, *The Self and the Object World*; Margaret Mahler, "On Human Symbiosis and the Vicissitudes of Individuation."

58. Kernberg, "Contrasting Viewpoints," pp. 256–57.

59. See Schwartz, "Narcissistic Personality Disorders," p. 292; Arnold Rothstein, *The Narcissistic Pursuit of Perfection*, pp. 37–43.

60. Kohut, *Restoration of the Self*, pp. 30–31.

61. Kohut, *How Does Analysis Cure?*, p. 64.

62. Ibid., p. 4.

63. Kernberg, "Contrasting Viewpoints," p. 265. Idem, *Borderline Conditions and Pathological Narcissism*, pp. 307–10.

64. Kohut, *How Does Analysis Cure?*, p. 208.

65. Kernberg "Contrasting Viewpoints," p. 259.

66. Ibid., p. 258.

67. Kernberg, *Borderline Conditions and Pathological Narcissism*, p. 231.

68. Kernberg, "Contrasting Viewpoints," p. 265.

69. Ibid., pp. 259, 261.

70. Ibid., p. 261.

71. Ibid., p. 264.

72. Kohut, *How Does Analysis Cure?*, p. 193.

73. Kohut, *Restoration of the Self*, p. 287.

74. Kernberg, *Borderline Conditions and Pathological Narcissism*, p. 223.

75. Rothstein, *Narcissistic Pursuit of Perfection*, p. 28.

76. Ibid., p. 38.

77. Ibid., pp. 41–42.

78. Ibid., pp. 17–25.

79. Ibid., p. 114.

80. Ibid., pp. 124–35.

81. Grunberger, *Narcissism*, pp. 75–76.

82. Ibid., pp. 2–3.

83. Ibid., pp. 20–21.

84. Freud, *Civilization and its Discontents*, pp. 11–12; Grunberger, *Narcissism*, p. 104. On this point, see also Chasseguet-Smirgel, "Some Thoughts on the Ego Ideal," p. 367.

85. Lou Andreas-Salomé, *The Freud Journal of Lou Andreas-Salomé*, p. 164; quoted by Grunberger, *Narcissism*, p. 24.

86. Grunberger, *Narcissism*, p. 31. See also p. 93.

87. Mahler, "On Human Symbiosis," pp. 77–88. See also Greenberg and Mitchell, *Object Relations*, pp. 288–89.

88. Grunberger, *Narcissism*, p. 267.

89. Mahler, "On the Three Subphases of the Separation-Individuation Process," p. 338.

90. Freud, "Instincts and their Vicissitudes," pp. 134–35.

91. Grunberger, *Narcissism*, p. 61; from Kafka's fable "A Country Doctor."

92. Grunberger, *Narcissism*, pp. 204–05.

93. Marion Oliner, Foreword to *Narcissism*, by Grunberger, p. xii.

94. Grunberger, *Narcissism*, p. 203.

95. Ibid., p. 245.

96. Freud, *Civilization and its Discontents*, pp. 36, 47–49.

97. Grunberger, *Narcissism*, p. 268, note.

98. Ibid., p. 195.

99. Ibid., p. 290.

100. Ibid., pp. 290–93.

101. See Chasseguet-Smirgel, *The Ego Ideal*, pp. 232–38. Lasch, in his bibliographic essay at the conclusion of *Minimal Self*, has a section on the psychoanalytic literature on the ego ideal (pp. 284–86). The key point is how much disagreement exists over the term: some see the ego ideal as more primitive than the superego, some as the highest stage of superego development, still others as identical with the superego (see *Minimal Self*, pp. 178–85). As Chasseguet-Smirgel points out in her Appendix to *The Ego Ideal*, Freud is of little help here (pp. 220–45). All three views can be found in Freud. Lasch concludes that the difficulty in characterizing the ego ideal reflects its dialectical character, its linking of the most base with the most sublime, the fact that it is both primitive and mature (*Minimal Self*, pp. 179–80). But it is definitely not identical with the superego, even though it may become well integrated with it. As we shall see, this is basically Chasseguet-Smirgel's position.

102. Freud, "On Narcissism," pp. 93–94.

103. Chasseguet-Smirgel, *Ego Ideal*, p. 44.

104. Fairbairn, *An Object Relations Theory of the Personality*, p. 154.

105. Chasseguet-Smirgel, *Ego Ideal*, p. 184. See also p. 8.

106. Ibid., pp. 181–82.

107. Ibid., pp. 187–88.

108. Ibid., p. 33.

109. Kohut, "Thoughts on Narcissism and Narcissistic Rage," pp. 397–98.

110. Lasch, *The Culture of Narcissism*, pp. 389–90.

111. Chasseguet-Smirgel, *Ego Ideal*, pp. 218–19.

112. Greenberg and Mitchell, *Object Relations*, pp. 403–07.

113. Andreas-Salomé, *Freud Journal*, p. 164.

114. Kernberg, *Borderline Conditions and Pathological Narcissism*, chap. 10.

Chapter 3:   Socrates, Eros, and the Culture of Narcissism

1. References to classical sources are given in the text in the form that is usual in classical studies.

2. This pattern is identified by Werner Jaeger, *Paideia*, vol. 1, pp. 65, 433. See too George Boas, "Love." For Thucydides' views on the socially disruptive character of eros, see Steven Forde, "Thucydides and the Causes of Athenian Imperialism," *American Political Science Review* 80 (1986): 433–48, esp. pp. 440–44.

3. Hans Kelsen, "Platonic Love," pp. 75–76.

4. Max Horkheimer, *Eclipse of Reason*, p. 11.

5. Kelsen, "Platonic Love," pp. 4–50. K. J. Dover's *Greek Homosexuality*, perhaps the best book on this topic ever written, does not really support Kelsen. Dover contends that homosexuality was the norm among young men. However, George Devereux's "Greek Pseudo-Homosexuality and the 'Greek Miracle'" casts this norm in an interesting light. By calling the phenomenon "pseudo-homosexuality," Devereux means to suggest that it served an important cultural and psychological function for adolescent boys in a society in which the father was generally absent. As Devereux puts it, because the Greeks "overvalued, discussed ad infinitum, and ostentatiously practiced homosexual courtship" does not mean that it possessed deep psychological significance for the individuals involved. It may have been "a kind of luxury product," a "'conspicuous display' in Veblen's sense" (pp, 81–82). Nothing in my argument depends on the intensity of homosexuality in Athens. Even "pseudo-homosexuality," centering on the praise of homosexuality, rather than its practice, is significant, insofar as it idealizes a narcissistic object choice. Indeed, this is precisely what one sees in Plato's *Symposium*.

6. H. Gomperz, "Psychologische Beobachtungen an griechischen Philosophen," p. 70; cited in Kelsen, "Platonic Love," p. 45.

7. Although it is possible to cross-check Plato's Socrates with Socrates as he is portrayed by Xenophon, Aristophanes (especially in *Clouds*), and other lesser sources, such as Aristoxenos, it is not necessary for our purpose.

8. Philip Slater, *The Glory of Hera*, pp. 420–22.

9. Christopher Lasch, *The Culture of Narcissism*, chap. 5, esp. p. 374.

10. A. H. M. Jones, *Athenian Democracy*, pp. 82–83; A. W. Gomme, *The Population of Athens in the Fifth and Fourth Centuries B.C.*, pp. 67–70. Jones's estimate is for the late fifth century. For more details on the population and death rate, see my "Plato's *Protagoras*: An Institutional Perspective."

11. Alvin Gouldner, *Enter Plato*, pp. 60–64.

12. Ibid., p. 61. Adkins, *Merit and Responsibility*, pp. 48ff. Dover (*Greek*

Homosexuality, pp. 201–03) makes a similar point regarding its psychological function.

13. Adkins, "Arete, Techne, Democracy and Sophists: Protagoras 316b–328d"; idem, *Merit and Responsibility*; idem, *Moral Values and Political Behavior in Ancient Greece*.

14. Michel Foucault, *The Use of Pleasure*, pp. 242–53.

15. Socrates clearly rejects this for himself (Plato *Symposium* 216c–219e). Though he is tolerant of active homosexuality in his friends (*Meno* 70b; *Republic* 474d–475a), he appears to regard its physical manifestation as base (Xenophon *Memorabilia* 1. 2.29ff). See Dover, *Greek Homosexuality*, p. 160. I follow Dover (pp. 153–70) closely here.

16. Sigmund Freud, *Three Essays on the Theory of Sexuality*, Preface to the 4th edition, p. xviii.

17. *Lysis* is not really an exception. As Paul Friedlaender observes, "behind the Philia of this dialogue is really hidden Eros. . . . From the first words the atmosphere of . . . [eros] is perceptible" (*Platon*, vol. 2, pp. 95–96); translated and quoted by Kelsen, "Platonic Love," p. 22. Both authors suggest that in this (presumably) early work Plato is still attempting to formulate his views on eros, views that will undergo several changes: to his later embrace of the divine madness of eros over friendship in *Phaedrus* and his still later explicit fear of the power of eros in the *Laws* (8.835d–8.842a). See too the *Timaeus*, also generally regarded as a late work, in which Plato treats erotic intemperance as a disease of the soul (86b–87c; 90e–91d).

18. Boas, "Love," p. 94.

19. F. M. Cornford, "The Doctrine of Eros in Plato's *Symposium*," pp. 71, 78.

20. Marion Oliner, Foreword to *Narcissism*, by Grunberger, p. xii.

21. Freud, "Instincts and their Vicissitudes," p. 81, my emphasis; quoted by Thomas Gould, *Platonic Love*, p. 13.

22. Freud, "On Narcissism," pp. 90–91.

23. Raymond Larson, trans. and commentator, *The Apology and Crito of Plato and the Apology and Symposium of Xenophon*, p. 121, n. 26. Xenophon *Symposium* 8. 2–3. See also Plato *Lysis* 205e–206b.

24. Dover, *Greek Homosexuality*, pp. 29–32.

25. Freud, "On Narcissism," pp. 87–88.

26. Léon Robin, *La théorie platonicienne de l'Amour*, p. 9; cited by Gould, *Platonic Love*, p. 23.

27. Jaeger, *Paideia*, vol. 2, pp. 174ff.

28. Stanley Rosen, *Plato's Symposium*, p. xvii and passim.

29. Freud, *Beyond the Pleasure Principle*, p. 80.

30. Ibid., pp. 80–81.

31. In the discussion which follows I assume that Diotima (from whom

Socrates claims he learned his account of love) serves a strictly literary function, by saving Socrates from being put in the position of praising himself. For he clearly represents what Diotima praises; thus, Diotima = Socrates. Thus, I will interchange the names Socrates and Diotima, according to which seems most appropriate in the particular context. Not all scholars treat Diotima in this fashion, however; see e.g., Rosen, *Plato's Symposium*, pp. 197–277. Rosen also finds much of value in Agathon's speech (pp. 159–73).

32. Rosen, *Plato's Symposium*, pp. 3, 309. See also idem, "The Role of Eros in Plato's Republic," p. 453.

33. Rosen, *Plato's Symposium*, p. 8.

34. Lasch, *The Minimal Self*, p. 169.

35. Rosen, *Plato's Symposium*, p. 155; idem, "The Role of Eros in Plato's Republic," p. 472. Contrast Harry Neumann, "Diotima's Concept of Love," p. 37.

36. Eric Havelock, *Preface to Plato*, p. 269 and n. 34.

37. Neumann, "Diotima's Concept of Love," p. 47.

38. Jaeger, *Paideia*, vol. 2, p. 189; Neumann, "Diotima's Concept of Love," p. 47.

39. Grunberger, *Narcissism*, p. 290.

40. That identification is less mature is suggested by Freud, "Group Psychology and the Analysis of the Ego," pp. 105–11.

41. Grunberger, *Narcissism*, p. 292.

42. Rosen, *Plato's Symposium*, p. 309.

43. Ibid., p. 317.

44. See Martha Nussbaum, *The Fragility of Goodness: Luck and Ethics in Greek Tragedy and Philosophy*, chap. 4, n. 5; chap. 5, n. 21; chap. 7, n. 5, on the order of composition. George Klosko generally supports Nussbaum's position on the order of composition (*The Development of Plato's Political Theory*, pp. 15–22). Though this is not the place to develop this point, I believe that it is impossible to understand Plato without making certain assumptions about the order of composition of the dialogues.

45. Nussbaum, *Fragility of Goodness*, pp. 200–03.

46. Theodor Adorno, *Negative Dialectics*, pp. 22–24. "Rage is the mark of each and every idealism" (p. 23).

47. Friedrich Nietzsche, *The Will to Power*, p. 519 (see also p. 576); quoted in Nussbaum, *Fragility of Goodness*, p. 161.

48. Arnold Rothstein, *The Narcissistic Pursuit of Perfection*, p. 300.

49. Nussbaum, *Fragility of Goodness*, pp. 181–83.

50. Ibid., p. 181.

51. Ibid., p. 199.

52. Ibid.

53. Ibid., p. 204.
54. Herbert Marcuse, *An Essay on Liberation*, p. 32.
55. Nussbaum, *Fragility of Goodness*, p. 220.

Chapter 4:   Adorno and the Retreat from Eros

1. Jürgen Habermas, *Toward a Rational Society*, pp. 85–86.
2. Theirs was a unique analysis, but not a unique approach. At about this time, Karl Popper, in *The Open Society and its Enemies*, attempted to trace facism and Stalinism back to the teachings of Plato.
3. Max Horkheimer and Theodor Adorno, *Dialectic of Enlightenment*, pp. 20–42.
4. Ibid., pp. 43–80.
5. David Held, *Introduction to Critical Theory: Horkheimer to Habermas*, p. 404.
6. Horkheimer and Adorno, *Dialectic of Enlightenment*, pp. 40–42.
7. Erich Fromm's *Escape From Freedom* is an excellent account of the psychological dimension of this process. Fromm was a member of the Frankfurt school during its early days.
8. Horkheimer, *Eclipse of Reason*, pp. 63–71.
9. Adorno, "Subject and Object," p. 499; quoted by Martin Jay, *Adorno*, pp. 63–64.
10. Jay, *Adorno*, p. 64.
11. Adorno, *Minima Moralia*, p. 50.
12. Herbert Marcuse, *Reason and Revolution*, p. xiv; quoted by Jay, *Marxism and Totality*, p. 208.
13. Gillian Rose, *The Melancholy Science: An Introduction to the Thought of Theodor W. Adorno*, p. 43. See also Jay, *Marxism and Totality*, p. 268.
14. Adorno, *Negative Dialectics*, pp. 22–24.
15. Ibid., p. 5.
16. Jay, *Marxism and Totality*, pp. 254–56; Susan Buck-Morss, *The Origin of Negative Dialectics*, p. 66.
17. Horkheimer, "Die Gegenwärtige Lage der Sozialphilosophie und die Aufgaben eines Instituts für Sozialforschung," p. 11; trans. and quoted by Jay, *Marxism and Totality*, p. 199.
18. Marcuse, *Reason and Revolution*, p. xiv.
19. Adorno, "The Actuality of Philosophy," p. 120; quoted by Jay, *Marxism and Totality*, p. 256.
20. Jean-François Lyotard, "Adorno as the Devil," pp. 132–33; trans. Robert Hurley; quoted by Jay, *Marxism and Totality*, p. 515.
21. Habermas, *The Theory of Communicative Action*, vol. 1, *Reason*

and the *Rationalization of Society*, pp. 382–83. The German terms are from the original, *Theorie des kommunikativen Handelns*, vol. 1, p. 512.

22. Habermas, "The Entwinement of Myth and Enlightenment: Rereading *Dialectic of Enlightenment*," p. 29.

23. Adorno, *Negative Dialectics*, p. 10.

24. Ibid., p. 181.

25. Ibid., p. 43.

26. Ibid., p. 45.

27. Habermas, *Theory of Communicative Action*, vol. 1, p. 382.

28. Adorno, "The Actuality of Philosophy," p. 131.

29. Buck-Morss, *Origin of Negative Dialectics*, pp. 72–88. Jay (*Adorno*, pp. 155–58) discusses the complexity of mimesis, also showing it to be an active, constructive force.

30. Adorno, *Kierkegaard: Konstruktion des Aesthetischen*, p. 142; quoted by Buck-Morss, *Origin of Negative Dialectics*, p. 73.

31. Adorno, *Negative Dialectics*, p. 19.

32. It might seem that science would remain a bastion of belief in an objective cosmological order. What else is Karl Popper's falsifiability criterion, for example, but an expression of the belief that an objective world exists and that it resists some experimental intrusions but not others? (*The Logic of Scientific Discovery*, pp. 40–42). But Adorno and Marcuse see modern science as an expression of what might be called "instrumental idealism," for science believes that its theories constitute reality. See Horkheimer and Adorno, *Dialectic of Enlightenment*, pp. 9–11; Marcuse, *One-Dimensional Man* (Boston: Beacon Press, 1964), pp. 146–52. See, too, Marcuse's "On Science and Phenomenology." For a criticism of this view, see my *Science and the Revenge of Nature: Marcuse and Habermas*, pp. 53–57.

33. Buck-Morss, *Origin of Negative Dialectics*, pp. 186–87; Jay, *Marxism and Totality*, pp. 274–75. But see also Buck-Morss's fascinating analysis of how the large-scale empirical study of which Adorno was co-director, *The Authoritarian Personality*, benefited from the method of negative dialectics (pp. 177–84).

34. Buck-Morss, *Origin of Negative Dialectics*, p. 186.

35. Jay, *Marxism and Totality*, p. 21.

36. Ibid., pp. 22–23.

37. Ibid., passim.

38. Ibid., p. 22.

39. Adorno, *Minima Moralia*, p. 247.

40. Ibid.

41. Adorno et al., *The Positivist Dispute in German Sociology*, p. 12, quoted by Jay, *Marxism and Totality*, pp. 266–67.

42. Adorno, *Prisms*, p. 34. But see Jay, *Marxism and Totality*, p. 243, n. 5, for Adorno's amendment of this view.

43. Adorno, *Minima Moralia*, p. 15.

44. Sigmund Freud, "Mourning and Melancholia," pp. 243–44. On the relationship of narcissism and melancholia, see ibid., p. 252.

45. Adorno, *Minima Moralia*, p. 247.

46. See original, in Adorno, *Gesammelte Schriften*, vol. 4, p. 281n. *Willkür* covers an enormous range of possibilities, from free will to arbitrary action. *Selbstherrlichkeit* and *Laune* are often employed in similar contexts. With such a wide range of dictionary meanings available, the translator must obviously choose according to the context.

47. Quoted by Jay, *The Dialectical Imagination*, p. 103.

48. Adorno, "Die revidierte Psychoanalyse," p. 40; my translation.

49. Freud, "Totem and Taboo," p. 106.

50. Horkheimer and Adorno, *Dialectic of Enlightenment*, p. 11; internal quote from Freud, "Totem and Taboo."

51. Their tone is ironic in precisely the same sense as the title of Marcuse's essay, "The Obsolescence of the Freudian Concept of Man"; Marcuse believes that the Freudian concept of man has become outdated, because men have changed, although he regrets this change.

52. Janine Chasseguet-Smirgel, *The Ego Ideal*, p. 218. See also Christopher Lasch, *The Minimal Self*, pp. 240–58.

53. Marcuse, *Eros and Civilization*, pp. 215–16.

54. See my *Science and the Revenge of Nature*, pp. 49–57.

55. Freud, "The Ego and the Id," pp. 51–57. Actually, Freud's argument regarding the superego is more complex than Horkheimer or Adorno suggest. It is not merely the mirror of the father's values. Freud came to see the superego as representing not the father punishing the son, but the son attempting to punish the father within him—that is, the father with whom he has identified. Conscience—morality—is our aggression toward those who stand in the way of our satisfaction turned back against ourselves. It is this that accounts for the discontent of civilization. See Freud, *Civilization and its Discontents*, p. 123. See also "Totem and Taboo," p. 156.

56. Horkheimer, "Authority and the Family," p. 101.

57. Jessica Benjamin, "The End of Internalization: Adorno's Social Psychology"; idem, "Authority and the Family Revisited: or, A World Without Fathers?"

58. Horkheimer, "Authority and the Family," p. 101.

59. Horkheimer, "Authority and the Family Today," p. 365.

60. Adorno, "Sociology and Psychology," part 2, p. 85.

61. Freud puts it this way: "In the absence of fear of castration, the chief motive is lacking which leads boys to surmount the Oedipus complex. Girls remain in it for an indeterminate length of time; they demolish it late, and even so, incompletely. In these circumstances the formation of the superego must suffer; it cannot attain the strength and independence which give

it its cultural significance, and feminists are not pleased when we point out to them the effects of this factor upon the average female character." ("Femininity," p. 129). This claim is related to Freud's assertion that women threaten civilization more than men, because they are less capable of sublimation. See idem, *Civilization and its Discontents*, p. 56; also "The Dissolution of the Oedipus Complex," p. 178.

62. Horkheimer, "Authority and the Family," p. 107.

63. Horkheimer, "Authority and the Family Today," p. 365; quoted by Benjamin, "Authority and the Family Revisited," p. 48.

64. Marcuse, *Five Lectures: Psychoanalysis, Politics, and Utopia*, p. 51.

65. Adorno, "Sociology and Psychology," part 2, p. 95.

66. Ibid., p. 88.

67. Adorno, however, is not always entirely clear or correct regarding narcissism. At one point he states that "the kind of instinctual energy on which the ego draws . . . is of the anaclitic type Freud called narcissistic" ("Sociology and Psychology," part 2, p. 88). In fact, narcissistic libido is precisely the opposite of anaclitic, or object-oriented, libido, as we have seen.

68. Horkheimer, "Authority and the Family Today," pp. 368–73; quoted in Lasch, *Haven in a Heartless World*, p. 92.

69. Lasch, *Haven*, pp. 91–94.

70. Ibid., pp. 165–83.

71. Ibid., p. 178.

72. Benjamin, "The End of Internalization," p. 61; Adorno, "Die revidierte Psychoanalyse," pp. 39–40. See also idem, "Sociology and Psychology," part 2, pp. 96–97, for a similar point. Actually, this "coldness" does not seem to have been as much a part of Freud's practice as of his theory (or Adorno's interpretation of his theory). In his account of his analysis with Freud, the "Wolf-Man" says that Freud often asked after his fiancée, remarked how attractive she was after meeting her, and loaned him considerable sums of money over a long period of time (*The Wolf-Man*, pp. 113, 142, 303).

Chapter 5:   Narcissism and Civilization: Marcuse

1. See, e.g., Barry Katz, *Herbert Marcuse and the Art of Liberation*, p. 151.

2. See Joel Kovel, "Narcissism and the Family," p. 91; Joel Whitebook, "Reason and Happiness: Some Psychoanalytic Themes in Critical Theory," pp. 22–23; Heinz Kohut, *The Restoration of the Self*, p. 271. But see also Colleen Clements, chap. 2, n. 3.

3. Christopher Lasch, *The Minimal Self*, pp. 227–34 and passim. Several reviewers have argued that Lasch does not give the Frankfurt school,

and especially Marcuse, sufficient credit as a source of his own views. See, e.g., Mark Crispin Miller's review of *The Minimal Self*, p. 148.

4. Stanley Aronowitz, "On Narcissism."

5. A representative of the "Marcuse sticks too closely to Freud" school is Anthony Wilden, "Marcuse and the Freudian Model," esp. p. 197. A representative of the "Marcuse doesn't stick closely enough to Freud" school is Morton Schoolman, *The Imaginary Witness*, chap. 3. Perhaps the most balanced treatment of this issue is that of Gad Horowitz, *Repression: Basic and Surplus Repression in Psychoanalytic Theory*.

6. Sigmund Freud, *Civilization and its Discontents*, p. 16; quoted by Herbert Marcuse, *Eros and Civilization*, p. 153; emphasis original.

7. Marcuse, *Eros*, pp. 153–54; my emphasis.

8. Ibid., p. 154.

9. Freud, "Group Psychology and the Analysis of the Ego," pp. 137–42.

10. Freud, "The Ego and the Id," p. 30.

11. Marcuse, *Eros*, p. 154.

12. Schoolman, *Imaginary Witness*, pp. 255–59; Heide Berndt and Reimut Reiche, "Die geschichtliche Dimension des Realitätsprinzips," pp. 108–10 and passim.

13. Freud, "The Ego and the Id," pp. 29–33.

14. Freud, *An Outline of Psycho-Analysis*, pp. 11–12.

15. Sidney Lipshires, *Herbert Marcuse: From Marx to Freud and Beyond*, p. 45.

16. Freud, "The Ego and the Id," pp. 28–31.

17. Marcuse, *Eros*, p. 149.

18. Ibid., pp. 24–27, 148–52.

19. Béla Grunberger, *Narcissism*, pp. 259–64.

20. Kohut, *How Does Analysis Cure?*, pp. 19–21.

21. Marcuse, *Eros*, p. 152.

22. Grunberger, *Narcissism*, pp. 2–3.

23. Marcuse, *Eros*, pp. 146–47.

24. Thomas Bulfinch, *Bulfinch's Mythology*, pp. 101–05, 185–89. The classic source of the Narcissus myth is Ovid's account in *Metamorphoses*, book 3. See the discussion of the myth in chap. 1, n. 5.

25. But see Marcuse, *Eros*, p. 155.

26. Ibid., pp. 74, 77, 199ff.; Ives Hendrick, "Work and the Pleasure Principle."

27. Marcuse, *Eros*, pp. 195–97; Barbara Lantos, "Work and the Instincts," p. 116.

28. Lantos, "Work and the Instincts," p. 116.

29. Marcuse, *Eros*, p. 195.

30. Ibid., p. 196.

31. Ibid., p. 179.

32. This reason is examined extensively in my book *Science and the Revenge of Nature*, chap. 3–4.

33. Marcuse, *Eros*, p. 76.

34. Freud, *Beyond the Pleasure Principle*, p. 43.

35. Marcuse, *Eros*, p. 76.

36. Ibid., pp. 31–33.

37. Ibid., p. 142; see also p. 178.

38. Janine Chasseguet-Smirgel, *The Ego Ideal*, pp. 218–19.

39. Marcuse, *An Essay on Liberation*, p. 31.

40. Lou Andreas-Salomé, "The Dual Orientation of Narcissism," p. 9.

41. Martin Jay, "Anamnestic Totalization: Reflections on Marcuse's Theory of Remembrance," pp. 9–11.

42. Marcuse, *An Essay on Liberation*, p. 90; Jay, "Anamnestic Totalization," pp. 10–11.

43. Marcuse, *Eros*, p. 165.

44. Ibid., pp. 177–78.

45. Lasch, *Minimal Self*, pp. 244–46; Chasseguet-Smirgel, *Ego Ideal*, pp. 217–22. See also Chasseguet-Smirgel, "Some Thoughts on the Ego Ideal," pp. 368–71.

46. Grunberger, *Narcissism*, p. 21.

47. Lasch, *Minimal Self*, pp. 233–34.

48. Ibid., p. 234.

49. Ibid., pp. 232–34.

50. Norman O. Brown, *Life Against Death: The Psychoanalytic Meaning of History* (Middletown, Conn.: Wesleyan University Press, 1959); Marcuse, "Love Mystified: A Critique of Norman O. Brown."

51. Marcuse, *Eros*, quoted by Lasch, *Minimal Self*, p. 235.

52. Lasch, *Minimal Self*, p. 235; all internal quotes are from Brown.

53. Lasch, *Minimal Self*, p. 282.

54. Lasch gives the Freudian sources, many of which we have considered (ibid., pp. 282–83).

55. Lasch, *Minimal Self*, pp. 236–37.

56. Ibid., pp. 281–82. Freud, *Civilization and its Discontents*, pp. 15–16; idem, *Beyond the Pleasure Principle*, pp. 47–57, esp. p. 56.

57. Freud, *Civilization and its Discontents*, pp. 36–37.

58. Marcuse, *the Aesthetic Dimension*, p. 72.

59. Grunberger, *Narcissism*, p. 268.

60. Freud, "On Narcissism," pp. 93–94. See also idem, "Group Psychology and the Analysis of the Ego," pp. 109–10; Chasseguet-Smirgel, *Ego Ideal*, p. 232.

61. Karl Marx, "The Economic and Philosophic Manuscripts of 1844," pp. 76–77.

62. Marcuse, "Protosocialism and Late Capitalism: Toward a Theoretical Synthesis Based on Bahro's Analysis."

63. William Galston, *Justice and the Human Good*, p. 15.

64. Freud, "On Narcissism," pp. 93–94; idem, "Group Psychology and the Analysis of the Ego," pp. 109–10.

65. Marion Oliner, Foreword to *Narcissism*, by Grunberger, p. xii.

Chapter 6: Habermas and the End of the Individual

1. Jürgen Habermas, "A Postscript to *Knowledge and Human Interests*," pp. 166–72, 182–85. Actually, the parallel between ideal speech and psychoanalysis is not perfect; Habermas characterizes the latter as an educative or therapeutic discourse. However, with regard to the issues with which we are concerned here, the parallel is most exact, as we shall see.

2. Stephen K. White, "Foucault's Challenge to Critical Theory," pp. 420–21.

3. Habermas, *Der philosophische Diskurs der Moderne*, pp. 70, 120, 311, 314, 359.

4. Jacques Lacan, *Speech and Language in Psychoanalysis*, idem, *Ecrits: A Selection*, chap. 3. On Habermas's view of the instinctual unconscious, see B. Frankel, "Habermas Talking: An Interview," p. 53.

5. Lacan, *Ecrits*, pp. 5–6. See also Martha Evans, "Introduction to Jacques Lacan's Lecture: The Neurotic's Individual Myth," pp. 394–400. The "mirror stage" runs from about 6 to 18 months.

6. Lacan, *Ecrits*, pp. 67, 199, 217, 310, 314, and p. xi (Translators Note). See also Ellie Ragland-Sullivan, *Jacques Lacan and the Philosophy of Psychoanalysis*, pp. 30–37.

7. Lacan, *Ecrits*, pp. 20–21; Ragland-Sullivan, *Lacan and Philosophy*, pp. 34–35.

8. Sigmund Freud, "The Ego and the Id," p. 29; quoted by Ragland-Sullivan, *Lacan and Philosophy*, p. 35.

9. Lacan, *Ecrits*, pp. 15, 80–88, 171. See also Ragland-Sullivan, *Lacan and Philosophy*, pp. 37–39; Evans, "Introduction to Lacan's Lecture," pp. 395–96, 398–99.

10. See Immanuel Kant, "What is Enlightenment?"

11. Habermas, *Theorié des kommunikativen Handelns*, vol. 1, pp. 42–43; see also the translation, *Theory of Communicative Action*, pp. 20–22.

12. Habermas, *Der philosophische Diskurs der Moderne*, pp. 255, 309.

13. Habermas, *Knowledge and Human Interests*, p. 218.

14. Ibid., p. 226; emphasis original.

15. Ibid., p. 227; emphasis original.

16. Ibid., p. 241.

17. Henning Ottmann, "Cognitive Interests and Self-Reflection," p. 86.

18. Russell Keat, *The Politics of Social Theory: Habermas, Freud, and the Critique of Positivism*, pp. 96, 107.

19. Habermas, *Knowledge*, pp. 309–11, 314–17. See also idem, "A Postscript to *Knowledge and Human Interests*," pp. 182–85.

20. Christopher Nichols, "Science or Reflection: Habermas on Freud"; Joel Whitebook, "Reason and Happiness: Some Psychoanalytic Themes in Critical Theory," esp. pp. 23–30.

21. Heinz Kohut, *The Restoration of the Self*, pp. 30–32; idem, *How Does Analysis Cure?*, pp. 70–71.

22. Habermas, *Theorie*, vol. 1, p. 523; my translation. See also McCarthy's translation, *Theory*, p. 390.

23. Habermas, *Theorie*, pp. 522–24.

24. Habermas, "Historical Materialism and the Development of Normative Structures," pp. 100–01.

25. Jean-Jacques Rousseau, "Discourse on the Origin and Foundations of Inequality Among Men," pp. 102–04.

26. Although they are different concepts, the *ego* and the *self* are frequently used interchangeably by object relations theorists. This is somewhat confusing, but it is done primarily to preserve continuity with Freud.

27. Whitebook, "Reason and Happiness," p. 25.

28. Habermas, "Moral Development and Ego Identity," p. 93.

29. Habermas, "Questions and Counterquestions," pp. 199–203. See also White, "Foucault's Challenge," pp. 426–27.

30. Habermas, "Questions and Counterquestions," p. 200.

31. Habermas, "Bewusstmachende oder rettende Kritik-Die Aktualität Walter Benjamins," pp. 322–32. See also idem, *Legitimation Crisis*, p. 78; Martin Jay, "Habermas and Modernism," pp. 126–27.

32. Habermas, *Theorie*, vol. 1, pp. 226–29.

33. Actually, to write of needs and experiences as "essentially linguistic" is not so much an explanation as a definition. One sees this, for example, in Habermas's earlier (1970) "Der Universalitätsanspruch der Hermeneutik." Here Habermas argues roughly in the form: that which is prelinguistic can later be integrated into language; that which is not cannot (pp. 270–76). How this could lead to a tautological explanation is apparent. The phrase "essentially linguistic" is used here only as a shorthand way of referring to Habermas's treatment of the issue. No ontological claim is at stake.

34. Jay, "Habermas and Modernism," pp. 136–39; White, "Foucault's Challenge," pp. 427–29.

35. Habermas, *Knowledge*, p. 310–17.

36. Whitebook, "Reason and Happiness," p. 26.

37. Habermas, "Moral Development and Ego Identity," pp. 93–94.

38. Herbert Marcuse, "On Hedonism," pp. 159–64.

39. Habermas, "A Reply to my Critics," p. 235; quoted by Jay, "Habermas and Modernism," p. 137.

40. Habermas, "Moral Development and Ego Identity," p. 93.

41. Habermas, "The New Obscurity: The Crisis of the Welfare State and the Exhaustion of Utopian Energies," pp. 16–17.

42. Habermas, "Moral Development and Ego Identity," p. 72.

43. Ibid.

44. Habermas, Legitimation Crisis, pp. 117–30.

45. For a succinct discussion of these conditions, see Thomas McCarthy, "A Theory of Communicative Competence," pp. 145–46.

46. Habermas, Legitimation Crisis, pp. 117–30.

47. Habermas, Knowledge, p. 314; my emphasis.

48. Nancy Chodorow, The Reproduction of Mothering: Psychoanalysis and the Sociology of Gender; Dorothy Dinnerstein, The Mermaid and the Minotaur: Sexual Arrangements and Human Malaise.

Chapter 7: Narcissism and Philosophy

1. Martha Nussbaum, Fragility of Goodness, p. 371.

2. Heinz Kohut, Restoration of the Self, p. 177.

3. Kohut, Self Psychology and the Humanities, chaps. 1 and 14.

4. Michel Foucault, The Archaeology of Knowledge, p. 203; quoted by Martin Jay, Marxism and Totality, p. 524.

5. Sigmund Freud, "On Narcissism," p. 94.

6. Anne Carson, Eros the Bittersweet, pp. 3–9.

7. Ibid., p. 173.

8. Ibid., pp. 30–31.

9. Ibid., p. 71.

10. Ibid., p. 68. Hephaestus was hurled out of heaven by his mother, Hera, because, alone of all the gods, he was born deformed and ugly. To punish his mother, Hephaestus chained her to a golden throne; but he freed her when she promised him Aphrodite as his wife. Aphrodite was an unwilling wife, however, and committed adultery with the handsome Ares. Whether Hephaestus was in fact impotent, as Carson claims, depends on how one interprets his unsuccessful advances toward Athena. In one account, he embraced her, she repulsed him, and his seed fell on her leg. See Catherine Avery, ed. The New Century Handbook of Greek Mythology and Legend, pp. 245–49.

11. Herbert Marcuse, "Love Mystified," p. 236.

12. Philippa Foot, review of After Virtue, by Alasdair MacIntyre.

13. Freud, "Group Psychology and the Analysis of the Ego," pp. 129–30.

14. Immanuel Kant, Critique of Judgment, pp. 318–24.

15. See William Galston, *Justice and the Human Good*, p. 12.

16. Nancy Chodorow, "Beyond Drive Theory," p. 293.

17. Ibid. Chodorow suggests that an alternative construction of narcissism that stresses the connections between individuals could encourage community (p. 306), but she does not elaborate.

18. Paul Zweig, *The Heresy of Self-Love: A Study of Subversive Individualism*, pp. 233–34.

19. Michael Balint, *The Basic Fault*, p. 20.

Bibliography

Note: Classical sources given in the text in the form that is usual in classical studies are not repeated here.

Adkins, A. W. H. "Arete, Techne, Democracy and Sophists: *Protagoras* 316b–328b." *Journal of Hellenic Studies* 93 (1973): 9–12.
———. *Merit and Responsibility.* Oxford: Clarendon Press, 1960.
———. *Moral Values and Political Behavior in Ancient Greece.* New York: W. W. Norton, 1972.
Adorno, Theodor. "The Actuality of Philosophy." *Telos* 31 (Spring 1977):120–33.
———. "Freudian Theory and the Pattern of Fascist Propaganda." In *The Essential Frankfurt School Reader,* ed. A. Arato and E. Gebhardt, pp. 118–37. New York: Urizen, 1978.
———. *Gesammelte Schriften,* ed. Rolf Tiedemann. 23 vols. Frankfurt am Main: Suhrkamp, 1970–.
———. *Kierkegaard: Konstruktion des Aesthetischen.* Tübingen: J. C. B. Mohr, 1966.
———. *Minima Moralia,* trans. E. F. N. Jephcott. London: New Left Books, 1974.
———. *Negative Dialectics,* trans. E. B. Ashton. New York: Seabury, 1973.
———. *Prisms,* trans. Samuel and Shierry Weber. Cambridge, Mass.: MIT Press, 1983.
———. "Die revidierte Psychoanalyse." In *Gesammelte Schriften,* vol. 8; pp. 3–42.

_____. "Sociology and Psychology," part 2. *New Left Review* 47 (1968):79–97.

_____. "Subject and Object." In *The Essential Frankfurt School Reader*, pp. 497–511.

Adorno, Theodor et al. *The Positivist Dispute in German Sociology*, trans. Glyn Adey and David Frisby. New York: Harper and Row, 1976.

Alford, C. Fred. "Plato's *Protagoras*: An Institutional Perspective." *The Classical World* 80 (1987–88), forthcoming.

_____. *Science and the Revenge of Nature: Marcuse and Habermas*. Gainesville, Fl.: University Presses of Florida, 1985.

American Psychiatric Association. *Diagnostic and Statistical Manual of Mental Disorders*, 3d ed. Washington, D.C.: American Psychiatric Association, 1980.

Andreas-Salomé, Lou. "The Dual Orientation of Narcissism," trans. S. Leavy. *The Psychoanalytic Quarterly* 31 (1962):3–30.

_____. *The Freud Journal of Lou Andreas-Salomé*. New York: Basic Books, 1964.

Aronowitz, Stanley. "On Narcissism." *Telos* 44 (Summer 1980): 65–74.

Avery, Catherine, ed. *The New Century Handbook of Greek Mythology and Legend*. New York: Appleton-Century-Crofts, 1972.

Balint, Michael. *The Basic Fault*. New York: Brunner/Mazel, 1979.

Benjamin, Jessica. "Authority and the Family Revisited: or, A World Without Fathers?" *New German Critique* 13 (Winter 1978): 35–57.

_____. "The End of Internalization: Adorno's Social Psychology." *Telos* 32 (Summer 1977):42–64.

Berndt, Heide, and Reiche, Reimut. "Die geschichtliche Dimension des Realitätsprinzips." In *Antworten auf Herbert Marcuse*, ed. J. Habermas, pp. 104–33. Frankfurt am Main: Suhrkamp, 1968.

Black, Max. *Models and Metaphors*. Ithaca, N.Y.: Cornell University Press, 1962.

Boas, George. "Love." In *Encyclopedia of Philosophy*, ed. Paul Edwards, vol. 5, pp. 89–95. New York: MacMillan, 1967.

Brodbeck, May. "Methodological Individualisms: Definition and Reduction." In *Readings in the Philosophy of the Social Sci-*

ences, ed. M. Brodbeck, pp. 280–303. New York: Macmillan, 1968.

Buck-Morss, Susan. *The Origin of Negative Dialectics*. New York: Free Press, 1977.

Bulfinch, Thomas. *Bulfinch's Mythology*. New York: Avenel Books, 1979.

Carson, Anne. *Eros the Bittersweet*. Princeton, N.J.: Princeton University Press, 1986.

Chasseguet-Smirgel, Janine. *The Ego Ideal*, trans. Paul Barrows. New York: W. W. Norton, 1984.

——. "Some Thoughts on the Ego Ideal." *Psychoanalytic Quarterly* 45 (1976):345–73.

Chodorow, Nancy. "Beyond Drive Theory." *Theory and Society* 14 (1985):271–319.

——. *The Reproduction of Mothering: Psychoanalysis and the Sociology of Gender*. Berkeley and Los Angeles: University of California Press, 1978.

Clements, Colleen. "Misusing Psychiatric Models: The Culture of Narcissism." *Psychoanalytic Review* 69 (1982):283–95.

Contemporary Psychoanalysis 23 (1987):6–59.

Cornford, F. M. "The Doctrine of Eros in Plato's *Symposium*." In *The Unwritten Philosophy*, ed. W. K. C. Guthrie, pp. 68–80. Cambridge: Cambridge University Press, 1950.

Devereux, George. *Basic Problems of Ethnopsychiatry*, trans. Basia Miller Gulati and George Devereux. Chicago: University of Chicago Press, 1980.

——. "Greek Pseudo-Homosexuality and the 'Greek Miracle.'" *Symbolae Osloenses*. 42 (1967):69–92.

Dinnerstein, Dorothy. *The Mermaid and the Minotaur: Sexual Arrangements and Human Malaise*. New York: Harper and Row, Colophon Books, 1976.

Dodds, E. R. *The Greek and the Irrational*. Boston: Beacon Press, 1957.

Dover, K. J. *Greek Homosexuality*. New York: Vantage Books, 1980.

Evans, Martha. "Introduction to Jacques Lacan's Lecture: The Neurotic's Individual Myth." *Psychoanalytic Quarterly* 48 (1979): 386–404.

Fairbairn, W. R. D. *An Object-Relations Theory of the Personality*. New York: Basic Books, 1954. (Originally published in 1952 in London by Routledge and Kegan Paul as *Psychoanalytic Studies of the Personality*.)

Foot, Philippa. Review of *After Virtue*, by Alasdair MacIntyre. *Times Literary Supplement*, 25 Sept. 1981, p. 1097.

Foucault, Michel. *The Archaeology of Knowledge*, trans. A. M. Sheridan Smith. New York: Pantheon Books, 1972.

———. *The Use of Pleasure*, trans. Robert Hurley. New York: Vintage Books, 1986. (Vol. 2 of *The History of Sexuality*.)

Frankel, B. "Habermas Talking: An Interview." *Theory and Society* 1 (1974):37–58.

Freud, Sigmund. *Beyond the Pleasure Principle*, trans. James Strachey. New York: Liveright Publishing Co., 1950.

———. *Civilization and its Discontents*, trans. James Strachey. New York: W. W. Norton, 1961.

———. "The Dissolution of the Oedipus Complex." In *The Standard Edition*, vol. 19; pp. 173–79.

———. "The Ego and the Id." In *The Standard Edition*, vol. 19; pp. 1–66.

———. "Female Sexuality." In *The Standard Edition*, vol. 21; pp. 221–43.

———. "Femininity." In *New Introductory Lectures on Psychoanalysis*, pp. 112–35.

———. *Five Lectures on Psycho-Analysis*, trans. James Strachey. New York: W. W. Norton, 1977.

———. "From the History of an Infantile Neurosis." In *The Standard Edition*, vol. 17; pp. 3–122.

———. "Group Psychology and the Analysis of the Ego." In *The Standard Edition*, vol. 18; pp. 67–143.

———. "Instincts and their Vicissitudes." In *The Standard Edition*, vol. 14, pp. 117–40.

———. "Mourning and Melancholia." In *The Standard Edition*, vol. 14, pp. 243–58.

———. *New Introductory Lectures on Psychoanalysis*, trans. James Strachey. New York: W. W. Norton, 1964.

_____. "On Narcissism." In *The Standard Edition*, vol. 14; pp. 73–107.

_____. *An Outline of Psycho-Analysis*, trans. James Strachey, rev. ed. New York: W. W. Norton, 1969.

_____. "Psychoanalytic Notes on an Autobiographical Account of a Case of Paranoia" [Schreber Case]. In *The Standard Edition*, vol. 12; pp. 9–82.

_____. *The Standard Edition of the Complete Psychological Works of Sigmund Freud*, ed. James Strachey. 24 vols. London: Hogarth Press, 1953–74.

_____. *Three Essays on the Theory of Sexuality*, trans. James Strachey. New York: Basic Books, 1962.

_____. "Totem and Taboo." In *The Standard Edition*, vol. 13; pp. 1–162.

Friedlaender, Paul. *Platon*, vol. 2, 2d ed. Berlin: De Gruyter, 1957.

Fromm, Erich. *Escape From Freedom*. New York: Avon Books, 1965.

Galston, William. "Aristotelian Morality and Liberal Society: A Critique of Alasdair MacIntyre's *After Virtue*." Paper read at the 1982 annual meeting of the American Political Science Association, Denver, Colo.

_____. *Justice and the Human Good*. Chicago: University of Chicago Press, 1980.

Gomme, A. W. *The Population of Athens in the Fifth and Fourth Centuries B.C.* Chicago: Argonaut, 1967.

Gomperz, H. "Psychologische Beobachtungen an griechischen Philosophen." *Imago* 10 (1942):63–76.

Gould, Thomas. *Platonic Love*. New York: The Free Press of Glencoe, 1963.

Gouldner, Alvin. *Enter Plato*. New York: Basic Books, 1965.

Greenberg, Jay R., and Mitchell, Stephen A. *Object Relations in Psychoanalytic Theory*. Cambridge, Mass.: Harvard University Press, 1983.

Grünbaum, Adolf. *The Foundations of Psychoanalysis: A Philosophical Critique*. Berkeley and Los Angeles: University of California Press, 1984.

Grunberger, Béla. *Narcissism: Psychoanalytic Essays*, trans. Joyce Diamanti. New York: International Universities Press, 1979.

Guntrip, Harry. *Personality Structure and Human Interaction*. New York: International Universities Press, 1961.

———. *Psychoanalytic Theory, Therapy, and the Self*. New York: Basic Books, 1971.

Habermas, Jürgen. "Bewusstmachende oder rettende Kritik—Die Aktualität Walter Benjamins." In *Kultur und Kritik*, pp. 302–44. Frankfurt am Main: Suhrkamp, 1973.

———. "The Entwinement of Myth and Enlightenment: Rereading *Dialectic of Enlightenment*," trans. Thomas Levin. *New German Critique* 26(1982):13–30.

———. "Historical Materialism and the Development of Normative Structures." In *Communication and the Evolution of Society*, trans. T. McCarthy, pp. 95–129. Boston: Beacon Press, 1979.

———. *Knowledge and Human Interests*, trans. J. Shapiro. Boston: Beacon Press, 1971.

———. *Legitimation Crisis*, trans. T. McCarthy. Boston: Beacon Press, 1975.

———. "Moral Development and Ego Identity." In *Communication and the Evolution of Society*. trans. T. McCarthy, pp. 69–94. Boston: Beacon Press, 1979.

———. "The New Obscurity: The Crisis of the Welfare State and the Exhaustion of Utopian Energies," trans. Phillip Jacobs. *Philosophy and Social Criticism* 11 (Winter 1986):1–18.

———. *Der philosophische Diskurs der Moderne*. Frankfurt am Main: Suhrkamp, 1985.

———. "A Postscript to *Knowledge and Human Interests*." *Philosophy of the Social Sciences* 3(1973):157–89.

———. "Questions and Counterquestions." In *Habermas and Modernity*, ed. R. Bernstein, pp. 192–216. Cambridge, Mass.: M.I.T. Press, 1985.

———. "A Reply to my Critics." In *Habermas: Critical Debates*, ed. J. B. Thompson and David Held, pp. 219–83. Cambridge, Mass.: MIT Press, 1982.

_____. *Strukturwandel der Öffentlichkeit*. Neuwied and Berlin: Luchterhand, 1962.

_____. *The Theory of Communicative Action*; vol. 1, *Reason and the Rationalization of Society*, trans. Thomas McCarthy. Boston: Beacon Press, 1984. (Translation of vol. 1 of *Theorie des kommunikativen Handelns*. 2 vols. Frankfurt am Main: Suhrkamp, 1981.)

_____. *Toward a Rational Society*, trans. Jeremy Shapiro. Boston: Beacon Press, 1970.

_____. "Der Universalitätsanspruch der Hermeneutik." In *Kultur und Kritik*, pp. 264–301. Frankfurt am Main: Suhrkamp, 1973.

Havelock, Eric. *Preface to Plato*. Cambridge, Mass.: Harvard University Press, Belknap Press, 1963.

Held, David. *Introduction to Critical Theory: Horkheimer to Habermas*. Berkeley and Los Angeles: University of California Press, 1980.

Hendrick, Ives. "Work and the Pleasure Principle." *Psychanalytic Quarterly* 12 (1943):311–29.

Horkheimer, Max. "Authority and the Family." In *Critical Theory*, trans. Matthew J. O'Connell et al., pp. 47–128. New York: Seabury, 1972.

_____. "Authority and the Family Today." In *The Family: Its Function and Destiny*, ed. Ruth Anshen, pp. 359–74. New York: Harper, 1949.

_____. *Eclipse of Reason*. New York: Seabury, 1974.

_____. "Die Gegenwärtige Lage der Sozialphilosophie und die Aufgaben eines Instituts für Sozialforschung." *Frankfurter Universitätsreden* 37 (Jan. 1931).

_____ and Adorno, Theodor. *Dialectic of Enlightenment*, trans. John Cumming. New York: Herder and Herder, 1972.

Horowitz, Gad. *Repression: Basic and Surplus Repression in Psychoanalytic Theory*. Toronto: University of Toronto Press, 1977.

Jacobson, Edith. *The Self and the Object World*. New York: International Universities Press, 1964.

Jacoby, Felix, ed. *Die Fragmente der griechischen Historiker*, vol. 1. Berlin: 1923.

Jaeger, Werner. *Paideia*, vols. 1–2, trans. Gilbert Highet. New York: Oxford University Press, 1945.

Jay, Martin. *Adorno*. Cambridge, Mass.: Harvard University Press, 1984.

———. "Anamnestic Totalization: Reflections on Marcuse's Theory of Remembrance." *Theory and Society* 11 (1982):1–15.

———. *The Dialectical Imagination*. Boston: Little, Brown and Co., 1973.

———. "Habermas and Modernism." In *Habermas and Modernity*, ed. R. Bernstein, pp. 125–39. Cambridge, Mass.: MIT Press, 1985.

———. *Marxism and Totality*. Berkeley and Los Angeles: University of California Press, 1984.

Jones, A. H. M. *Athenian Democracy*. Oxford: Basil Blackwell, 1957.

Kant, Immanuel. *Critique of Judgment*. In *The Philosophy of Kant: Immanuel Kant's Moral and Political Writings*, ed. C. Friedrich. New York: Modern Library, 1949.

———. "What is Enlightenment?" In *The Philosophy of Kant*, ed. C. Friedrich, pp. 132–39. New York: Modern Library, 1949.

Katz, Barry. *Herbert Marcuse and the Art of Liberation*. London: New Left Books, 1982.

Keat, Russell. *The Politics of Social Theory: Habermas, Freud, and the Critique of Positivism*. Chicago: University of Chicago Press, 1981.

Kelsen, Hans. "Platonic Love," trans. George Wilbur. *The American Imago* 3 (Apr. 1942):3–110.

Kernberg, Otto. *Borderline Conditions and Pathological Narcissism*. New York: Jason Aronson, 1975.

———. "Contrasting Viewpoints Regarding the Nature and Treatment of Narcissistic Personality Disorders." *Journal of the American Psychoanalytic Association* 22(1974):255–67.

Klein, Melanie. *The Writings of Melanie Klein*, ed. Roger Money-Kyrle. 4 vols. New York: Free Press, 1964–75.

Klosko, George. *The Development of Plato's Political Theory*. New York: Methuen, 1986.

Kohut, Heinz. *How Does Analysis Cure?* Chicago: University of Chicago Press, 1984.

_____. *The Restoration of the Self*. New York: International Universities Press, 1977.

_____. *Self Psychology and the Humanities*. New York: W. W. Norton, 1985.

_____. "Thoughts on Narcissism and Narcissistic Rage." *The Psychoanalytic Study of the Child* 27 (1973):360–400.

Kovel, Joel. "Narcissism and the Family." *Telos* 44 (Summer 1980): 88–100.

Lacan, Jacques. *Ecrits: A Selection*, trans. A. Sheridan. New York: W. W. Norton, 1977.

_____. *The Four Fundamental Concepts of Psycho-Analysis*, trans. A. Sheridan. New York: W. W. Norton, 1978.

_____. *The Language of the Self: The Function of Language in Psychoanalysis*, trans. with commentary by A. Wilden. Baltimore: Johns Hopkins University Press, 1968.

_____. *Speech and Language in Psychoanalysis*, trans. A. Wilden. Baltimore: Johns Hopkins University Press, 1968.

Lantos, Barbara. "Work and the Instincts." *International Journal of Psychoanalysis* 24 (1943):114–19.

Larson, Raymond, trans. and commentator. *The Apology and Crito of Plato and the Apology and Symposium of Xenophon*. Lawrence, Kans.: Coronado Press, 1980.

Lasch, Christopher. *The Culture of Narcissism*. New York: Warner Books, 1979.

_____. *Haven in a Heartless World*. New York: Basic Books, 1979.

_____. *The Minimal Self*. New York: W. W. Norton, 1984.

Lipshires, Sidney. *Herbert Marcuse: From Marx to Freud and Beyond*. Cambridge, Mass.: Schenkman Publishing Co., 1974.

Lyotard, Jean-François. "Adorno as the Devil." *Telos* 19 (Spring 1974):127–37.

MacIntyre, Alasdair. *After Virtue*. Notre Dame, Ind.: University of Notre Dame Press, 1981.

————. *Herbert Marcuse: An Exposition and a Polemic.* New York: Viking, 1970.

Mahler, Margaret. "On Human Symbiosis and the Vicissitudes of Individuation." In *Selected Papers*, vol. 2, pp. 77–98. New York: Jason Aronson, 1979.

————. "On the Three Subphases of the Separation-Individuation Process." *International Journal of Psychoanalysis* 53 (1972):333–38.

Marcuse, Herbert. *The Aesthetic Dimension.* Boston: Beacon Press, 1978.

————. *Eros and Civilization.* New York: Vintage Books, 1962.

————. *An Essay on Liberation.* Boston: Beacon Press, 1969.

————. *Five Lectures: Psychoanalysis, Politics, and Utopia,* trans. Jeremy Shapiro and Shierry Weber. Boston: Beacon Press, 1970.

————. "Love Mystified: A Critique of Norman O. Brown." In *Negations*, pp. 227–43.

————. *Negations*, trans. J. Shapiro. Boston: Beacon Press, 1968.

————. "The Obsolesence of the Freudian Concept of Man." In *Five Lectures*, pp. 44–61.

————. "On Hedonism." In *Negations*, pp. 159–200.

————. "On Science and Phenomenology." In *Boston Studies in the Philosophy of Science*, ed. Robert Cohen and Marx Wartofsky, vol. 2, pp. 270–90. New York: Humanities Press, 1965.

————. "Protosocialism and Late Capitalism: Toward a Theoretical Synthesis Based on Bahro's Analysis," trans. Michel Vale and Annemarie Feenberg. *International Journal of Politics* 10, nos. 2–3 (1980):25–48.

————. *Reason and Revolution,* 2d ed. Boston: Beacon Press, 1960.

Marx, Karl. "Economic and Philosophic Manuscripts of 1844." In *The Marx-Engels Reader*, ed. Robert Tucker, 2d ed., pp. 66–125. New York: W. W. Norton, 1972.

McCarthy, Thomas. "A Theory of Communicative Competence." *Philosophy of the Social Sciences* 3 (1973):135–56.

Miller, Mark Crispin. Review of *The Minimal Self*, by Christopher Larsch. *The Atlantic*, Nov. 1984, pp. 141–48.

Nagel, Ernest. *The Structure of Science.* New York: Harcourt, Brace and World, 1961.

Neumann, Harry, "Diotima's Concept of Love." *American Journal of Philology* 86 (1965):33–59.

Nichols, Christopher. "Science or Reflection: Habermas on Freud." *Philosophy of the Social Sciences,* vol. 2 (1970):261–70.

Nietzsche, Friedrich. *The Will to Power,* trans. W. Kaufmann and R. J. Hollingdale. New York: Random House, 1967.

Nussbaum, Martha. *The Fragility of Goodness: Luck and Ethics in Greek Tragedy and Philosophy.* Cambridge: Cambridge University Press, 1986.

Ottmann, Henning. "Cognitive Interests and Self-Reflection." In *Habermas: Criticial Debates,* ed. J. B. Thompson and David Held, pp. 79–97. Cambridge, Mass.: MIT Press, 1982.

Ovid, *The Metamorphoses,* trans. Horace Gregory. New York: Viking, 1958.

Popper, Karl. *Conjectures and Refutations.* New York: Harper and Row, 1965.

_____. *The Logic of Scientific Discovery.* New York: Harper and Row, 1968.

_____. *The Open Society and its Enemies.* 2 vols. 5th ed. Princeton: Princeton University Press, 1966.

Ragland-Sullivan, Ellie. *Jacques Lacan and the Philosophy of Psychoanalysis.* Urbana and Chicago: University of Illinois Press, 1986.

Riviere, Joan. "A Contribution to the Analysis of Negative Therapeutic Reaction." *International Journal of Psychoanalysis* 17 (1936):304–20.

Robin, Léon. *La théorie platonicienne de l'Amour.* Paris: Presses universitaires de France, 1933.

Rose, Gillian. *The Melancholy Science: An Introduction to the Thought of Theodor W. Adorno.* London: Macmillan, 1978.

Rosen, Stanley. *Plato's Symposium.* New Haven: Yale University Press, 1968.

_____. "The Role of Eros in Plato's *Republic.*" *Review of Metaphysics* 18 (Mar. 1965):452–75.

Rothstein, Arnold. *The Narcissistic Pursuit of Perfection,* 2d rev. ed. New York: International Universities Press, 1984.

Rousseau, Jean-Jacques. "Discourse on the Origin and Foundations of Inequality Among Men." In *The First and Second Discourses*, ed. Roger Masters, trans. Roger Masters and Judith Masters. New York: St. Martin's Press, 1964.

Schoolman, Morton. *The Imaginary Witness*. New York: Free Press, 1980.

Schwartz, Lester. "Narcissistic Personality Disorders—A Clinical Discussion." *Journal of the American Psychoanalytic Association* 22 (1974):292–305.

Segal, Hanna. *Melanie Klein*. Harmondsworth, Middlesex: Penguin Books, 1981.

Sennett, Richard. *The Fall of Public Man: On the Social Psychology of Capitalism*. New York: Vintage Books, 1978.

Slater, Philip. *The Glory of Hera: Greek Mythology and the Greek Family*. Boston: Beacon Press, 1968.

Spotnitz, Hyman and Philip Resnikoff. "The Myths of Narcissus." *The Psychoanalytic Review* 41 (1954):173–81.

Stern, Daniel N. *The Interpersonal World of the Infant: A View from Psychoanalysis and Developmental Psychology*. New York: Basic Books, 1985.

White, Stephen K. "Foucault's Challenge to Critical Theory." *American Political Science Review* 80 (1986):419–32.

Whitebook, Joel. "Reason and Happiness: Some Psychoanalytic Themes in Critical Theory." *Praxis International* 4 (1984): 15–31.

Wilden, Anthony. "Marcuse and the Freudian Model." In *The Legacy of the German Refugee Intellectuals*, ed. R. Boyers, pp. 196–245. New York: Schocken Books, 1979.

Wolf-Man. *The Wolf-Man*, ed. Muriel Gardiner. New York: Basic Books, 1971.

Zweig, Paul. *The Heresy of Self-Love: A Study of Subversive Individualism*. New York: Basic Books, 1968.

Index

Cornford, F. M., 80
Counteridentification, 59, 94
Cultural manifestations: and culture of emotivism, 9–14; and schizoid disorders, 19; and self psychology, 49–50
Cultural phenomena, and psychoanalytic categories, 14–20
Culture of Narcissism, The (Lasch), 1, 9–14, 18, 76

Death drive, 30
Dependence, 11–12, 39, 40–42, 67
Depressive position, 31–33, 130–31
Developmental stages, 31–33, 52, 53, 57, 173. *See also* Minoan-Mycenean stage; Oral stage
Devereux, George, 17–19
Diagnostic and Statistical Manual of Mental Disorders (American Psychiatric Association), 2
Dialectic of Enlightenment (Horkheimer and Adorno), 105–08, 124, 142
Dinnerstein, Dorothy, 182
Dover, K. L., 78
Drives: for Klein versus Freud, 37–38; and object relationships, 38–39; narcissism and, 56
Drive theory, 21, 39, 121. *See also* Libido theory
Dualisms, in Platonic philosophy, 72–73
Duality of narcissism: and progressive narcissism, 4–5, 98–99, 137; and maturity of ego ideal, 27; and Grunberger, 54, 55, 68–69, 70, 184–85; in Marcuse, 141–42; and balance in pursuit of whole, 192–97; and mutuality, 202–03
"Dual Orientation of Narcissism, The" (Andreas-Salomé), 54, 55

Eclipse of Reason (Horkheimer), 73
"Economic and Philosophic Manuscripts of 1844" (Marx), 156
Ego, 29–30, 40–42, 67. *See also* Ego ideal
"Ego and the Id, The" (Freud), 139, 168
Ego ideal, 25; and primary narcissism,

26; and superego, 26, 60–61, 62–63, 66–67; mature, 26, 62–63; and group psychology, 26–27; and Freud, 59–60; for Chasseguet-Smirgel, 59–65; and object mastery, 60–65, 69; and eros, 62–63; and reconciliation with ego, 88–89, 143, 154–59, 188–89; character of, 148; content of, 199–200
Emotivism, 9–14, 163
Enter Plato (Gouldner), 77
Envy, 32–34, 91
Erikson, Erik, 117
Eros: and ego ideal, 62–63; in pre-Socratic philosophy, 72–73; and reason, 72–74, 90–93, 104, 112, 119, 120–21; and Frankfurt school, 73; and sublimation, 79–83; roots of, 81–83; and quest for wholeness, 83–86, 185; Socrates' account of, 86–88; hubris of, 90–91; selfishness of, 92–93, 195; physical, 100–102, 194; and Adorno, 112, 115–21, 185–86; and nirvana principle, 143; and labor, 143–45; and Marcuse, 143–45, 161–62; in Freudian versus narcissism theory, 187–88; intellectual expression of, 194; and boundaries, 195–96, 197
Eros and Civilization (Marcuse), 58, 123, 136–62, 203
Eros the Bittersweet (Carson), 193
Erotic labor, 144
Erotic utopia, 137, 147, 148–49, 153–59, 201–03
Ethnic unconscious, 17–19
Ethnopsychiatric paradigm, 17–20
Exact fantasy, 113–14

Fairbairn, W. R. D., 19, 38–43, 66, 67, 203
Family, 50, 129–32, 181–83
"Female Sexuality" (Freud), 28
Foot, Philippa, 199
Foucault, Michel, 78
Fragility of Goodness: Luck and Ethics in Greek Tragedy and Philosophy, The (Nussbaum), 97–102
Frankfurt school: and eros, 73; and quest for the whole, 109–10; and philosophy versus psychoanalysis,

Kernberg, Otto: approach of, 16, 43–50; and Rothstein's view, 23, 50–53; and pathological narcissism, 23, 68, 70; and object relations theory, 36–37
Klein, Melanie, 29–38, 67, 120–21
Knowledge and Human Interests (Habermas), 169–73
Kohlberg, Lawrence, 174–75
Kohut, Heinz, 43–53, 68, 167, 172

Labor, 143–45, 146, 155–56
Lacan, Jacques, 166–69
Ladder of love, 73, 86–90, 194
Language: and psychopathology, 169–73; and development, 173, 174; and autonomy, 176–81, 187
Lantos, Barbara, 144
Larson, Raymond, 82
Lasch, Christopher: *The Minimal Self*, 1, 4, 18; *The Culture of Narcissism*, 1, 9–14, 18, 76; Clements's criticism of, 15–16; and Freud, 27–28, 29; and development of autonomy, 129–32; and Marcuse, 150–53
Libido theory, 36, 121, 174. See also Drive theory
Life Against Death (Brown), 151
Lipshires, Sidney, 140
Lyotard, Jean-François, 111, 118

Mahler, Margaret, 23, 44, 48, 55–56, 61
Marcuse, Herbert: *Eros and Civilization*, 58, 123, 136–62, 203; and Adorno, 108, 110, 121, 123, 128; criticism of, 150–53, 201–03; and Habermas, 177, 179, 181
Marx, Karl, 156
Marxism and Totality (Jay), 116–17
Mature narcissism: and normal development, 46; and Socrates, 74, 80–81, 86–90, 92–93, 95–97; and ladder of love, 89–90; and mastery, 157; and harmony, 203–04
Mimesis, 106–07, 112–15, 119
Minimal philosophy, 191–92
Minimal self, 10–11, 130–32, 191–92. See also Lasch, Christopher

Minoan-Mycenean stage, 4, 28–29, 67, 71, 152, 185
Mitchell, Stephen A., 35, 36, 37, 40, 65, 67
Moral autonomy, 126
Moral development, 174
"Moral Development and Ego Identity" (Habermas), 178
Mutuality, 201, 202–03
Mythic culture heroes, 142–43

Narcissism: as term, 36; myth of, 142, 147
Narcissistic injury: and Grunberger, 55–57; and object mastery, 68–69, 134, 143; Aristophanes' account of, 83–86; and radical social change, 129; culture-based solutions to, 190
Narcissistic investment, mode of, 51–53, 70
Narcissistic Pursuit of Perfection (Rothstein), 23
Narcissistic rage, 69–70
Narrative selfhood, 10, 12–14
Narrative unity, 160, 189–99, 196
National socialism, 63–64
Nature: reconciliation with, 107–08, 114–15, 172; domination of, 149
Nature romanticism, 103–04
Needs, 160–61, 174–78
Negative dialectics, 111–12, 132–35
Negative Dialectics (Adorno), 111–12
Negative therapeutic reaction, 34
Negativity versus totality, 117–18
Neo-Freudian revisionism, 152
Nirvana principle, 28, 141, 154
Nussbaum, Martha, 97–102

Object love, versus narcissism, 25–26, 27
Object mastery: and reconciliation, 60, 62, 68–69, 70; and narcissistic wound, 68–69, 134, 143; and alienated labor, 143–45; and erotic utopia, 149; and civilization, 153–59; and pleasure and reality principles, 188–89; and narcissistic ideal, 197. See also Contingency, transcendence of
Object relationships: for Fairbairn, 38–43, 66; and ego, 40–42, 67

Object Relations in Psychoanalytic Theory (Greenberg and Mitchell), 35, 36, 67

Object relations theory: narcissism in, 21, 65; and Klein, 37; and Chasseguet-Smirgel, 60–61, 67; and autonomy, 127–28, 203

Odysseus, 106, 133–34

Oedipal conflict: and neurosis, 42–43; and narcissism, 58–59, 89; and sexuality, 61; for Chasseguet-Smirgel, 61–62; and Frankfurt school, 124–25; and Horkheimer,125–29; and ego development, 125–29, 130

Oliner, Marion, 57, 81, 160

"On Hedonism" (Marcuse), 177

"On Human Symbiosis and the Vicissitudes of Individuation" (Mahler), 55–56

"On Narcissism" (Freud), 24–25, 59, 66

Oral stage, 42. *See also* Minoan-Mycenean stage

Ottmann, Henning, 171

Ovid, 2

Paranoid-schizoid position, 31–33, 48–49

Parental relationships, and autonomy, 127–28, 129–32

Parsons, Talcott, 12

Pathological narcissism, 2–4, 14, 141; and survival mentality, 11; continuity with normal, 22, 23, 66, 69, 70; and internal objects, 39, 40–42, 67; in self theory, 44–45, 69–70; and grandiosity, 46–48; and early oral stages, 67; as a defense, 69–70; for Lacan, 168. *See also* Regressive narcissism

Pederasty. *See* Homosexual eros

"Pervert's mother," 63, 64

Phaedrus (Plato), 100–102, 112, 191

Philosophical narcissism, 100–102

Philosophical phenomena, and psychoanalytic categories, 14–20

Plato: sublimation of, 5, 79–83, 186, 189, 190; *Symposium*, 74, 83–100, 188, 189; and homosexual eros, 75–

79, 82–83; and value of individual, 97–100, 191; *Phaedrus*, 100–102, 112, 191; and goal of mature narcissism, 193–96

Play, 144

Pleasure principle, 150

Popper, Karl, 24

Position, as term, 31–32

Postmodernism, 165–69

Primary narcissism: as objectless state, 25, 27, 65; rejection of, 34–35; and fusion, 56, 61; and non-repressive sublimation, 138–40

Progressive narcissism, 4–5, 96–98, 119, 137

Projective identification, 31

Pseudo-narcissism, 70

Psychoanalytic theory: and cultural phenomena, 14–20; views of narcissism in, 21–22; and metapsychological aspects, 24; in theory of narcissism, 71, 169–73, 183, 184, 187

Psychopathology, 40–42, 169–73. *See also* Pathological narcissism; Schizoid phenomena

Radical individualism, 201–03

Reality principle, 146, 149, 153

Reason. *See* Instrumental reason; Reconciling reason

Reconciliation of ego and ego ideal, 60–65, 69, 81, 188–89

Reconciling reason, 108–21

Regressive narcissism: and "pervert's mother," 63, 64; and national socialism, 63–64; and Greek culture, 74, 77; and Socrates-Alcibiades relationship, 93–97; and nirvana principle, 141; in Marcuse, 141–45, 148–49, 161–62; and aesthetic experience, 148–49; and intensity of quest, 189; infantile origins of, 190

Reparation, 33–34

Restoration of the Self (Kohut), 49

Riviere, Joan, 23, 44, 48

Robin, Léon, 84

Rosen, Stanley, 84, 91

Rothstein, Arnold, 23, 50–53